CONSTRAINTS AND DATABASES

edited by

Raghu Ramakrishnan
University of Wisconsin

and

Peter Stuckey
University of Melbourne

*Reprinted from
a Special Issue of
CONSTRAINTS
An International Journal
Volume 2, Nos. 3 & 4
December 1997*

SPRINGER SCIENCE+BUSINESS MEDIA, LLC

CONSTRAINTS

An International Journal

Volume 2, Nos. 3/4, December 1997

Special Issue on Constraints and Databases
Guest Editors: Raghu Ramakrishnan and Peter J. Stuckey

ISBN 978-1-4613-7520-3   ISBN 978-1-4615-5515-5 (eBook)
DOI 10.1007/978-1-4615-5515-5

Library of Congress Cataloging-in-Publication Data

A C.I.P. Catalogue record for this book is available
from the Library of Congress.

Constraints: An International Journal, 2, 243 (1997)

Introduction to the Special Issue on Constraints and Databases

RAGHU RAMAKRISHNAN   raghu@cs.wisc.edu
Computer Sciences Dept., University of Wisconsin-Madison, 1210 West Dayton Street,
Madison, WI 53706, USA

PETER J. STUCKEY   pjs@cs.mu.oz.au
Dept. of Computer Science, University of Melbourne, Parkville 3052, Australia

This special issue of the journal is dedicated to the memory of Paris C. Kanellakis, who pioneered the area of constraint databases in a seminal paper with Kuper and Revesz. Paris died in a tragic air accident, leaving a void in the many research communities in which he was a leader; looking at the work that he did and influenced emphasizes just how significant this void is.

This issue contains papers on a range of topics involving constraints and databases, demonstrating the breadth of this research area. The papers by Brodsky, Chen, Exarkhapoulou, Jaffar, Maher, and Segal address the precise topic studied by Kanellakis, namely, databases that store and manipulate constraints in tuples.

The paper by Brodsky, Segal, Chen and Exarkhapoulou describes the design and implementation of an object-oriented constraint database, while the paper by Brodsky, Jaffar and Maher investigates efficient query evaluation strategies for databases storing linear arithmetic constraints.

The papers by Fribourg and Olsen, and by Toman both discuss efficient evaluation for recursive programs with constraint tuples. Fribourg and Olsen consider a class of programs related to Petri nets, while Toman gives an evaluation method parametric in the constraint domain. The paper by Revesz describes an application of constraint databases for refining genome maps.

Constraints have long been associated with databases for maintaining integrity of the data. The paper by Huyn discusses integrity constraint maintenance over distributed databases.

Finally, the paper by Morimoto, Fukuda, Morishita, and Tokuyama uses numeric constraints to create efficient decision trees for large datasets.

Constraints: An International Journal, 2, 245–277 (1997)

The CCUBE Constraint Object-Oriented Database System

ALEXANDER BRODSKY   brodsky@isse.gmu.edu

VICTOR E. SEGAL   vsegal@isse.gmu.edu

JIA CHEN   jchen1@isse.gmu.edu

PAVEL A. EXARKHOPOULO   pexarkh@isse.gmu.edu

Dept. of Information and Software Systems Engineering, George Mason University, Fairfax, VA 22030, USA

Abstract. Constraints provide a flexible and uniform way to represent diverse data capturing spatio-temporal behavior, complex modeling requirements, partial and incomplete information etc, and have been used in a wide variety of application domains. Constraint databases have recently emerged to deeply integrate data captured by constraints in databases. This paper reports on the development of the first constraint object-oriented database system, CCUBE, and describes its specification, design and implementation. The CCUBE system is designed to be used for the implementation and optimization of high-level constraint object-oriented query languages as well as for directly building software systems requiring extensible use of constraint database features. The CCUBE data manipulation language, *Constraint Comprehension Calculus*, is an integration of a *constraint calculus* for extensible constraint domains within *monoid comprehensions*, which serve as an optimization-level language for object-oriented queries. The data model for the constraint calculus is based on constraint spatio-temporal (CST) objects that may hold spatial, temporal or constraint data, conceptually represented by constraints. New CST objects are constructed, manipulated and queried by means of the constraint calculus. The model for the monoid comprehensions, in turn, is based on the notion of monoids, which is a generalization of collection and aggregation types. The focal point of our work is achieving the right balance between the expressiveness, complexity and representation usefulness, without which the practical use of the system would not be possible. To that end, CCUBE constraint calculus guarantees polynomial time data complexity, and, furthermore, is tightly integrated with the monoid comprehensions to allow deeply interleaved global optimization.

Keywords: constraint databases, constraint languages, constraint database optimization

1. Introduction

Constraints provide a flexible and uniform way to conceptually represent diverse data capturing spatio-temporal behavior, complex modeling requirements, partial and incomplete information etc, and have been used in a wide variety of application domains. Constraint databases (CDBs) have recently emerged to deeply integrate data captured by constraints in databases. Although a relatively new realm of research, constraint databases have drawn much attention and increasing interest, mostly in aspects of expressibility and complexity, but also in algorithms and optimization.

Constraint databases are very promising for applications required to support large heterogeneous data sets that can be uniformly captured by constraints. This includes (1) engineering design; (2) manufacturing and warehouse support; (3) electronic trade with complex objectives; (4) command and control (such as spatio-temporal data fusion and

7

sensor management [2] and maneuver planning [5]); (5) distribution logistics; and (6) market analysis.

While many fundamental research questions are yet to be answered, we believe that the area of constraint databases became mature for a reliable research prototype that could serve as a stable platform for experimentation with algorithms and optimization techniques as well as for real-life case studies of a number of promising application domains. We believe that building such a system is a crucial step toward proving the validity of constraint databases as a technology with a significant practical impact.

The contribution of the work reported in this paper is the development, i.e. the specification, design and implementation, of the *first constraint object-oriented database system*, CCUBE.

Motivation and Design Goals

Until now, most of the work on CDBs has been theoretical (see Related Work section). CDB researchers are being challenged by the question whether the CDB technology can really work on real-life, real-size, real-performance applications, or it is just an intellectual toy that will eventually fade away. This parallels, in a sense, to the state of relational databases before the first two prototypes, Ingres and System-R, were developed. Our view is that the viability test for the CDB technology will be the ability to achieve competitive performance and scalability. Therefore, algorithms, data structures and optimization techniques are the most critical issues.

At the beginning of the CCUBE work we had two main choices regarding the design objectives: (1) to naively implement a high-level and purely declarative constraint DB language, such as $\mathcal{LyriC}$, focusing on its interface, but ignoring the performance and scalability, or (2) to develop an extensible infrastructure (i.e. an intermediate, optimization-level language, in which evaluation plans can be explicitly expressed) suitable for developing and testing optimization techniques, algorithms and data structures.

The first choice would lead to a much faster and simpler implementation, and, in fact, this is the way most research prototypes are implemented. The second choice, clearly, is considerably more work- and time-intensive, but is essential for our overall objectives. Of course, ideally, we would like to have both a high-level language and a full-scale optimizer in place, but this would not be possible without developing first the optimization infrastructure of (2). This direction was indeed our choice.

The following were our main design principles:

1. In terms of constraint domains and operators, a careful balance between expressiveness and complexity must be achieved. It is easy to fall into a trap of highly expressive constraint domains for almost any imaginable types of data, but with absolutely impractical complexity.

2. The language and the model should be object-oriented, since many object-oriented features are important for the target applications (e.g. [2]).

3. The language should be suitable for explicitly expressing highly optimized evaluation plans (preserving their I/O time and space complexity). It must be flexible enough to support object-oriented optimization (e.g. ENCORE [58], O2 [21], POSTGRES [54]), constraint database optimization (e.g. [10]) and constraint indexing and filtering (e.g. [14]).

4. The system should be extensible with respect to (constraint and other) data types, operators and predicates, and special data structures and algorithms.

5. The system should allow an easy interaction with an underlying programming language in order to be usable directly by system or application programmers

6. Provided the previous principles are met, the language should ideally be as high-level and easy-to-use as possible.

CCUBE Features and Architecture

The CCUBE data manipulation language, *Constraint Comprehension Calculus* is an integration of a *constraint calculus* for extensible constraint domains within *monoid comprehensions*, which were suggested as an optimization-level language for object-oriented queries [22]. In the following, when no misinterpretation arises, we will be using the same name CCUBE for both the system and the language of the constraint comprehension calculus. [1]

The data model for constraint calculus is adapted from *constraint spatio-temporal* (CST) objects [11], that may hold spatio-temporal constraint data, conceptually represented by constraints (i.e. symbolic expressions). In the current version, linear arithmetic constraints (i.e. inequalities and equations) over reals [2] are implemented. New CST objects are constructed using logical connectives, existential quantifiers and variable renaming, within a multi-typed constraint algebra.[3] The constraint module also provides predicates such as for testing satisfiability, entailment etc, that are used as selecting conditions in hosting monoid comprehension queries.

CST objects possess great modeling power and as such can serve as a *uniform data type* for conceptual representation of heterogeneous data, including spatial and temporal behavior, complex design requirements and partial and incomplete information. Moreover, the constraint calculus operating on CST is a highly *expressive* and *compact* language. For example, just linear arithmetic CSTs and its calculus currently implemented in the system, allow description and powerful manipulation of a wide variety of data, including (1) 2- or 3-D geographic maps; (2) geometric modeling objects for CAD/CAM; (3) fields of vision of sensors; (4) 4-D (3 + 1 for time) trajectories of objects moving in a 3-D space, based on the movement equations; (5) translations of different system of coordinates; and (6) operations research type models such as manufacturing patterns describing interconnections between quantities of manufactured products and resource materials. It is important to note that the conceptual and physical representations of CST objects are orthogonal: while conceptually constraints are viewed as symbolic expressions, the physical representation is typically chosen to facilitate efficient storage and manipulation.

The general framework of the CCUBE language is the *monoid comprehensions* language, in which CST objects serve as a special data type, and are implemented as a library of interrelated C++ classes. The data model for the monoid comprehensions is based on the notion of *monoid*, which is a conceptual data type capturing uniformly aggregations, collections, and other types over which one can "iterate". This includes (long) disjunctions and conjunctions of constraints.

The ability to treat disjunctive and conjunctive constraints uniformly as collections is a very important feature of CCUBE: it allows to express and implement many constraint operations through nested monoid comprehensions, i.e. in the same language as hosting queries. For example, the satisfiability test of a disjunction of conjunctions of linear inequalities is expressed as a monoid comprehension query that iterates over the disjuncts (each being a conjunction), and tests the satisfiability of every conjunction (using the simplex algorithm).

In turn, the ability to express a constraint operation as a sub-query in the hosting query is crucial for what we call *deeply interleaved optimization*: it gives the flexibility to re-shuffle and interleave parts of the constraint algorithm (sub-query) with the hosting query. This re-shuffling can be done by additional global query transformations (discussed in the paper) involving approximations, indexing, re-grouping, pushing cheaper selections earlier, replacing sub-queries with special-purpose algorithms, and so forth. Figuratively speaking, constraint operations are not treated in CCUBE as *black boxes* plugged into a query, which would severely restrict optimization opportunities, but rather as *white boxes with black holes*.

The CCUBE system architecture supports:

1. Besides CST objects, any data structures expressible in C++.

2. An extensible family of parameterized and possibly nested collection monoids currently including sets, bags, lists, as well as (long) disjunctions and conjunctions of CST objects.

3. An extensible family of aggregation monoids such as *sum, count, some* and *all*.

4. An extensible family of search structures implemented as parameterized monoids and currently including B-trees, hashing and kD-trees for multidimensional rectangles. Because the search structures are implemented as monoids, they can be used uniformly anywhere in queries where monoids are allowed.

5. An extensible family of special-purpose algorithms, such as the sort-join and the constraint join [10], which are implemented as parameterized monoids. These special algorithms are important for performance because they cannot be matched, in terms of I/O complexity, by standard monoid comprehension algorithms with dynamic buffer management (although many other algorithms, such as the loop join and standard selections, can). Since the special algorithms are expressed as monoids, they can be easily plugged in monoid comprehension queries to replace equivalent sub-queries.

6. Approximation-based filtering, indexing and regrouping based on internal components of nested collection monoids. These features are especially important for achieving deeply interleaved optimization in presence of constraint operations.

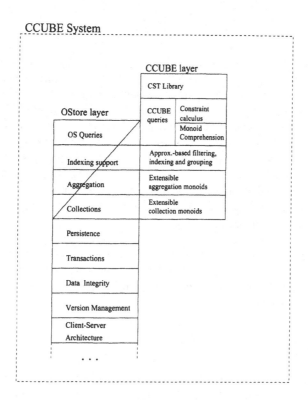

Figure 1. CCUBE Functional Components

7. Orthogonal features inherited from the commercial OODB ObjectStore, including persistence, dynamic buffer management, transaction management, data integrity, crash recovery, version management, and multi-client/multi-server architecture.

The functionality of the CCUBE system, depicted in Figure 1, is a combination of the new CCUBE layer and ObjectStore. Note that CCUBE as a virtual system (1) inherits "lower" features of ObjectStore, (2) replaces "middle" ObjectStore's features with those of the CCUBE layer, and (3) adds "upper" features of the CCUBE layer. The implementation of the CCUBE layer, in turn, uses ObjectStore and the linear programming package CPLEX. We feel important to note that while CCUBE is a research prototype, we believe that it is a scalable system designed to carry out implementations of serious, massive data applications. That is partly due to the use of commercially available components (i.e. ObjectStore and CPLEX).

CCUBE, similar to ObjectStore, can be better viewed as a powerful extension of C++ with constraint database features, rather than a full-scale DBMS, and is currently to be used from within a hosting C++ program. As a C++ extension, CCUBE uses the native C++ data structures and its type system. In fact, in the current implementation only the monoid comprehensions are pre-compiled, and all the other CCUBE features, including the

the constraint calculus, are implemented as C++ libraries; hence the native C++ syntax is preserved.

The use of the "dirty" C++ data model, as opposed to "clean" and formally defined models such as of ODMG OQL [3] or XSQL [37] was our pragmatic choice due to the intended purpose of CCUBE: an intermediate optimization-level language, i.e. one in which an optimizer or a programmer can (explicitly) write highly optimized queries, using appropriate order, nesting, special operators (e.g. for the sort join) and built-in optimization primitives. Because of the intended use as an intermediate language, we prefer to regain the flexibility of and the uniformity with the underlying programming language, C++. We designed CCUBE to be used both for the implementation and optimization of high-level constraint object-oriented query languages such as $\mathcal{L}yri\mathcal{C}$ or constraint extensions of OQL, and for directly building software systems (by application or system programmers) requiring extensible use of constraint database features.

The focal point of our work is achieving the right balance between the expressiveness, complexity and representation usefulness [9] without which the practical use of the system would not be possible. To that end, the CCUBE constraint calculus guarantees polynomial data complexity, and, furthermore, is tightly integrated with the monoid comprehensions to allow deeply interleaved global optimization.

Organization of Paper

The paper is organized as follows. Following the introduction, Section 2 informally discusses the CCUBE language, including CST objects, the constraint calculus and the monoid comprehensions language by examples. In Section 3, we review formal definitions of monoid comprehensions, explain the implementation of monoids in CCUBE and the syntax and the semantics of CCUBE queries. Section 4 describes the design and implementation of the CST multi-typed algebra, on which the constraint calculus is based. The CCUBE primitives for optimization using approximation-based filtering, regrouping and indexing are discussed in Section 5. Section 6 briefly surveys the related work. Finally, in Section 7 we conclude and mention some topics of future work.

2. CST Objects and CCUBE Queries by Example

In this section we informally discuss CCUBE queries, including CST objects, the constraint calculus and monoid comprehensions using an architectural design example similar to the one in [11]. We assume, briefly, that a database stores a collection of office objects such as desks, file cabinets etc, which have extents (or shapes) and moving parts, such as drawers, as well as other attributes. A designer then may ask queries such as: Given a room and the locations of a number of objects in it, can we put an additional desk such that its drawer will not touch any other object in the room, and still have an unoccupied 4×4 feet space? Can we put in a room two desks, two file cabinets and two chairs such that (1) no two objects or their opened drawers will touch each other or the walls, and (2) there will be at least 4 feet between the front of each desk and the opposite wall? Can the system give constraints

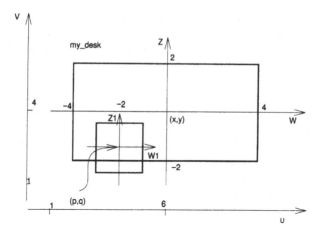

Figure 2. An instance of a desk with drawer in the room

describing possible interconnections of the centers of objects such that the above goals are achieved? What would be the location of the above mentioned objects if we wanted to maximize the size of a square of the available empty space? Given a collection of objects in the room, show a projection of their cut at the height of 1/2 feet. Those queries can be efficiently answered in CCUBE without using user implemented predicates or functions.

2.1.   Constraints, CST objects and Schema by Example

Consider a two-dimensional desk ''my-desk'' depicted in Figure 2 as the larger rectangle. The smaller square is the desk's drawer, which may open, i.e. move relatively to the desk. Similarly, the desk may be moved in the room. There are three systems of coordinates used in Figure 2: U, V, the room's (or global) system; W, Z, the desk's coordinate system used to describe the desk's shape independently of the location of the desk in the room; and $W1, Z1$, the drawer's coordinate system. The pair of variables (x, y) describes the center of the desk in the room's coordinates; similarly, (p, q) describe the center of the drawer in the desk's coordinates.

The basic idea in constraint databases is the introduction of constraint formulae as a basic data type in databases. For example, a constraint (formula)

$$(-4 \leq w \leq 4) \wedge (-2 \leq z \leq 2)$$

with the variables ranging over reals can be viewed as a set of points

$$\{(w, z) | (-4 \leq w \leq 4) \wedge (-2 \leq z \leq 2)\}$$

in two-dimensional space and describes, say, the extent of my-desk (Figure 2) given in the desk's coordinates. More accurately, the constraint formula $(-4 \leq w \leq 4) \wedge (-1 \leq z \leq 2)$

will be interpreted as an infinite relation over the schema W, Z, that contains all tuples (w, z) satisfying the constraint.

Similarly, the extent of the desk's drawer in the drawer's coordinates can be described by the constraint $(-1 \leq w1 \leq 1) \wedge (-1 \leq z1 \leq 1)$. The possible locations (p, q) of the drawer's center in the desk's coordinates can be described by $p = -2 \wedge -3 \leq q \leq -1$; note that the horizontal component of the center, p, equals to a constant since the drawer in the example cannot move left or right; note also that the vertical component, q, is between -3, when the drawer is fully open, and -1 when it is closed.

The translation between the desk's W, Z and the room's U, V systems of coordinates can be captured by the constraint $u = x + w \wedge v = y + z$, meaning that if the desk's center is at (x, y), then a point (w, z) in desk's coordinates is (u, v) in the global room's coordinates. Suppose that the desk's center has room's coordinates $(6, 4)$, i.e. $x = 6 \wedge y = 4$. Then, for example, we can find the extent of the desk in the room's coordinates by simplifying the following formula:

$$(\exists x, y, w, z)[[(-4 \leq w \leq 4) \wedge (-2 \leq z \leq 2)] \wedge [u = x + w \wedge v = y + z] \wedge [x = 6 \wedge y = 4]]$$

where the first []-component is the desk's extent in the local coordinates, the second is the translation between the coordinate systems and the third is the position of the desk's center. Finally, since we are only interested in the free variables u, v, representing 2D-points in the room's coordinates, we existentially quantify all the other variables. If we substitute the constants into x, y we get $u = 6 + w \wedge v = 4 + z$, and then, by using it in the first inequality we finally get $(2 \leq u \leq 10) \wedge (2 \leq v \leq 6)$. From Figure 2 we can easily see that this is exactly the extent of my-desk described in the room's coordinate system.

In the CCUBE syntax the above formula will look as follows:

```
(u,v) |   ((-4 <= w <= 4) && (-2 <= z <= 2) &&
          (u == x + w && v == y + z) &&
          (x == 6 && y == 4))
```

The (u,v) | ... notation is a projection, where we indicate all free variables in the result, rather than variables to be existentially quantified. We also use && and == instead of $\wedge$ and $=$, correspondingly, to preserve the C++ style. Interestingly, the above constraint syntax is native in C++, which is achieved by exploiting the C++ operators' overloading mechanism. How this is done is explained in more detail in Section 4.3. Users can intuitively think of a constraint with d free variables as a (possibly) infinite relation of d-tuples, as an object in d-dimensional space (i.e. a set of points), or as a symbolic expression, interchangeably, depending on the application and the context of its use. Thus, we will be referring to a constraint by a generic name CST (i.e. *constraint spatio-temporal*) object.

Consider now an architectural design example schema depicted in Figure 3. We assume that the database keeps a bag collection (multiset) all-office-objects, i.e. it is declared as Bag<OFFICE_OBJECT*>, where "*" denotes a reference (i.e. a C++ pointer) to. Similarly, all-desks and all-file-cabinets are kept, which are declared as Bag<DESK*> and Bag<FILE_CABINET*> correspondingly. Note that the same object may appear more than once in the bag.

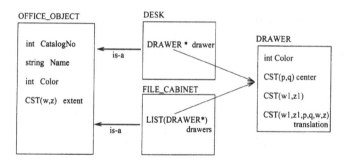

Figure 3. An Object-Oriented Database Schema

Objects of the class OFFICE_OBJECT have standard attributes such as catalog#, name and color, and also the extent attribute, describing the object's shape. The extent attribute is declared as CST(w,z), to indicate that it must be represented as a constraint with free variables w and z. Note that, unless otherwise stated, we use the term "class" in this paper in the C++ sense. For instance, there is no class extent automatically associated with each class, as usually assumed in OO database models.

The classes DESK and FILE_CABINET are subclasses of OFFICE_OBJECT, and, therefore, inherit all its attributes. This is indicated by the thick arrows in Figure 3. In addition, the class DESK has an attribute drawer, which is declared as reference to an object of the class DRAWER. Similarly, an additional attribute of the class FILE_CABINET is drawers that is declared as a list of references to objects of class DRAWER. Note, that the thin arrows in Figure 3 indicate the composition hierarchy.

Each drawer, in turn, is characterized by possible locations of its center, declared as CST(p,q); its extent declared as CST(w1,z1); and translation, declared as CST(w1, z1,p,q,w,z), which would hold an equation describing the interconnection between $(w1, z1)$, a point in the drawer's coordinates and (w, z), the same point in the desk's coordinates, provided the center of the drawer is at (p, q) in the desk's coordinates.

Below is an example of the CCUBE (in fact, C++) definition of my_desk of the class DESK:

```
DESK my_desk = DESK(
  22354,                            // catalog#
  ''one-drawer-desk'',              // name
  ''red'',                          // color
  (-4 <= w <= 4 && -2 <= z <= 2),   // extent
  *new  DRAWER(                      // drawer
      ''blue'',                         // color
      (p == -2 && -3 <= q <= -1),       // center
      (-1 <= w1 <= 1 && -1 <= z1 <= 1), // extent
      (w == w1 + p && z == z1 + q)      // translation
  )
);
```

2.2.   CCUBE Queries by Example

Consider the following CCUBE query, yet without CST objects, which finds a bag of all
red file cabinets, that have at least one blue drawer:

```
SELECT fc                               // for file cabinet
INTO {Bag<FILE_CABINET*>} result        // result is a bag-collection
FROM all_file_cabinets
          AS {FILE_CABINET*} fc         // iterator: fc iterates
                                        //              over BAG
WHERE fc->color == ''red''              // predicate, i.e. condition
FROM  fc->drawers AS {DRAWER*} dr       // iterator: dr iterates
                                        //              over LIST
WHERE dr->color == ''blue''             // predicate
```

The SELECT clause is followed by a possibly interleaved list of the FROM-clause iterators
and WHERE-clause conditions. Any order of iterators and predicates, in which variables
are only used after they are bound is allowed. However, in general, different orders may
lead, as we shall see, to different resulting collections. In the SELECT clause we may have
any C++ expression, possibly using variables bounded in the iterators, or invoking another
monoid comprehension.

The semantics of the query is best understood, intuitively, through the following nested
loop program, which is a conceptual skeleton of the actual algorithm evaluating monoid
comprehensions.[4]

```
result = empty_bag;
FOREACH fc IN {BAG} all_file_cabinets DO
    IF fc->color == ''red'' THEN
        FOREACH dr IN {LIST} fc->drawers DO
            IF dr->color == ''blue'' THEN
                INSERT fc INTO result
```

If the bag collection all_file_cabinets contains a file cabinet fc which has 3 blue
drawers, it will be inserted in result 3 times, creating 3 copies of fc in the result bag
collection. However, if the collection type of result were SET, then the insertion of fc
into result more than once would be equivalent to a single insertion. If, on the other
hand, the result collection were of the type LIST, the order in which the insertions are
made would also impact the result collection.[5] Also important to note is that a query can
be always written with just one FROM clause containing all the iterators, followed by just
one WHERE clause with all the conditions. However, we allow any order of interleaved
iterators and conditions, in order to control the evaluation of the query, as is necessary for
optimization-level languages such as CCUBE.

The next query demonstrates construction of CST objects in the SELECT clause; it finds,
for each desk in all_desks, its extent in the rooms coordinates, assuming the center of the
desk is located at the point $(6, 4)$ and the desk orientation is aligned with the room's walls,
i.e. the translation equation is $u = w + x \land v = z + y$.

```
SELECT new CST( (u,v) | (dsk->extent &&         // recall: in var's
                                                 //    w and z
                 u == w + x && v == z + y &&     // translation of
                                                 //    coord.
                 x == 6 && y == 4) )             // location of
                                                 //    the center
INTO   {Bag<CST*>} result
FROM   all_desks AS {DESK*} dsk                  // iterates over
                                                 //    a bag
```

Note that Bag<CST*> in the INTO clause indicates the type of result. The next query finds all pairs (dsk, dsk->extent) for all desks that, if centered at $(6, 4)$, would intersect the area (3 <= u <= 4 && 8 <= v <= 10) in the room's coordinates.

```
SELECT new pair(dsk,dsk->extent)
INTO   {Bag<pair*>} result
FROM   all_desks AS {DESK*} dsk
DEFINE area   AS {CST} (3 <= u <= 4 && 8 <= v <= 10)
DEFINE transl AS {CST} (u == x + w && v == y + z)
WHERE  SAT(area && dsk->extent && transl && x == 6 && y == 4)
```

Here, pair(dsk, dsk->extent) is a constructor of the class pair; expressions DEFINE expr1 AS expr2 cause the replacement expr1 by expr2 in the remainder of the comprehension; they are used simply as shortcuts. SAT stands for the satisfiability test of the constraint expression inside the parentheses which checks whether area intersects the desk's extent.

The following query exemplifies the use of the ENTAIL predicate in the WHERE clause and some geometrical manipulation of CST objects in the SELECT clause. For all desks that, if located at $(6, 4)$, contain the area 3 <= u <= 4 && 8 <= v <= 10, it finds the desk's extent above the diagonal (45 degree) through its center.

```
SELECT new CST(dsk->extent && w <= z)     // Note: w <= z
                                          // for above
INTO   {Bag<CST*>} result                 // 45 degree diagonal
FROM   all_desks AS {DESK*} dsk
DEFINE area   AS {CST} (3 <= u <= 4 && 8 <= v <= 10),
DEFINE transl AS {CST} (u == x + w && v == y + z),
DEFINE dsk_ext_in_room AS
  {CST} (u,v) | (dsk->extent && transl && (x == 6 && y == 4))
WHERE  ENTAIL(area, dsk_ext_in_room) // To test containment
                                     // of area in dsk_ext_in_room
```

Note that dsk_ext_in_room stands for the desk's extent in the room's coordinates. Finally, the last query finds all desks whose drawer may intersect, if closed or partly or fully open, the desk area (-1 <= w <= 1 && -1 <= z <= 1)

```
SELECT dsk
```

```
INTO   {Bag<DESK*>} result
FROM   all_desks AS {DESK*} dsk
DEFINE dr_ext    AS {CST} dsk->drawer->extent,
DEFINE dr_loc    AS {CST} dsk->drawer->center,
DEFINE dr_transl AS {CST} dsk->drawer->translation,
DEFINE dr_ext_in_dsk AS
                 {CST} (w,z) | (dr_ext && dr_loc && dr_transl),
WHERE  SAT(dr_ext_in_dsk && -1 <= w <= 1 && -1 <= z <= 1)
```

3. CCUBE Monoids and Monoid Comprehensions

In this section we describe the syntax, semantics and implementation of the CCUBE monoids and monoid comprehensions. The formal counterpart of the CCUBE monoid comprehensions is *monoid comprehensions* of [22], which is a restricted version of *monoid homomorphizms* [6, 8, 7] written using the syntax of *monad comprehensions* [56], as is done by [15]. We first review the formal definition of monoids and monoid comprehensions borrowing heavily from [22] and [14].

3.1. Review of Monoid Comprehensions

```
BAG { fc | fc ← all_file_cabinets,
           fc->color == ''red'',
           dr ← fc->drawers,
           dr->color == ''blue'' }
```

This is the original monoid comprehension syntax for the first CCUBE query in Subsection 2.2. Here, BAG indicates the type of the resulting collection (monoid); fc to the left of | is what we SELECT; ← is used to denote an *iterator*, i.e. the statement in the FROM clause; and the rest is *predicates*, i.e. logical conditions appearing anywhere in the WHERE clauses. The intuitive meaning is given by the nested loop program in Subsection 2.2.

In addition to collections, we can also compute aggregation functions. For example,

```
SUM { 1 | fc ← all_file_cabinets,
          fc->color == ''red'',
          dr ← fc->drawers,
          dr->color == ''blue'' }
```

will count the number of file_cabinets in the result.

More formally, a set of basic data types given, e.g., int, real and char, and a set of type constructors, e.g., set, list, bag. A *data type* is defined recursively as a basic data type or a constructed type $T(\alpha)$ determined by the type parameter α.

A *monoid* is a triple $(T, \text{zero}, \text{merge})$, where T is a data type and merge is an associative function, of type $T \times T \rightarrow T$, with left and right identity zero. For example, $sum = (int, 0, +)$ is a monoid. A *collection monoid* is a quadruple $(T(\alpha), \text{zero}, \text{unit}, \text{merge})$, where (1) $T(\alpha)$ is a constructed type determined by the type parameter α, (2) $(T(\alpha), \texttt{zero}, \texttt{merge})$ is a monoid, and (3) $\texttt{unit}$ is a function of type $\alpha \rightarrow T(\alpha)$. As an example, $(list(int), [], f, ++)$, where $[]$ is the empty list, $f(i) = [i]$ for each i and $++$ is the concatenation operation on lists.[6] Finally, a *primitive monoid* is a quadruple $(T, \texttt{zero}, \texttt{unit}, \texttt{merge})$, where $(T, \texttt{zero}, \texttt{merge})$ is a monoid and $\texttt{unit}$ is the identity function of type $T \rightarrow T$. Examples of primitive monoids include $prod = (int, 1, id, *)$, where $id(i) = i$ for each integer.

Intuitively, a monoid $\mathcal{M} = (T, \texttt{zero}, \texttt{merge})$ is an abstract definition of a data type. Collection monoids capture the bulk types, and primitive monoids capture the basic types. Each instance of the collection type $\mathcal{M} = (T(\alpha), \texttt{zero}, \texttt{unit}, \texttt{merge})$ is expressed as compositions of functions $\texttt{zero}$, $\texttt{unit}$ and $\texttt{merge}$ on instances of type α. As an example, the monoid $(list(int), [], f, ++)$ given earlier defines a data type of the integer lists. An instance of the type is intuitively a list of integers and the list is expressed as a composition of functions $[]$, u and $++$ applying on integers. For example, the list $\{1, 2, 3, 1\}$ can be expressed as $++(u(1), ++(u(2), ++(u(3), ++(u(1), []))))$.

A monoid $(T, \texttt{zero}, \texttt{merge})$ is called *commutative* (*idempotent*, resp.) if function $\texttt{merge}$ is commutative (idempotent, resp.). For example, the monoid $set^\alpha = (set(\alpha), \{\}, f', \cup)$, where $f'(i) = \{i\}$ for each instance i of type α, is a commutative and idempotent monoid, and $bag^\beta = (bag(\beta), \{\!\{\ \}\!\}, f'', \hat{\cup})$, where $f''(i) = \{\!\{i\}\!\}$ for each instance i of type β and $\hat{\cup}$ is the additive bag union, is a commutative monoid. Intuitively, less properties correspond to more structure. For example, the monoid *bag* has more structure than the monoid *set* because repetitions in a *bag* do matter (since it is not idempotent), whereas in a *set* do not (since it is idempotent). Similarly, the monoid *list*, being not commutative, has more structure then the monoid *bag*, which is commutative. For monoids $\mathcal{M}$ and $\mathcal{N}$, we say $\mathcal{N} \preceq \mathcal{M}$ if that $\mathcal{N}$ is commutative (idempotent, resp.) implies that $\mathcal{M}$ is commutative (idempotent, resp.), i.e. $\mathcal{N}$ has the same or less properties than $\mathcal{M}$. This exactly corresponds to the intuitive notion that $\mathcal{N}$ has more structure than $\mathcal{M}$. It is easily seen that $bag^\beta \preceq set^\alpha$. If $\mathcal{N} \preceq \mathcal{M}$, then an instance of type $\mathcal{N}$ can be "translated" deterministically, by using the merge function of the monoid $\mathcal{M}$, into an instance of the type $\mathcal{M}$, but not necessarily vice versa.

Queries on monoids are expressed as monoid comprehensions. A *monoid comprehension* over the monoid $\mathcal{M}$ takes the form

$$\mathcal{M}\{e \mid r_1, \ldots, r_n\}$$

where e is an expression called the *head* of the comprehension, and $r_1, \ldots, r_n$ is a list of *qualifiers*, each of which is either

- an *iterator* of the form $v \leftarrow e'$, where v is a variable, and e' is an expression that evaluates to an instance of a collection monoid of type which is $\preceq \mathcal{M}$ or

- a *selection-predicate*, which is an expression that evaluates to $\texttt{true}$ or $\texttt{false}$.

The expressions in turn can include monoid comprehensions. An important condition for the monoid comprehension is that for each $1 < i \leq n$, each free variable (i.e., free variables in the expressions and predicates) appearing in $r_i, \ldots, r_n$ must appear as the variable of an iterator among $r_1, \ldots, r_{i-1}$, and each free variable in the e must appear as the variable of a iterator among $r_1, \ldots, r_n$.

It is assumed that each instance of a monoid appearing as argument in a monoid comprehension is represented as an expression involving merge, unit and zero functions. For example BAG$\{1, 2, 1, 3\}$ can be represented as

```
merge( merge(unit(1),unit(2)),
       merge(unit(1),unit(3)))
```

or, since merge is associative and zero is a left (and right) identity, as

```
merge( merge( merge( merge( zero,
                            unit(1)),
                     unit(2)),
              unit(1)),
       unit(3))
```

We will assume that every monoid instance is (conceptually) represented this way, and, thus, the notation $\mathcal{N}\{a_1, a_2, \ldots, a_n\}$ will denote the expression

$$\texttt{merge}(\ldots \texttt{merge}(\texttt{merge}(\texttt{zero},\texttt{unit}(a_1)),\texttt{unit}(a_2)), \ldots,\texttt{unit}(a_n))$$

Furthermore, $\mathcal{N}\{\}$, and $\mathcal{N}\{a_1, a_2, \ldots, a_n\}$ where $n = 0$ will both denote $\texttt{zero}^{\mathcal{N}}$, i.e. the empty monoid instance.

A monoid comprehension M over a monoid $\mathcal{M} = (T, \texttt{zero}, \texttt{unit}, \texttt{merge})$(collection or primitive), defines an instance of type T [7] by first initializing result with $\texttt{zero}^{\mathcal{M}}$, and then invoking the procedure insert_MC(result,M) defined recursively by the following reduction rules:

> (r1)   insert_MC(result,$\mathcal{M}\{e \mid\}$)
> $\rightarrow$ result := $\texttt{merge}^{\mathcal{M}}$(result,$\texttt{unit}^{\mathcal{M}}(e)$)
> (r2)   insert_MC(result,$\mathcal{M}\{e \mid \texttt{false}, \vec{r}\}$)
> $\rightarrow$ nil (i.e. do nothing)
> (r3)   insert_MC(result,$\mathcal{M}\{e \mid \texttt{true}, \vec{r}\}$)
> $\rightarrow$ insert_MC(result,$\mathcal{M}\{e \mid \vec{r}\}$)
> (r4)   insert_MC(result, $\mathcal{M}\{e \mid x \leftarrow \mathcal{N}\{a_1, \ldots, a_n\}, \vec{r}\}$)
> $\rightarrow$ for $i = 1$ to n do insert_MC(result,$\mathcal{M}\{e \mid \vec{r}\}[x/a_i]$)

where $\mathcal{N}$ is a collection monoid $(S, \texttt{zero}^{\mathcal{N}}, \texttt{unit}^{\mathcal{N}}, \texttt{merge}^{\mathcal{N}})$ with the condition $\mathcal{N} \preceq \mathcal{M}$. Note that $\mathcal{M}\{e \mid \vec{r}\}[x/a_i]$ denotes the replacement of x with a_i in $\mathcal{M}\{e \mid \vec{r}\}$. Note also that the last rule is deterministic as far as the resulting monoid instance is concerned.

3.2. Monoids in CCUBE

To understand the minimum requirements for primitive and collection monoids, consider the recursive rules defining the result of a monoid comprehension. For the monoid $\mathcal{M}$ to appear in the result of the monoid comprehension, we only need to (1) use $\texttt{zero}^{\mathcal{M}}$ and (2) know how to perform

$$\texttt{result} = \texttt{merge}^{\mathcal{M}}(\texttt{result},\texttt{unit}^{\mathcal{M}}(e))$$

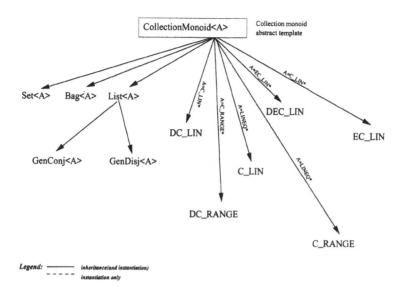

Figure 4. Collection Monoids in CCUBE

which is, in fact the $\text{insert}^{\mathcal{M}}(\text{result}, e)$ operation (i.e. we define $\text{insert}^{\mathcal{M}}$ this way).
[8] In order for the collection monoid $\mathcal{N}$ to appear inside the comprehension, we only need
to be able to *iterate* over $\mathcal{N}\{a_1, \ldots, a_n\}$, i.e. to perform the **for** loop.

The representation (and implementation) of collection monoids in CCUBE is based on
two C++ template classes, parameterized with the type A of collection elements:
CollectionMonoid and Iterator:

```
template < class A > class CollectionMonoid
{
friend class Iterator<A>;
public:
    CollectionMonoid();              //   C++ constructor used as zero
    virtual void Insert( A& ) = 0;
    virtual Iterator<A>* CreateIterator() = 0;
private:                             //   specific subclasses contain
                                     //   actual implementation
};
```

The class CollectionMonoid reflects the minimum requirements: it has zero, implemented as a class constructor, and Insert and CreateIterator member functions. An
Iterator object, created by CreateIterator, has First, More and Next member functions which can be directly used in the C++ **for**-loop. Specific collection monoids implemented in CCUBE, depicted in Figure 4, are implemented each with two classes derived
from the classes CollectionMonoid and Iterator, correspondingly. The collection
monoids list, set, and bag are currently implemented using the ObjectStore collections.

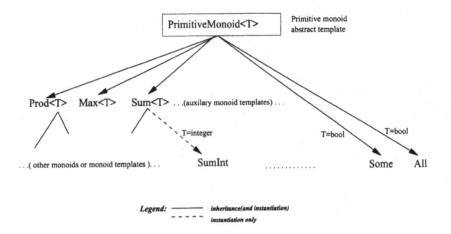

Figure 5. Primitive Monoids in CCUBE

As opposed to collection monoids, primitive ones only require `zero` and the `insert` member function, since they are not used in the query iterators.

```
template < class T > class PrimitiveMonoid
{
public:
   PrimitiveMonoid( );                     // Note: creates zero of monoid
   virtual void Insert( T& ) = 0;
   operator T ();
   static T zero;
protected:
   T value;
};
```

The extensible family of primitive monoids and monoid templates in CCUBE, depicted in Figure 5, includes Prod<T>, Max<T>, Sum<T>, Some and All. Note, that the type used in Some and All is bool. These monoids work as disjunction and conjunction of conditions, respectively.

3.3. Syntax and Semantics of CCUBE queries

The syntax of the CCUBE comprehensions has been explained by examples. More accurately, it is of the form:

```
SELECT C++expr
INTO [{monoid_type}] [result]
[from-where-define-list]
```

`C++expr` in the SELECT clause is an arbitrary C++ expression that evaluates to the type of `result`'s elements. Note that `C++expr` may involve variables instantiated in the FROM clauses and may also contain nested monoid comprehensions. The first (optional) parameter in the INTO clause specifies the type of `result`. If this argument is omitted, the system assumes that `result` is defined elsewhere in the C++ program. When the monoid comprehension is nested, `result` argument may be omitted. The `from-where-define-list` is a sequence of the FROM, DEFINE and WHERE clauses (explained earlier by examples) in any order. Note that any number of iterators, separated by commas, may appear in each FROM clause; further, any number of predicates (conditions) may appear in each WHERE clause. Also important is that nesting is recursively allowed anywhere in the monoid comprehension, provided that nested monoid comprehensions return appropriate types. For instance, collection monoid comprehensions may stand anywhere a collection monoid can; or, monoid comprehensions returning TRUE or FALSE may stand in place of any predicate. This flexibility also enables the use of special algorithms (such as for the constraint and sort join, indexing or regrouping), provided that they produce the appropriate types (e.g. collection monoid) as their outputs.

The semantics of CCUBE monoid comprehension queries is defined by the corresponding formal monoid comprehension. Furthermore, the basic evaluation is by the nested loop algorithm with dynamic buffer management. Important, however, is that the nested monoid comprehension in the FROM clause does not create physical intermediate results, but rather supports the pipe-lining.

4. CST Objects and Constraint Calculus

4.1. Framework for Constraint Algebra and Calculus

CCUBE uses the multi-typed algebra framework of [9], which we review here. As seen in the examples, the notion of CST data relies on a simple and fundamental duality: a constraint (formula) ϕ in free variables $x_1, \ldots, x_n$ is interpreted as a set of tuples $(a_1, \ldots, a_n)$ over the schema $x_1, \ldots, x_n$ that satisfy ϕ; and, conversely, a finitely representable object in $(x_1, \ldots, x_n)$ space can be viewed as a constraint. That is, the syntax is constraints, i.e. symbolic expressions; the semantics are the corresponding, possibly infinite, relations.

CST objects are represented by a sub-family of the first order logic, (i.e. with the logical connectors $\wedge$, $\vee$, $\neg$ and $\exists$) and by a family of atomic constraints, such as linear arithmetic over reals, polynomial or dense order. CST objects are manipulated by means of a *constraint algebra*, whose operators are expressed using a sub-family of the first-order logic, renaming of variables, and atomic (e.g. arithmetic) constraints. For example, if P and Q are CST objects in $x_1, \ldots, x_n$, their intersection can be represented by $P \wedge Q$; union by $P \vee Q$; the test of containment of P in Q by $\forall x_1, \ldots, \forall x_n (P \longrightarrow Q)$ (this is, in fact, the entailment test, ENTAIL); emptiness of P by $\neg \exists x_1, \ldots, \exists x_n P$ (this is, in fact the satisfiability test, SAT); disjointness of P and Q by $\neg \exists x_1, \ldots, \exists x_n (P \wedge Q)$; the projection of P on axes $x_1, \ldots, x_i, 1 \leq i < n$, by $\exists x_{i+1} \ldots \exists x_n P$ etc. If we only use linear constraints over reals, as implemented in CCUBE, within the first-order logic we can express any linear transformation such as rotation, translation and stretch; check convexity, discreteness and boundness [55]; compute the convex hull, augment objects, change coordinate systems; etc.

Thus, constraint objects can be manipulated by a very *expressive language*. Moreover, since this language uses only a small number of operators (i.e. logical connectors and quantifiers), it is also very *compact*, as compared to using a separate operator for each specific type of transformation, which is typically done in extensible or spatial database systems. It is also claimed, that for linear constraints, query languages manipulating constraint objects are deeply *optimizable*, in terms of indexing and filtering (e.g. [12, 35, 51]), and constraint algebra algorithms and global optimization (e.g. [10, 23]).

More specifically, constraint algebras operate on a family $\mathcal{F}$ of canonical representations of constraint expressions (objects). For constraint objects $C_1, \ldots, C_n$ a first-order logic formula $\phi(C_1, \ldots, C_n)$ such as $\exists y (C_1[u_1/y, v_1/z] \wedge \ldots \wedge C_n[u_n/y, v_n/z])$, where $[u_i/y, v_i/z]$ denotes the variable replacement, defines the following constraint algebra operator op: (1) replace each C_i by the corresponding constraint expression, (2) do all variable replacements and (3) transform the resulting constraint expression into the required (equivalent) canonical representation in $\mathcal{F}$. Thus op can be seen as a function from $\mathcal{F} \times \ldots \times \mathcal{F}$ to $\mathcal{F}$. On the other hand, the operator op has the interpretation $\mathcal{I}(op)$, which is a query that maps n relations to one. Given $\mathcal{I}(C_1), \ldots, \mathcal{I}(C_n)$, where $\mathcal{I}(C_i)$, $1 \leq i \leq n$, is the relational interpretation of C_i and $x_1, \ldots, x_m$ are all free variables, $\mathcal{I}(op)$ computes the following relation:

$$\{(x_1, \ldots, x_m) \mid \phi(C_1, \ldots, C_n)\}$$

Clearly, the duality between constraints and point sets carries over to the constraint algebra/calculus, that is, the following commutative property holds:

$$\mathcal{I}(op(C_1, \ldots, C_n)) = \mathcal{I}(op)(\mathcal{I}(C_1), \ldots, \mathcal{I}(C_n))$$

A constraint family $\mathcal{F}$ is defined by choosing (1) an atomic constraint domain, (e.g. polynomial over reals or linear over integers), (2) the structure of the logical formula allowed (e.g. disjunction of conjunctions or existentially quantified disjunction) and (3) the required canonical form (e.g. whether to eliminate existential quantifiers, eliminate each redundant disjunct, extract all implicit equalities in conjunction or eliminate redundancy in conjunctions). The definition of a constraint algebra amounts to choosing the structure of first-order formulae and the atomic constraints allowed in the query.

The challenge here (and a major area of research) is the development of constraint families and algebras, that strike, for each application realm, a careful balance between (1) *expressiveness*, (2) *computational* complexity and, very importantly, (3) *representation usefulness*.

As one extreme, if the entire first-order logic (as studied in [1, 55]), and the same atomic constraints are allowed in both the constraint family $\mathcal{F}$ and the algebra, we get a very expressive algebra with the low data complexity, since no actual manipulation of constraints would be required. However, the representation of the result might consist of a very large unsimplified constraint expression that might not be useful for the user. For instance, the answer to a query "is constraint object C empty" would be $\exists x_1 \ldots \exists x_n C$, where $x_1, \ldots, x_n$ are all free variables, whereas the user expects a true or false answer.

An example of a very expressive, but having high (exponential) time data complexity is the DISCO (Datalog with Integer and Set order COnstrains) query language [16]. Constraint representation is DISCO is useful in many, but not all applications. For example, to express satisfiability of a simple propositional formula, the user needs to encode the formula by a datalog (with constraints) program, in a fairly unnatural way.

Close to the other end, the framework [34] requires a fairly restricted sub-family of first-order logic in constraint objects: disjunction of (unquantified) conjunctions of atomic constraints (the algebra, however, allows more, including quantifier elimination). This representation is useful for many, but not all applications: for example a constraint representation of a triangle given by vertices $(a_1, b_1), (a_2, b_2), (a_3, b_3)$,

$$\exists t_1 \exists t_2 \exists t_3 (x = a_1 t_1 + a_2 t_2 + a_3 t_3 \wedge y = b_1 t_1 + b_2 t_2 + b_3 t_3 \wedge t_1, t_2, t_3 \geq 0 \wedge t_1 + t_2 + t_3 \leq 1)$$

is not directly representable in that framework. Still, for some atomic constraint families, such as linear inequalities over reals, this framework may be computationally unmanageable: the quantifier elimination may result in a constraint exponential in the size of the original conjunction, although for many sub-families more efficient algorithms were developed (e.g. [23, 32, 30, 40]). A more flexible first-order logic structure that allows the entire linear constraints over reals while controlling computational complexity was described in [10, 11].

4.2. CCUBE Constraint Families and Canonical Forms

In CCUBE we concentrate on linear constraint over reals, which are expressive and useful in a variety of application domains. However, in order to control the computational complexity, we design a more flexible first-order logic structure by constructing a number of interrelated constraint families. This continues the line of work in [10, 11].

The six interrelated constraint families in CCUBE are depicted in Figure 6. The four main families are for unrestricted linear constraints over reals: C_LIN, for Conjunctive Linear, stands for constraints represented in the form $\wedge_{i=1}^{n} C_i$, where C_i is a linear inequality; EC_LIN, for Existential Conjunctive, corresponds to the form $\exists \vec{x} \wedge_{i=1}^{n} C_i$; DC_LIN, for Disjunctions of Conjunctions, corresponds to the form $\vee_{i=1}^{m} \wedge_{i=1}^{n} C_{ij}$; and DEC_LIN, for Disjunctions of Existential Conjunctive, corresponds to the form $\exists \vec{x} \vee_{i=1}^{m} \wedge_{j=1}^{n} C_{ij}$. The other two families are for range constraints, i.e. of the form a op x op b, where op is either $<$ or $\leq$ and a and b are either real numbers or $-\infty$ or ∞. Namely, C_RANGE, for Conjunctive Range, stands for constraints represented in the form $\wedge_{i=1}^{n} C_i$, where C_i is a range constraint; and DC_RANGE corresponds to the form $\vee_{i=1}^{m} \wedge_{j=1}^{n} C_{ij}$.

We use the CCUBE notation for operations: not, &&, ||, and (...) for projection. We distinguish between projections on one variable, denoted (one); on zero attributes, denoted (), i.e. all free variables are existentially quantified; on all variables, denoted (all+), i.e. no variables are quantified; and, on any number of attributes, denoted (any), for arbitrary projection. The user is recommended to use the most specific projection operator in order to achieve the strongest (i.e. lowest) resulting types.

25

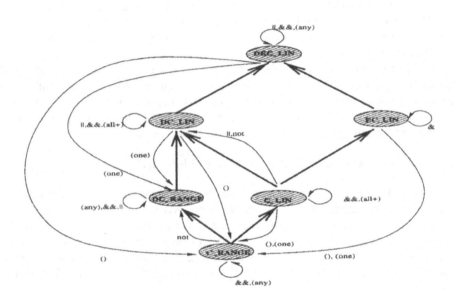

Figure 6. Families of CST Objects

Not only the projections in CCUBE can eliminate existing free variables, but they can also add new ones. For example, a CST $(1 \le x \le 5)$ can be transformed by the "projection" on (x,y) into $(x,y) \mid (1 \le x \le 5)$, thus adding the new free variable y, and getting a new interpretation as a relation over x,y of all tuples with x as required and an arbitrary real number y. However, in the classification of the projection cases discussed earlier, we only consider free variables physically appearing in the constraint expressions.

Thick arrows indicate type hierarchy. For example, C_LIN is a sub-type of DC_LIN, EC_LIN and, transitively, DEC_LIN, meaning that a CST object of type C_LIN may be used as an argument wherever its supertypes are allowed.

Thin arrows indicate, for each constraint family, the allowed operations and the type of the result, which may belong to a different constraint family. For example, && is allowed on C_LIN, returning the result in the same family, while (), and (one) return the result in C_RANGE (which is also in C_LIN as a supertype of C_RANGE). Note, that the result of || on arguments from C_LIN will be in DC_LIN, not in C_LIN. Some of the operations are implicit: for instance, while || does not explicitly appear in C_LIN, it can be applied since it is allowed for its supertype DC_LIN.

Operators may be overloaded: for example && in C_LIN is different from && in DC_LIN; they are implemented differently and return the results of different types (with different representations). The actual operator applied depends on the types of its arguments. As an example, &&(C_LIN,C_LIN) will use the C_LIN operator; whereas, &&(DC_LIN,DC_LIN),

as well as `&&(C_LIN,DC_LIN)` will use the operator from `DC_LIN`. In general, for the application of `op(arg1,arg2)` we use the lattice structure of the type hierarchy, where sub-type $\preceq$ super-type (i.e. the higher the bigger). The actual op chosen is the one of the CST type that is the **least upper bound** of `type(arg1)` and `type(arg2)` on which op is defined. Note, that the CST families are constructed in such a way that, for every op used, such least upper bound, if exists, is unique; hence, there is no ambiguity. If no such bound exists, op is not allowed on `arg1` and `arg2` and would result in a compile-time error.

For users of the CCUBE CST library it is easy to remember what's allowed and what's not. `&&`, `||`, and `()` can be freely applied on arguments of any CST family. Only not is restricted: it can only be applied to arguments of the type `C_LIN` (and thus its sub-type `C_RANGE`). The system will always produce the strongest (i.e. least) type possible for the resulting constraint.

In addition to the logical algebraic operators, all families have the following operators:

1. `RENAME(CST_obj,''x1/e1,...,xN/eN'')` where `x1,...,xN` are the names of the variables to be replaced with the variables `e1,...,eN`.

2. `SAT(CST_obj)` to check satisfiability of the argument, i.e. whether there exists an assignment of real constants into its free variables that makes it true. There is also `MUT_SAT(CST_obj_1, CST_obj_2)` which is equivalent to `SAT(CST_obj_1 && CST_obj_2)`.

3. `TRUTH_VALUE(Var_Assign,CST_obj)` returns the truth value of the CST under the assignment `Var_Assign` of constants into the `CST_obj` free variables.

4. `MIN_POINT(lin_func,CST_obj)` and `MAX_POINT(lin_func,CST_obj)` where `lin_func` is a linear function with real coefficients. Returned is the assignment of constants into the variables of `lin_func` that maximizes it subject to the constraints in the CST.

5. `MIN(var_name,CST_obj)` and `MAX(var_name,CST_obj)` that return MIN and MAX of the first argument subject to the constraints in the second.

Note that the MIN and MAX operators correspond to the problem of linear programming. In addition, `ENTAIL(DC_LIN,C_LIN)` operator is allowed.[9]

Finally, since all the disjunctive CST objects can be considered as collections of disjuncts and all the conjunctive CST objects as collection of conjuncts, we make these CST families CCUBE collection monoids by implementing the required iterators and member functions.

The six CST families are carefully constructed with the complexity consideration in mind as follows. First, all operations allowed on the families have polynomial data complexity. This is the reason, for example, that `C_LIN` is not closed under the general projection: transforming the result into `C_LIN` will require quantifier elimination and thus the size of the result (and, of course, time complexity) may be exponential in the number of variables eliminated. Whereas, `EC_LIN` is closed under the general projection since the general projection in `EC_LIN` is *lazy*: `EC_LIN` allows quantifiers in the internal representation and hence no physical quantifier elimination is performed. Similar, not is allowed on conjunctive CST families, `C_RANGE` and `C_LIN`, but not on, say, `DC_LIN`. The reason is that transforming an expression of the form $\neg \vee \wedge C$ or, of the form $\wedge \vee \neg C$, into DC_LIN may result in an expression of an exponential size, which we would like to avoid. We discuss what operators involve computationally in more detail in the next subsection.

The CST families use canonical forms, i.e. useful standard forms of constraints, that we adopt in CCUBE from [41, 10] and review here from [10]. For CST objects in the disjunctive families, some disjuncts might be redundant in the sense that omitting them results in an equivalent constraint. Clearly, a canonical form that eliminates such disjuncts would be desirable. However, the problem of detecting such tuples is co-NP-complete [51], and so we will perform only one simplification of disjunctions: the deletion of inconsistent disjuncts.

For CST objects in the conjunctive families, there are a number of simplifications that can be requested by the user. One choice is to write all the equations in the form $\{x_i = t_i \mid i = 1, \ldots, n\}$ where x_i's are distinct and appear nowhere else in the constraint. A second choice is whether all equations which are implicit in the inequality constraints should be represented explicitly. (As a simple example of this, consider the constraints $x + y \leq 2, x + y \geq 2$.) A third is the extent to which redundancy within the inequalities should be removed. [41] presents a classification of redundancy that suggests simple forms of redundancy removal. A fourth choice is whether to keep the inequalities in a different form, such as the simplex tableau form. In the current CCUBE implementation, the only simplification is the removal of inconsistent disjuncts in the disjunctive families; however, a range of simplifications on the conjunctions is presently being implemented.

4.3. Implementation of CST families

On the conjunctive families, the && operator simply combines its arguments and is constant time; (one)| C, which is a projection on a single variable, involves applying a linear program (using the simplex algorithm of CPLEX) twice for finding the minimum and the maximum of the variable subject to C; ( )|C, which is eliminating all variables in C works as a satisfiability test, using the first phase of the simplex, as does the SAT predicate.

On the disjunctive families, the || operator is constant-time, while D1 && D2, where $D1 = \vee_{i=1\ldots n}C1_i$ and $D2 = \vee_{j=1\ldots m}C2_j$ is more involved:

$$D1 \wedge D2 = \bigvee_{i=1,\ldots,n} C1_i \wedge \bigvee_{i=1\ldots m} C2_j = \bigvee_{i=1\ldots n, j=1\ldots m} (C1_i \wedge C2_j)$$

that is, the result consists of all combinations of $C1_i$ and $C2_j$ that are mutually consistent (i.e. their conjunction is satisfiable). Since the CST families are monoids, D1 && D2 is implemented as the following CCUBE query:

```
SELECT *c1 && *c2
INTO   {DEC_LIN} conj_D1_and_D2
FROM   D1 AS {EC_LIN*} c1,
       D2 AS {EC_LIN*} c2
WHERE SAT(*c1,*c2)
```

We show how such queries are optimized using the approximation-based filtering, indexing and re-groupings in the next section. Similar, SAT(D), where D is of the type DEC_LIN (as well as other disjunctive families) is represented as

```
SELECT SAT(*c)
INTO   {Some} satisf_flag
FROM   D AS {EC_LIN*} c
```

Note, that c is of the type EC_LIN and so SAT in the WHERE clause works on conjunctions. Further recall that Some is a primitive monoid whose merge operator is a logical or; thus, the satisf-flag will be true if and only if at least one component is true. Finally, ENTAIL(D,C), where D is DC_LIN and C is C_LIN, is represented as

```
SELECT ENTAIL(*c,C)
INTO   {Some} imply_flag
FROM   D AS {C_LIN*} c
```

Beyond the algorithms for constraint operations discussed, there are two subtle design problems that we address in CCUBE: compile-time maintenance of the type lattice and a lazy evaluation. Support for the lazy evaluation of constraint (i.e. involving CST) expressions is necessary for efficiency. For example, if we are interested in the SAT test of an expression involving logical connectors, it is typically wasteful to perform simplifications of subexpressions.

To exemplify the problem arising from the type lattice maintenance, consider the && operator. In fact, while && has one conceptual meaning, it works differently in every CST family. Moreover, since && is defined on DEC_LIN, the arguments may be any subtypes of DEC_LIN. Thus, every ordered pair of (sub) types for arguments of && works uniquely: we need to find the least upper bound type, to perform corresponding type conversions, and then to apply the physical algorithm of the resulting CST family. One possibility is implementing a separate function for each pair of subtypes, but this would result in a quadratic number of functions for each logical operator: 30 for the six families, and impractically many for future extensions of CCUBE with new CST families. On the other hand, the direct implementation of a subtype relationship using the C++ inheritance mechanism does not work, since each family has its own implementation, data-structures etc, which should not be inherited by its subclasses. Of course, there is also a possibility of maintaining just one global CST type, and to distinguish individual subfamilies only at run time. This, however, would eliminate the capability of the compile-time type checking, an important feature of CCUBE.

To solve the type lattice problem we designed a two-layer architecture for the CST families: the lower layer, called basic_CST, supports the physical representation and manipulation of the CST families; the upper layer, called lazy_typed_CST, is responsible for the type lattice management and the lazy evaluation, while the actual evaluation is passed to the lower, basic_CST layer.

The basic_CST layer is composed of the six classes basic_C_LIN, basic_DC_LIN etc., each maintaining its own data structures to represent the underlying constraints; and one super (base) class, basic_CST. No automatic type casts are supported on this layer. However, each basic family has member functions for explicit type conversions into basic types that are higher in the type hierarchy. For example, transforming basic_C_LIN into basic_DC_LIN creates a basic_DC_LIN object (disjunction) that has a single disjunct in it.

The lazy_typed_CST layer, on the other hand, does support automatic sub-typing and the ability to determine the least upper bounds of operators' arguments at compile-time. The six families lazy_typed_C_LIN, lazy_typed_DC_LIN etc., are implemented as six classes with a class hierarchy that exactly matches the type hierarchy of the CST families. However, all the lazy_typed classes have similar internal representation, which is inherited from the abstract class lazy_typed_CST. The representation is basically an expression tree (hence "lazy"), with internal nodes storing the constraint operators (such as && or ||) and encoding the strongest type to which the subtree can be converted; the leaves are objects of the lower layer, basic_CST. It is important to emphasize that the CST type checking we do in CCUBE heavily uses capabilities of C++ and would be impossible (at compile-time without any precompiling) in languages such as C.

The CCUBE system also supports two generic parameterized CST families: Gen_Conj<T> for generic conjunctions and Gen_Disj<T> for generic disjunctions, where T is an arbitrary, possibly complex, CST type. Both are collection monoids and support the TRUTH_VALUE function; further, SAT is supported by Gen_Disj<T> provided it is supported by T. Also ENTAIL(Gen_Disj<T>,T) is defined provided it is defined on T. These operations are represented again with monoid comprehension queries. For example, SAT(D), where D is of the type Gen_Disj<T>, is represented as

```
SELECT SAT(c)
INTO   {Some} satisf_flag
FROM   D AS {T} c
```

Finally, we explain how the native C++ syntax is preserved in constraint formulas, such as in 2 <= z <= 5 && x + z <= 7. The logical connective && is supported by the C_LIN class. In turn, each of the C++ expressions 2 <= z <= 5 and x + z <= 7 must yield an object of type C_LIN. This is done by overloading operators <= and +. Clearly, in such an expression, x and z must be C++ variables that have already been declared within an appropriate C++ scope (the usual C++ scoping rules apply). The type for the C++ variables x and z is a special class, called CST_Var, which keeps inside the constraint variable name, i.e. a string. It is convenient, although not required, to use the same name for a constraint variable name and the corresponding C++ variable into which the constraint variable is assigned. Each CST object keeps inside its free constraint variables that can be also shared among different CST objects.

5. Optimization by Approximation-based Filtering and Indexing

General optimization of object-oriented queries (e.g. ENCORE [58], O2 [21], POSTGRES [54]) and monoid comprehensions in particular, (e.g. [22]), as well as optimization in presence of expensive predicates [17, 29] is outside the scope of this paper; We concentrate here on approximation-based filtering, regrouping and indexing [14], that

CCUBE is designed to support. More specifically, we describe, mostly by examples, the CCUBE primitives for *approximation* and *inverse groupings* [14], *indices* and special purpose algorithms.

To understand the idea, we use a modification of an example from [14] of the query: "find all trajectories passing over the Fairfax county". It will be assumed here that a set of 4D aircraft trajectories as well as a map is stored in the database. A trajectory is assumed to have a piece-wise linear representation, i.e. it is represented as a DC_LIN CST object

$$\bigvee_{i=1}^{n} (t_{i-1} \le t < t_i \wedge x = a_{i,1}t + b_{i,1} \wedge y = a_{i,2}t + b_{i,2} \wedge z = a_{i,3}t + b_{i,3})$$

Where x, y, z are variables for a location, t is a time variable, and $t_{i-1}, a_{i,1}, b_{i,1}, a_{i,2}, b_{i,2}, a_{i,3}, b_{i,3}, 1 \le i \le n$, are constants. Note that for each i, $(t_{i-1} \le t < t_i \wedge x = a_{i,1}t + b_{i,1} \wedge y = a_{i,2}t + b_{i,2} \wedge z = a_{i,3}t + b_{i,3})\}$ describe the movement equations for the time interval $[t_{i-1}, t_i)$, for the constant 3-D velocity vector $(a_{i,1}, a_{i,2}, a_{i,3})$, starting from the point $(b_{i,1}, b_{i,2}, b_{i,3})$. All_trajectories is a variable of type SET<DC_LIN*>, i.e. a set of pointers to trajectories. The Fairfax county is assumed to be represented as a polygon,[10] i.e. as a C_LIN CST object Fairfax_area in variables x and y. The query can be directly expressed in CCUBE as

```
SELECT traj
INTO {Set<DC_LIN*>} result
FROM All_Trajectories AS {DC_LIN*} traj
WHERE  MUT_SAT(*traj, Fairfax_area )          // Note: MUT_SAT
                                              //    on DC_LIN
```

or, if MUT_SAT is expressed, in turn, as a monoid comprehension:

```
SELECT traj
INTO {Set<DEC_LIN*>} result
FROM All_Trajectories AS {DC_LIN*} traj
WHERE SELECT MUT_SAT(*segment,Fairfax_area)   // Note: MUT_SAT
         INTO {Some}                          //    on C_LIN
         FROM *traj AS {C_LIN*} segment       // SELECT returns
                                              //    True of False
```

which is an expensive query if evaluated directly.

Inverse Grouping(IG)

To optimize the last query, we can first use the *inverse grouping*, described graphically in Figure 7. Intuitively, each trajectory can be viewed as composed of 4D-segments, and each segment has a projection, say an xy-segment on the horizontal plane x,y.

Now, consider a collection of all xy-segments that originate from all the trajectories. The *inverse grouping primitive* tracks back, for each xy-segment in the collection, the set of all the trajectories from which this xy-segment came.

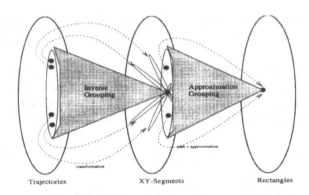

Figure 7. Inverse and Approximation Grouping

The correspondence between an xy-segment and the set of trajectories is captured through a parameterized C++ class G_Pair<T1,T2> which represents a pair containing a reference to an object of type T1 (C_LIN* in our case) as its first element and a reference to a set of objects of type T2 (DC_LIN* in our case) as its second element. The inverse grouping is captured through a special C++ class which essentially represents a set of G_Pair-s. To create an inverse grouping the user must create an instance of that class, passing the original collection as a constructor parameter. Assuming that All_Traj_IG has been created as the inverse grouping for the All_Traj collection, we can now re-write the previous query as follows:

```
SELECT traj
INTO {Set<DC_LIN*>} result
FROM  All_Traj_IG AS {G_Pair<C_LIN*,DC_LIN*>*} G_pair
//
DEFINE xy_segment AS {C_LIN*} G_pair->first
WHERE MUT_SAT( *xy_segment, Fairfax_area )          // Note: MUT_SAT
                                                    //   on C_LIN

DEFINE trajectories_of_xy_segment
        AS {Set<DC_LIN*>*} G_pair->second
FROM  *trajectories_of_xy_segment AS {DC_LIN*} traj
```

First note that the new query is equivalent to the previous one. The reason is that a trajectory passes over the Fairfax_area if and only if one of its xy-segment intersects the Fairfax_area. The new query, however, is likely to perform better. Note that different trajectories may "share" the same xy-segment, for example if one passes exactly above another. Therefore, the previous query will apply the MUT_SAT (i.e. intersection) test multiple times for every shared xy-segment. Whereas, in the last query we eliminate such duplication by checking MUT_SAT for each xy-segment only once and then quickly retrieving the corresponding trajectories using the inverse grouping.

Approximation Grouping(AG)

Even though we have minimized the number of the MUT_SAT checks, we know that MUT_SAT on C_LIN is relatively expensive. To optimize further, we can approximate each xy-segment with a minimum bounded box (MBOX), which is of type C_RANGE. Then, before testing MUT_SAT on C_LIN it can be tested first on MBOXes, which is cheaper. Also, it opens opportunities for indexing. This is the purpose of the *approximation grouping* primitive, which we introduce next. Intuitively, approximation grouping takes a collection of objects and creates another collection. The elements of the latter are approximations of the objects from the original one (see dashed lines in Figure 7). The approximation grouping, similar to the inverse one, must track back, for each approximation, the set of original objects that yield this approximation.

The implementation of the approximation grouping is similar to that of inverse grouping. It uses the same class G_Pair<T1,T2> which now represents the relationship between an approximation and the corresponding objects. The approximation grouping is constructed by creating an object of a special class, passing the original collection and the approximation method as constructor parameters. As in the case of inverse grouping, the object being created represents a set of G_Pair-s. To continue the optimization of the last query the original collection in our case would be the inverse grouping collection All_Traj_IG. Recall that All_Traj_IG is a set of inverse grouping pairs G_Pair<C_LIN*,DC_LIN*>. If we define an approximation of an inverse grouping pair as an approximation of its first element (i.e. xy-segment) then we can create an approximation grouping object All_Traj_IG_AG which would be a set of G_Pair<C_RANGE*,G_Pair<C_LIN*,DC_LIN*>*>-s.

We can now re-write the last query as follows:

```
SELECT traj
INTO {Set<DC_LIN*>} result
//
FROM All_Traj_IG_AG AS {G_Pair<C_RANGE*,G_Pair<C_LIN*,
                                              DC_LIN*>*>*} AG_pair
 DEFINE min_box_of_xy_segment AS {C_RANGE*} AG_pair->first
 WHERE  MUT_SAT(*min_box_of_xy_segment,  // On C_RANGE;
                min_box_of_Fairfax)      // precomputed outside
                                         // of the query
 DEFINE Candidate_Traj_IG AS {Set<G_Pair<C_LIN*,DC_LIN*>*>*}
                                              AG_pair->second
//
FROM  *Candidate_Traj_IG  AS {G_Pair<C_LIN*,DC_LIN*>*} IG_pair
DEFINE xy_segment  AS {C_LIN*} IG_pair->first
WHERE Mut_Sat( *xy_segment, Fairfax_area )    // Note: MUT_SAT
                                              //   on C_LIN
DEFINE trajectories_of_xy_segment
AS{Set<DC_LIN*>*}\\ IG_pair->second
FROM *trajectories_of_xy_segment AS traj
```

Indexed Approximation Grouping(IAG)

The last query involves the retrieval of rectangles that are mutually consistent with a given one. Another optimization possibility is to maintain an index on the collection of rectangles. This is done using the *indexed approximation grouping*, instead of the approximation grouping. The IAG has the same functionality as the approximation grouping with the following differences: 1) the first element of an IAG pair is always a rectangle (i.e. of type C_RANGE) and 2) there is a kD-tree index imposed on the rectangles. The IAG is constructed by creating an object of a special class which, in addition to the approximation grouping functionality, contains member functions for search. In our example we create an indexed approximation grouping object named All_Traj_IG_IAG. As in the case of approximation grouping, All_Traj_IG_IAG is a set of G_Pair<C_RANGE*,G_Pair<C_LIN*,DC_LIN*>*>-s. In the query we invoke the MUT_SAT(C_RANGE) method on that object. The method returns, for each MBOX (of type C_RANGE), the set of all G_Pair<C_LIN*,DC_LIN*>*-s for which the corresponding rectangles intersect that MBOX.

Note, that the returned set is not a physical set collection, but rather a structure allowing to iterate over its elements (and thus no intermediate evaluation is necessary when used within monoid comprehension). The last query can be re-written as follows:

```
SELECT traj
INTO {Set<DC_LIN*>} result
//
FROM All_Traj_IG_IAG.MUT_SAT(min_box_of_Fairfax)
  AS {Set<G_Pair<C_LIN*,DC_LIN*>*>*} Candidate_Traj_IG
//
FROM  *Candidate_Traj_IG  AS {G_Pair<C_LIN*,DC_LIN*>*} IG_pair
DEFINE xy_segment  AS {C_LIN*} IG_pair->first
WHERE Mut_Sat( *xy_segment, Fairfax )              // Note: MUT_SAT
                                                   //  on C_LIN
//
DEFINE trajectories_of_xy_segment AS {Set<DC_LIN*>*} IG_pair->second
FROM  *trajectories_of_xy_segment AS traj
```

It is important to note, that, while we intuitively explained the use of the IG, AG and IAG by examples, these primitives can be applied to any CollectionMonoid<A>. For the IG the user needs to provide a transformation producing, for each element of type A an instance of (another) commutative and idempotent monoid (see [14] for details). For the AG and IAG, an approximation of elements of type A must be provided by the user. The IG, AG and IAG are used to facilitate the query transformation rules supporting approximation-based filtering (by using less expensive predicates first) and indexing (see [14]).

6.   Related Work

No technology for declarative and efficient querying of databases involving constraint objects exists today. Applications of the kind discussed are typically implemented by special purpose programs; while these programs may use database and constraint programming tools, they typically require a considerable programming effort and are not flexible to changes. In addition, they do not perform overall optimization that interleaves database, mathematical programming and computational geometry manipulation techniques. Existing DBMS do not manage constraints as persistently stored data.[11] Constraint Logic Programming [31, 20, 19], on the other hand, was not designed to deal with large amounts of persistent data. Extensions of DBMS with spatio-temporal operators [46, 26, 57, 27] typically (1) are limited to low (two- or, at most three-) dimensional space, (2) have query languages restricted to predefined spatio-temporal operators, and (3) lack global economical filtering and deep optimization.

There has been work on the use of constraints in databases, earlier of which include [38, 28, 18, 48, 13]. The pioneering work [34] proposed a framework for integrating abstract constraints into database query languages by providing a number of design principles, and studied, mostly in terms of expressiveness and complexity, a number of specific instances. The work [28] considered polynomial equality constraints, adopting local propagation steps for reasoning on constraints. A restricted form of linear constraints, called *linear repeating points*, was used to model infinite sequences of time points [33, 4, 45]. More recent works on deductive databases [44, 52, 36, 42] considered the manipulation and repositioning of constraints for optimizing recursion. Algorithms for constraint algebra operators such as constraint joins, and generic global optimization were studied in [10], and constraint approximation-based optimization in [14]. The work [35] proposed an efficient data structure for secondary storage suitable for indexing constraints, that achieves not only the optimal space and time complexity as priority search trees [43], but also full clustering. The work [12] proposed an approach to achieve the optimal quality of constraint and spatial filtering. A number of works consider special constraint domains: integer order constraints [49]; set constraints [50]; dense-order constraints [24]. Linear constraints over reals drew special attention [2, 1, 10, 11, 12, 25, 55]. The use of constraints in spatial database queries was addressed in [47]. The work [53] used constraints to describe incomplete information. Constraint aggregation was studied in [39].

DISCO (Datalog with Integer and Set order Constraints) is a constraint database system being developed at the university of Nebraska [16]. DISCO incorporates a highly expressive family of constraints. However, its query language has time complexity exponential in the size of a database; hence DISCO's applicability to real-size database problems is not clear. Further, DISCO does not support the standard database features such as persistent storage, transaction management and data integrity.

7. Conclusions and Future Work

We first summarize some lessons we learned while building the CCUBE system.

The two-layer implementation of the constraint algebra was a simple and extensible solution to the problem of finding the appropriate C++ structures. The experiences learned while implementing the algebra can be applied to the C++ implementation of other similar multi-typed algebras.

Using ObjectStore and CPLEX as underlying components allowed us to concentrate on issues related to constraint implementation and to ignore many common aspects such as the simplex algorithm, persistence, data integrity etc.

However, in the process of development many problems came up while coding and maintaining some ObjectStore-specific parts. The goal was to put the library on a higher level, making it more flexible and uniform to use. Also, we did not want to tie the library design to the specific components used underneath. Rather, we aimed to make it portable enough to be easily transfered on the top of another object manager and/or LP package. This has been achieved by implementing an intermediate interface between CCUBE and the underlying components, which isolated the developers and users of the system from ObjectStore technicalities. In order to use a different object manager/LP package, only a relatively small part of the code will have to be re-written. A lot of effort has gone in making this interface both portable and easy to use.

Still, a fair amount of time has been spent on the implementation of the supporting structures such as search trees and sparse matrices. Even though there are some C++ packages that handle these issues, none of them was flexible enough to be directly plugged in CCUBE.

Currently CCUBE does not parse the full C++ grammar. Instead, there is a pre-compiler that passes its output over to the C++ compiler. CCUBE queries are embedded in hosting C++ programs and are allowed to use variables declared in the appropriate scope (with some restrictions). During the implementation of this scheme we encountered some non-trivial technical problems that required much effort to resolve.

It is important to note that C++ was the best pragmatic choice for our purposes. Its compactness and expressivness power enabled us to make things that would be hardly possible in any other programming language. The library extensively uses templates, operator overloading and multiple inheritance. Those features also provided higher reusability of components which allowed us to reduce the total amount of the source code (around 11,000 lines now, not including the commercial components).

Even though the query language we presented is an optimization-level language in which evaluation plans can be explicitly expressed, we found that the optimization primitives are not currently automated to the extent they can possibly be. For example, similar to a regular index, the grouping primitives require dynamic maintenance. If there is an update in the original collection, the corresponding change must be made in the grouping structures. CCUBE does not support the dynamic updates in the current implementation. The work in this direction is currently being performed.

We have described the work on the development of the first constraint object-oriented database system. Our work aims at the developing a practical and useful technology for a wide variety of important application realms, for which no existing technology is applicable. For example, CCUBE can be directly used to implement the real-life data fusion and sensor management system for air-space command and control [2]. CCUBE is a deeply optimizable and extensible system, striking the balance between expressiveness and computational complexity.

Many research questions remain open (see [9] for an overview): in constraint modeling and canonical forms, data models and query languages, indexing and approximation-based filtering, and, most importantly, special constraint algebra algorithms for specific domains and global optimization.

Acknowledgments

The authors wish to thank the anonymous referees for the time they spent on the insightful comments that were very helpful in improving this paper. This work was supported in part by NSF RIA grant No. 92-122, Office of Naval Research under prime grant No. N00014-94-1-1153.

Notes

1. In fact, the name CCUBE was originated from the shorthand C^3 for Constraint Comprehension Calculus.

2. using finite precision arithmetic

3. As explained in later sections, users can view the constraint layer as either calculus, or algebra, interchangeably.

4. The real algorithm also deals with many other issues such as persistence, dynamic buffer management, type management and interface with C++ etc.

5. In fact, as discussed in further sessions, the formal definition of monoid comprehension disallows to create LIST collection in result in our example, since it has more "structure" than BAG, on of the collection types used inside; we, however, do allow such situation.

6. We use $[a_1, \ldots, a_n]$ to denote a list and $\{\!\{a_1, \ldots, a_k\}\!\}$ to denote a bag.

7. Our definition here is different from, but equivalent to the original one; ours is closer to the implementation.

8. For a primitive monoid the name insert is probably strange; we really mean by insert exactly result := merge(result, unit$^\mathcal{M}$(e)). For example, for primitive monoid sum $(int, +, 0, \text{identity})$, insert$^\mathcal{M}$(result, 5) is result:=result+ 5.

9. and, of course, for all subtypes of C_LIN and DC_LIN

10. in fact, it is not convex, but we'll assume that to simplify the example

11. Note, integrity constraints used in conventional databases are not data, but rather something the data must satisfy.

References

1. F. Afrati, S. Cosmadakis, S. Grumbach & G. Kuper.(1994). Linear versus polynomial constraints in database query languages. In A. Borning, editor, *Proc. 2nd International Workshop on Principles and Practice of Constraint Programming*, volume 874 of *Lecture Notes in Computer Science*, pages 181–192, Rosario, WA. Springer Verlag.

2. T. Aschenbrenner, A. Brodsky & Y. Kornatzky.(1995). Constraint database approach to spatio-temporal data fusion and sensor management. In *Proc. ILPS95 Workshop on Constraints, Databases and Logic Programming*, Portland, OR.

3. T. Atwood, D. Barry, J. Dubl, J. Eastman, G Ferran, D. Jordan, M. Loomis & D. Wade.(1996). *The Object Database Standard: ODMG-93*. Morgan Kaufmann.

4. M. Baudinet, M. Niezette & P. Wolper.(1991). On the representation of infinite temporal data and queries. In *Proc. ACM SIGACT-SIGART-SIGMOD Symp. on Principles of Database Systems*.

5. M. Benjamin, T. Viana, K. Corbett & A. Silva.(1993). Satisfying multiple rated-constraints in a knowledge based decision aid. In *Proc. IEEE Conf. on Artificial Intelligence Applications*, Orlando, FL.

6. V. Breazu-Tannen, P. Beneman & S. Naqvi.(1991). Structural recursion as a query language. In *Proc. Third International Workshop on Database Programming Languages*.

7. V. Breazu-Tannen, P. Buneman & L. Wong.(1992). Naturally embedded query languages. In *Proc. 4-th International Conference on Database Theory*.

8. V. Breazu-Tannen & R. Subrahmanyan.(1991). Logical and computational aspects of programming with sets/bags/lists. In *Proc. 18-th International Colloquium on Automata, Languages and Programming*.

9. A. Brodsky.(1996). Constraint databases: Promising technology or just intellectual exercise? In Proc. ACM workshop on strategic directions in Computing Research, MIT, Boston. Also, ACM Computing Surveys, electronic version, and Constraints Journal, to appear.

10. A. Brodsky, J. Jaffar & M.J. Maher.(1993). Toward practical constraint databases. In *Proc. 19th International Conference on Very Large Data Bases*, Dublin, Ireland.

11. A. Brodsky & Y. Kornatzky.(1995). The lyric language: Quering constraint objects. In Carey and Schneider, editors, *Proc. ACM SIGMOD International Conference on Management of Data*, San Jose, CA.

12. A. Brodsky, C. Lassez, J.-L. Lassez & M. J. Maher.(1995). Separability of polyhedra for optimal filtering of spatial and constraint data. In *Proc. ACM SIGACT-SIGMOD-SIGART Symposium on Principles of Database Systems*. ACM Press.

13. A. Brodsky & Y. Sagiv.(1989) Inference of monotonicity constraints in datalog programs. In *Proc. ACM SIGACT-SIGART-SIGMOD Symp. on Principles of Database Systems*, pages 190–199, Philadelphia, PA.

14. A. Brodsky & X. S. Wang.(1995). On approximation-based query evaluation, expensive predicates and constraint objects. In *Proc. ILPS95 Workshop on Constraints, Databases and Logic Programming*, Portland, OR.

15. P. Buneman, L. Libkin, D. Suciu, V. Tannen & L. Wong.(1994). Comprehension syntax. *SIGMOD Record*.

16. J.-H. Byon & P. Revesz.(1995). Disco: A constraint database system with sets. In *CONTESSA Workshop on Constraint Databases and Applications*.

17. S. Chauduri & K. Shim.(1993). Query optimization in the presence of foreign functions. In *Proc. 19th International Conference on Very Large Data Bases*.

18. J. Chomicki & T. Imielinski.(1989). Relational specifications of infinite query answers. In *Proc. ACM SIGMOD International Conference on Management of Data*, pages 174–183.

19. A. Colmerauer.(1990). An introduction to prolog 3. *Communications of the ACM* 33:69-90.

20. M. Dincbas, P. Van Hentenryck, H. Simnis, A. Aggoun, T. Graf & F. Berthier.(1988). The constraint logic programming language chip. In *Proc. Fifth Generation Computer Systems*, Tokyo, Japan.

21. O. Deux et. al.(1990). The story of o2. *IEEE Transactions on Knowledge and Data Engineering*.

22. L. Fegaras & D. Maier.(1995). Toward an effective calculus for object query processing. In *Proc. ACM SIGMOD Conf. on Management of Data*.

23. D. Q. Goldin & P.C. Kanellakis.(1996). Constraint query algebras. *Constraints* 1:45–83.

24. S. Grumbach & J. Su.(1995). Dense-order constraint databases. In *Proc. ACM SIGACT-SIGMOD-SIGART Symp. on Principles of Database Systems*.

25. S. Grumbach, J. Su & C. Tollu.(1994) Linear constraint query languages: Expressive power and complexity. In D. Leivant, editor, *Logic and Computational Complexity*, Indianapolis. Springer Verlag. LNCS 960.

26. R.H. Guting.(1989). Gral: An extensible relational database system for geometric applications. In *Proc. 19th Symp. on Very Large Databases*.

27. L.M. Haas & W.F. Cody.(1991). Exploiting extensible dbms in integrated geographic information systems. In *Proc. Advances in Spatial Databases, 2nd Symposium*, volume 525 of *Lecture Notes in Computer Science*. Springer Verlag.

28. M.R. Hansen, B.S. Hansen, P. Lucas & P. van Emde Boaz.(1989). Integrating relational databases and constraint languages. *Computer Languages* 14:63–82.

29. J.M. Hellerstein & M. Stonebraker.(1993). Predicate migration: optimizing queries with expensive predicates. In *Proc. ACM SIGMOD Conf. on Managment of Data*.

30. T. Huynh, C. Lassez & J-L. Lassez.(1990). Practical issues on the projection of polyhedral sets. *Annals of Mathematics and Artificial Intelligence* (forthcoming). Also IBM Research Report RC 15872, IBM T.J. Watson RC.

31. J. Jaffar & J-L. Lassez.(1987). Constraint logic programming. In *Proc. Conf. on Principles of Programming Languages*, pages 111–119.

32. J. Jaffar, M.J. Maher, P.J. Stuckey & R.H.C. Yap.(1992). Output in clp(r). In *Proc. Int. Conf. on Fifth Generation Computer Systems*, volume 2, pages 987–995, Tokyo, Japan.

33. F. Kabanza, J.-M. Stevenne, & P. Wolper.(1990) Handling infinite temporal data. In *Proc. ACM SIGACT-SIGMOD-SIGART Symp. on Principles of Database Systems*.
34. P. Kanellakis, G. Kuper & P. Revesz.(1990). Constraint query languages. *J. Computer and System Sciences* (forthcoming). A preliminary version appeared in *Proc. 9th PODS*, pages 299–313, 1990.
35. P. Kanellakis, S. Ramaswamy, D.E. Vengroff & J.S. Vitter.(1993). Indexing for data models with constraints and classes. In *Proc. ACM SIGACT-SIGMOD-SIGART Symposium on Principles of Database Systems*.
36. D. Kemp & P. Stuckey.(1992). Bottom up constraint logic programming without constraint solving. Technical report, Dept. of Computer Science, University of Melbourne.
37. (1992) M. Kifer, W. Kim & Y. Sagiv.(1992). Querying object-oriented databases. In *Proc. ACM SIGMOD Intl. Conf. on Management of Data*, pages 393–402.
38. A. Klug.(1988). On conjunctive queries containing inequalities. *Journal of ACM* 35:146–160.
39. G. M. Kuper.(1993) Aggregation in constraint databases. In *Proc. Workshop on Principles and Practice of Constraint Programming*.
40. (1991). C. Lassez & J-L. Lassez. Quantifier elimination for conjunctions of linear constraints via a convex hull algorithm. Technical Report RC16779, IBM T.J. Watson Research Center.
41. J-L. Lassez, T. Huynh & K. McAloon.(1989). Simplification and elimination of redundant linear arithmetic constraints. In *Proc. North American Conference on Logic Programming*, pages 35–51, Cleveland, OH.
42. A. Levy & Y. Sagiv.(1992). Constraints and redundancy in datalog. In *Proc. 11-th ACM SIGACT-SIGMOD-SIGART Symp. on Principles of Database Systems*.
43. E.M. McCreight.(1985). Priority search trees. *SIAM Journal of Computing* 14:257–276.
44. I.S. Mumick, S.J. Finkelstein, H. Pirahesh & R. Ramakrishnan.(1990). Magic conditions. In *Proc. ACM SIGACT-SIGMOD-SIGART Symposium on Principles of Database Systems*, pages 314–330.
45. M. Niezette & J.-M. Stevenne.(1992). An efficient symbolic representation of periodic time. In *Proc. of First International Conference on Information and Knowledge management*.
46. J.A. Orenstein & F.A. Manola.(1988). Probe spatial data modeling and query processing in an image database application. *IEEE Trans. on Software Engineering* 14:611–629.
47. J. Paredaens, J. Van den Bussche & D. Van Gucht.(1994). Towards a theory of spatial database queries. In *Proc. ACM SIGACT-SIGMOD-SIGART Symp. on Principles of Database Systems*.
48. R. Ramakrishnan.(1991). Magic templates: A spellbinding approach to logic programs. *J. Logic Programming* 11:189–216.
49. P. Z. Revesz.(1993) A closed form for datalog queries with integer order. *Theoretical Computer Science* 116:pp.
50. P. Z. Revesz.(1995). Datalog queries of set constraint databases. In *Proc. International Conference on Database Theory*.
51. D. Srivastava.(1992) Subsumption and indexing in constraint query languages with linear arithmetic constraints. *Annals of Mathematics and Artificial Intelligence*. .
52. D. Srivastava & R. Ramakrishnan.(1992). Pushing constraint selections. In *Proc. 11th ACM SIGACT-SIGMOD-SIGART Simposium on Principles of Database Systems*, pages 301–315.
53. D. Srivastava, R. Ramakrishnan & P. Revesz.(1994) Constraint objects. In *Proc. 2nd Workshop on the Principles and Practice of Constraint Programming*, Orcas Island, WA.
54. M. Stonebraker, M. Rowe & L. Hiroshama.(1990). The implementation of Postgress. *IEEE Transactions on Knowledge and Data Engineering*.
55. L. Vandeurzen, M. Gyssens & D. Van Gucht.(1995). On the desirability and limitations of linear spatial query languages. In M. J. Egenhofer and J. R. Herring, editors, *Proc. 4th Symposium on Advances in Spatial Databases*, volume 951 of *Lecture Notes in Computer Science*, pages 14–28. Springer Verlag.
56. P. Wadler.(1990) Comprehending monads. In *Proc. ACM Symposium on Lisp and Functional Programming*.
57. A. Wolf.(1989) The dasdba geo-kernel, concepts, experiences, and the second step. In *Design and Implementation of Large Spatial Databases, Proc. 1st Symp. on Spatial Databases*. Springer Verlag.
58. S. Zdonik.(1989). Query optimization in object oriented databases. In *Proc. 23rd annual Hawaii International Conference of System Sciences*.

Constraints: An International Journal, 2, 279–304 (1997)

Toward Practical Query Evaluation for Constraint Databases

ALEXANDER BRODSKY[*]   brodsky@isse.gmu.edu
Dept. of Information and Software Systems Engineering, George Mason University, Fairfax, VA 22030, USA

JOXAN JAFFAR   joxan@iscs.nus.sg
Dept. of Information Systems and Computer Science, National University of Singapore, Lower Kent Ridge Road, Singapore 119260

MICHAEL J. MAHER   mjm@cit.gu.edu.au
School of Computing and Information Technology, Griffith University, Nathan, 4111, Australia

Abstract.

Linear constraint databases (LCDBs) extend relational databases to include linear arithmetic constraints in both relations and queries. A LCDB can also be viewed as a powerful extension of linear programming (LP) where the system of constraints is generalized to a database containing constraints and the objective function is generalized to a relational query containing constraints. Our major concern is query optimization in LCDBs. Traditional database approaches are not adequate for combination with LP technology. Instead, we propose a new query optimization approach, based on statistical estimations and iterated trials of potentially better evaluation plans. The resulting algorithms are not only effective on LCDBs, but also applicable to existing query languages. A number of specific constraint algebra algorithms are also developed: select-project-join for two relations, constraint sort-join and constraint multi-join.

Keywords: constraint programming, datbases, database optimization, linear programming

1. Introduction

Linear programming/linear constraints is a technology widely used in applications of economics and business, e.g. allocation of scarce resources, scheduling production and inventory, cutting stock and many others. This paper proposes a merger of linear programming (LP) and relational database technologies in the framework of *linear constraints databases* (LCDBs), that extend relational databases to include linear arithmetic constraints in both relations and queries. The motivation comes from the fact that classical LP applications do not stand alone, but rather operate over a large amount of stored data and usually require not just to optimize one objective function, but to answer more complex queries involving manipulation of both regular data and constraints. A second application realm is

---

[*] Much of this research was conducted while the authors were employed at the I.B.M. Thomas J. Watson Research Center.

41

that of engineering design systems, which may operate over large catalogs of components, devices etc., and enable queries about design patterns that are described using constraints. LCDB technology, in particular, is important because it can enhance many existing software platforms such as relational DBMS, object oriented DBMS, operation research packages, constraint logic programming (CLP) systems etc.

Traditionally, there have been two major approaches to query optimization. One is based on compile-time algebraic simplification of a query using heuristics as in [20, 40, 44, 52, 43, 59, 12, 60, 3]. The other is based on cost estimation of different strategies as in [1, 16, 13, 14, 39, 58]. The heuristics of the algebraic simplification approach, such as performing selections as early as possible, assume that the selection conditions are readily available. In fact, extracting such conditions from the constraints of a query involves linear programming techniques which are, in general, expensive because there may be, for example, thousands of variables. The cost estimation approach, on the other hand, has the similar problem of extracting explicit constraints on attributes which are needed for the estimation. Even if these constraints were readily available, there is a second problem: it is typically necessary to make assumptions about the distribution of data (like uniformity within, and independence of, attributes), and these appear unlikely to hold in LCDBs. In short, traditional optimization approaches are inadequate for LCDBs.

In this paper, we propose a new generic approach to query optimization, that is not only effective on LCDB, but also on existing query languages. The underlying philosophy is that expenditure of computational cost is necessary in order to obtain information required to estimate which is the best evaluation plan. We use statistical sampling for the cost estimation of specific plans, which has the advantage of avoiding dependence on data distribution. Since it is impractical to consider all possible plans in the search for the best one (because cost estimation of each plan might be expensive), trials of evaluation plans are performed, one at a time, "gambling" some work required for the cost estimation of the plan in an attempt to discover a better plan. We bound the amount we can gamble, based on the best estimated cost so far. The gambling algorithm is then used for optimization of generalized select-project-join queries involving up to two generalized relations. This requires to develop algorithms for estimating costs of possible evaluation plans, based on statistical methods. The problem of how to perform reasonably accurate and computationally cheap cost estimations for a more general class of queries requires more study. As additional contribution, we developed two specific algorithms: first, adapting the algorithm of [15, 50] for n-dimensional rectangle intersection, we show how to perform an analog of the sort-join. Second, we developed a filtering algorithm for constraint multi-join suitable for long joins with small overall number of attributes. For a bounded number of attributes, this algorithm provides filtering in $O(nN^d \log N)$ time, where N is a bound on the number of tuples in relations, d is the number of attributes, and n is the number of joined relations.

There has been work on specific uses of constraints in databases, the earlier of which includes [27, 21, 11, 8, 37, 46, 22]. The pioneering work [28] proposed a framework for integrating abstract constraints into database query languages by providing a number of design principles, and studied, mostly in terms of expressiveness and complexity, a number of specific instances. The work of [21] considered optimiziting in the context arithmetic equations. However, constraint solving was limited to local propagation and hence not suitable for LP problems. A restricted form of linear constraints, called linear repeating points, was used to model infinite sequences of time points [33, 7, 42] More recent work on deductive databases [41, 55, 30, 31, 36] concentrate on optimizing by repositioning constraints and assume the implementation of selection, projection and join and optimization of expressions involving these operators. Constraint algebra algorithms for specific constraint families was considered in [18] and constraint approximation-based optimization in [10]. The work [5] proposed an approach to achieve the optimal quality of constraint and spatial filtering. A number of works consider special constraint domains: integer order constraints [47]; set constraints [48]; dense-order constraints [19]. Linear constraints over reals drew special attention [2, 6, 51, 57]. The use of constraints in spatial databases was addressed in [45], and to describe incomplete information in [56]; constraint aggregation was studied in [29].

The remainder of the paper is organized as follows. Motivating examples and discussion are next, in Section 2, and the definitions of our data model and query language appear in Section 3. An important aspect of our work, which pertains to practical use, is the use of the notion of constraint canonical forms. Section 4 covers relevant computational issues in constraint manipulation, which are fundamental to constraint query evaluation. Section 5 discusses why traditional optimization methods are inadequate, elaborating on the discussion above. Section 6 and beyond form the core technical presentation: we deal first with the selection/projection queries in Section 6, which motivates our generic "gambling" algorithm presented in Section 7. Section 8 gives an algorithm for sort join on constraint attributes and Section 9 presents an algorithm for filtering multi-joins. Section 10 presents the application of the gambling algorithm to optimizing select-project-join queries.

An earlier version of this paper was presented at the VLDB 93 conference [4].

2. Introductory Examples

Suppose a company manufactures two products using two resources. Its database has the relations *orders1* and *orders2* for orders of its first and second products respectively. Each relation has the attributes *Order#*, *Customer* and *Product_quantity*. Another relation *product_resource*($P1$, $P2$, $R1$, $R2$) specifies a relationship between quantities of resources and products: $P1$ and $P2$ represent quantities of the first and second products respectively to be produced, while $R1$ and $R2$ represent amounts of the first and second resources available. A possible manufacturing process can be specified by (a conjunction of) the following constraints:

$$P1 + 100\,P2 \leq R1$$
$$100\,P1 + P2 \leq R2$$
$$P1, P2, R1, R2 \geq 0$$

This says that the amount of the first resource needed to produce $P1$ and $P2$ units of the first and the second products must not exceed the amount $R1$ of this resource available, and similarly about the second resource. Suppose that there is another manufacturing processes:

$$1.7\,P1 + 13.1\,P2 \leq R1$$

$$28.3\,P1 + 11.5\,P2 \leq R2$$
$$P1, P2, R1, R2 \geq 0$$

Now, the relation *product_resource* is a disjunction of two conjunctions of (three) constraints, a finite description of the infinite number of tuples $(P1, P2, R1, R2)$ of values satisfying the disjunction. Similarly to [28], we define a *constraint tuple* to be a (possibly existentially quantified[1]) conjunction of constraints, and *constraint relation* to be disjunction of constraint tuples.

In addition to regular relational queries, one may have queries like: "if profit per unit of the first product is \$15 and of the second is \$4, and there are 100 and 10000 units of the first and second resources respectively, what is the maximum profit the company can make with each manufacturing pattern?" or "given certain quantities of resources, what are the ranges of and the connection between the quantities of the two products that can be produced with each manufacturing process?".

Typically the evaluation of queries involves both "regular" information and constraints, for example:

CONSTRUCT	*orders1_resources*$(O, C, R1, R2)$
FROM	*orders1*$(O, C, P1)$,
	products_resources$(P1, P2, R1, R2)$
WHERE	$P2 = 0$

Note that in our notation the arguments $O, C, R1, R2, P1$ and $P2$ in the query are variables, not attribute names, but we sometimes use the same name for a variable and an attribute when the distinction is not important. Suppose the relation *orders1* consists of the two tuples $(1, 'Smith', 154.3)$ and $(2, 'Stone', 17.2)$, and two constraint tuples of the relation *products_resources* correspond to the manufacturing processes above. The answer to the query can be computed by considering all four pairs of tuples obtained from *orders1* and from *products_resources*. In each pair, set $P1$ to the value given by *orders*, set $P2$ to 0, and finally, simplify the constraints for $R1$ and $R2$. Figure 1 depicts the results.

Note that we produce here a relation that is only partly constraint. *Order#* and *Customer* are regular and R_1 and R_2 are *constraint* attributes.

Clearly, regular relational database queries cannot produce this sort of relation as an answer. Although constraint logic programming [23] can, in principle, implement this sort of query, it is not efficient. Consider another example query:

CONSTRUCT	*both_products*$(O1, O2)$
FROM	*orders1*$(O1, C, P1)$,
	orders2$(O2, C, P2)$
WHERE	$P1 + 100\,P2 \leq R1$,
	$100\,P1 + P2 \leq R2$,
	$P1, P2, R1, R2 \geq 0$,
	$R1 = 100$,
	$R2 = 10000$

Order#	Customer	R_1 R_2
1	'Smith'	$R_1 \geq 262.31 \wedge R_2 \geq 4366.69$
1	'Smith'	$R_1 \geq 154.3 \wedge R_2 \geq 15430.0$
2	'Stone'	$R_1 \geq 49.708 \wedge R_2 \geq 486.76$
2	'Stone'	$R_1 \geq 17.2 \wedge R_2 \geq 1720.0$

Figure 1. Relation *orders1_resources*

Note that the first three lines in the WHERE clause correspond to the first manufacturing pattern given above.

Note also that attributes (such as $R1$ and $R2$) do not have to appear in a relation.

In order to estimate the size of the answer to the query and its evaluation time, let $orders$ denote either $orders1$ or $orders2$, and make the following 3 assumptions. (1) The relation $orders$ has 10^6 tuples. (2) The image size (that is, the number of different values) of $Customer$ in $orders$ is 10^5 and all values of $Customer$ are equally likely to occur. Hence there are approximately $10^6/10^5 = 10$ tuples having a particular value of $Customer$. (3) The range of P in $orders$ is $[0, 10^5]$ and then, assuming values are uniformly distributed, there are approximately $size(orders) * (b - a)/10^5$ tuples having a P value in the range $[a, b]$.

These assumptions are made purely to simplify the comparison of different evaluation methods.

The table in Figure 2 depicts the costs of naive evaluation, CLP($\mathcal{R}$), SQL and the ideal possible evaluation. The naive evaluation simply considers all pairs of tuples. In CLP($\mathcal{R}$) the only tuples of $order1$ that are consistent with the constraints are checked against $order2$. SQL takes advantage of using index on $Customer$ in $orders2$ for join operation.

The ideal evaluation does much better, as shown in Figure 2, as follows. First observe that we can deduce that $P1$ is in the range $[0.0, 100.0]$ and $P2$ is in the range $[0.0, 1.0]$. By the assumptions, there are about 10 relevant tuples in $orders2$ and 1000 relevant tuples in $orders1$. If we can estimate this comparison, we will perform a selection on $orders2$. Assuming an index on $P2$ is maintained in $orders2$, the selection of 10 tuples will take about 10 *look-at* operations, in addition to some overhead of one indexed access. Instead of selecting about 1000 tuples from $orders1$, find a natural join on C of the tuples selected from $orders2$ and the relation $orders1$. By assumption 2, the result has approximately 100 tuples and, assuming an index is maintained on $Customer$ in $orders1$, this join will take about 100 *look-at* operations. Finally, check every tuple in the join to see that it satisfies the constraints.

We can see, in this example, the advantages of deducing ranges on attributes and of estimating costs before making a decision. Our approach attempts to balance these advantages with the costs of range deduction and estimation.

	look -at	simple checks of constr.	proj. on single var.	satisf. tests
Naive	10^{12}	10^7	–	–
CLP($\mathcal{R}$)	10^9	10^4	–	10^6
SQL	10^7	10^7	–	–
Possible	10^2	10^2	2	–

Figure 2. Both products: evaluation costs

3. Data Model and Query Language

3.1. Data Model

A *constraint tuple* has the form $(t_1, \ldots, t_n)$ WHERE c in which the t_i's are either variables or constants and c is an existentially quantified conjunction of constraints, with free variables from $t_1, \ldots, t_n$. By using equality constraints we can write the tuple into the standard form $(x_1, \ldots, x_n)$ WHERE c', in which the x_i's are variables. When it is convenient, we will identify the constraint tuple with the constraint c'. A *constraint relation* (or simply relation) is a collection of constraint tuples. It can be understood as a finite representation for a possibly infinite regular relation; every assignment of values to variables which satisfies the constraint in a constraint tuple corresponds to a regular tuple.

A *constraint relation scheme* associates a type to each attribute of the relation, and specifies a canonical form for constraints. The type specifies the kind of values (integer, real, string, etc.) that the attribute may take and whether the value must appear explicitly in each constraint tuple (as is usual for databases), or may be represented implicitly by constraints. In this paper, only one type allows constraints, *constrained reals*. All other types (reals, integers, etc.) are *regular* database types. The constraints in each constraint tuple in the relation are required to be presented in the canonical form. We discuss canonical forms in the next section.

Thus our data model is almost an instance of the framework of [28]. The difference is that we consider explicitly the form in which constraints are presented and allow existentially quantified constraints to appear in constraint tuples.

3.2. Query Language

In general, a query will take the form

CONSTRUCT $a(X_1, \ldots, X_n)$
$\quad$ FROM $b_{1\,1}(args), \ldots, b_{1\,k_1}(args)$
$\quad$ WHERE $cons_1(args)$

OR

$\quad$ FROM $b_{2\,1}(args), \ldots, b_{2\,k_2}(args)$
$\quad$ WHERE $cons_2(args)$

OR $\quad\quad \ldots$

where each occurrence of $args$ denotes a sequence of variables from the set $\{X_1, \ldots, X_n, \ldots, X_m\}$. For convenience we assume that in each FROM clause no equality between two distinct variables is explicitly implied by $cons$ in the WHERE clause. (If this happen it is always possible to replace one variable by the other.) The query defines a relation a which contains the tuple $(v_1, \ldots, v_n)$ iff there are values $v_1, \ldots, v_n, \ldots, v_m$ such that for some i and for each j such that $1 \leq j \leq k_i$, the appropriate projections are tuples in $b_{i\,j}$. Since a is written with variable arguments, we sometimes abuse terminology and call an attribute a variable, or vice versa. This query incorporates selection, projection, join and union operations.

A *linear arithmetic constraint* has the form $r_1 X_1 + \cdots + r_m X_m \, relop \, r$, where $r, r_1, \ldots, r_m$ are real number constants and $relop$ is one of $=, <, \leq, >, \geq$. An arithmetic constraint is *pseudo-linear* with respect to a set of variables $\tilde{y}$ if, whenever the variables $\tilde{y}$ are replaced by real number constants, the resulting constraint is linear. We require that every constraint appearing in a WHERE clause be pseudo-linear with respect to those variables in the corresponding FROM clause which have regular types.

A straightforward extension of this language can incorporate views, cascades of views, complex types, and function symbols. These additional features do not significantly affect the issues we address in this paper. Other additional capabilities, such as recursion and the use of aggregation operators, introduce further complications, and we will not address them here.

Instead we direct our attention to a subset of this query language in which all constraints appearing in a query are linear. We consider selections and projections of relations, and the join of two relations, but we do not explicitly discuss the union operation.

4. Canonical Forms and Constraint Manipulation

In this paper, the constraint c associated with a constraint tuple is a (possibly existentially quantified) conjunction of linear equations and inequalities. In this section, we briefly discuss some computational issues on the manipulation of such constraints.

A *canonical form* for constraints is a useful standard form of the constraints, and is generally computed by simplification and the removal of redundancy. In addition to the advantages of a standard presentation of constraints, canonical forms can provide savings of space and time. In the class of linear arithmetic constraints there are many plausible canonical forms. However, they can be costly to compute.

Corresponding to a constraint relation is a disjunction of the constraints in each tuple. Some of these tuples might be redundant in the sense that omitting them does not alter the regular relation represented by the constraint relation. Clearly, a canonical form that eliminates such tuples would be desirable. However, the problem of detecting such tuples is co-NP-complete [54], and so we will perform only two simplifications of disjunctions: the deletion of each tuple with an inconsistent constraint, and the deletion of duplicates when all values are regular.

Similarly, while it is theoretically possible to eliminate all existential quantifiers from our constraints (as required in the framework of [28]), the cost of this elimination and the size of the resulting constraint can grow exponentially in the size of the original constraint. Since we expect applications with large constraints, it is unrealistic to expect that all quantifiers can be eliminated. We suggest a method of only performing simplifying quantifier eliminations, similar to what is done in CLP($\mathcal{R}$) [26].

The conjunctive constraints offer the greatest scope in choosing a canonical form. One choice is to write all equations in the form $\{x_i = t_i \mid i = 1, \ldots, n\}$ where the x_i's are distinct and appear nowhere else in the constraint (*parameterized form*). A second choice is whether all equations which are implicit in the inequality constraints should be represented explicitly. (As a simple example of this, consider the constraints $x + y \leq 2, x + y \geq 2$.) A third is the extent to which redundancy within the inequalities should be removed. [35] presents a classification of redundancy that suggests simple forms of redundancy removal. A fourth choice is whether to keep the inequalities in a different form, such as simplex tableau form.

A fifth option is the addition of redundant information to the constraints. In particular, since range constraints will play an important role in our optimization and implementation methods, we consider a canonical form that requires explicit ranges for some variables. (A *range constraint* is a constraint on a single variable using inequalities or equations. A range constraint is *trivial* if it has the form $-\infty < X$ or $X < \infty$.) More specifically, we require the "tightest" such range, which can be obtained for each variable by projecting the conjunctive constraint onto the variable. Placing constraints in canonical form and, in particular, testing the satisfiability (or consistency) of constraints requires, in general, linear programming techniques.

For the purposes of this paper we consider just one class of canonical forms. We assume that there are no implicit equations, that equations are presented in parameterized form (as described in the first choice above), some simple redundancy in the inequalities is removed, and there are explicit range constraints for some variables.

In addition to choosing canonical forms for constraint relations, we must also consider the manipulations of constraints necessary in the evaluation of queries. The most important computation with query constraints is the extraction of a range on a variable. The extraction of a lower bound (for example) on x is exactly the linear programming problem of minimizing x subject to the constraints. The detection of implicit equalities in the query constraint is also a linear programming problem [34] as is, of course, testing for consistency.

5. Optimization: Differences in Approach

In this section we highlight differences between constraint databases and regular databases, which make the straightforward application of usual database techniques difficult or impossible. Consider, first, a simple problem of selection, that is, the query of the form

CONSTRUCT	$a(X_1, \ldots, X_n)$
FROM	$b(X_1, \ldots, X_i, \ldots, X_n)$
WHERE	$cons(X_i, \ldots, X_n, \ldots, X_m)$

Each constraint tuple of a can be constructed by taking a conjunction of a constraint tuple from b and $cons$, testing whether it is satisfiable, and if it is, finding a required canonical form for it. Note that, depending on the canonical form for existential quantifiers, this may involve elimination of the implicit existential quantifiers over the variables $X_{n+1}, \ldots, X_m$. Thus, in general, processing a tuple in a constraint selection is significantly more expensive than in a regular selection.

To avoid unnecessary computation, we want to use the idea of *filtering*, similar to one used in spatial databases, that is, the discarding of irrelevant tuples of b by a computationally cheap test. Suppose we have a range $c \leq X_k < d$ for X_k in $cons$, where c might be $-\infty$ and d might be ∞. If X_k is also a regular variable in b, we can discard all tuples in b whose X_k value does not lie in the range, since clearly those tuples are inconsistent with $cons$. Similarly, if X_k is a constrained variable and a range for X_k is stored for each tuple of b, then we can discard all tuples for which the ranges for X_k are disjoint.

(There is a larger class of constraints of use in filtering. A constraint is *simply checkable* wrt a relation r if every variable in the constraint also occurs in the relation in an attribute that either is regular or has a range constraint in the canonical form for tuples of r. While testing such a constraint is a little more expensive, in general, than testing ranges, the cost still compares very favorably with the use of linear programming.)

We can do filtering more efficiently using indices. Indexing on regular attributes is the same as usual, whereas indexing on a constraint attribute X of r works as follows. For each inserted constraint tuple t the range of X is extracted using linear programming techniques. This interval is inserted into an index structure maintaining intervals and has a reference to the corresponding tuple. Selection of all tuples t in r consistent with a given set of constraints c is done as follows. First the range I of X is extracted from c. Second, using the interval index all tuples whose corresponding ranges of X intersect I are retrieved. Third, the retrieved tuples are checked for consistency with c using linear programming methods. Of course, many different indices can be maintained and used for selection. Moreover, in order to improve filtering additional attributes can be defined as linear combinations of constraint attributes, as proposed in [5].

In general we need to have index structures supporting storage of values and intervals, and value and range queries. Two efficient access structures for intervals are the interval tree [15] and the priority search trees [38]. In one dimension, finding all intervals intersecting a given interval or containing a given point, takes at most $O(n \log n + k)$ time, where n is the size of the relation and k is the size of the output. Moreover, it requires only linear space in the size of a relation, and thus seems to be ideal as an indexing structure. The work in

[32] proposes an efficient data structure for secondary storage, having the same space and time complexity and full clustering. There are different data structures to support access to multidimensional intervals, in particular based on combination of interval, segment and range trees [15, 50]. For 2-dimensional intervals (rectangles) R, R^+, R^* trees [17, 49, 53] are widely used in spatial databases.

In order to perform indexing and filtering, it is necessary to extract ranges of variables from *cons*. This extraction involves techniques of linear programming and can be very expensive, especially in applications coming from operational research in which *cons* might involve over a thousand constraints and variables. Thus, there is a trade-off to be made between an improvement gained by filtering and indexing and the cost paid for extracting ranges from *cons*.

Consider now projections, that is, the queries of the form

$$\text{CONSTRUCT} \quad a(X_1, \ldots, X_n)$$
$$\text{FROM} \quad b(X_1, \ldots, X_n, \ldots, X_m)$$

Computing a projection may involve, depending on the required canonical form, quantifier elimination of (some of) the variables $X_{n+1}, \ldots, X_m$. In contrast to the usual database case, in which projection is a trivial operation, when constraints are involved it can be computationally expensive.

Consider now a "constraint" join, where the query is of the form

$$\text{CONSTRUCT} \quad a(X_1, \ldots, X_i, \ldots, X_j, \ldots, X_n)$$
$$\text{FROM} \quad b(X_1, \ldots, X_j),$$
$$c(X_i, \ldots, X_n)$$

In principle, each tuple in the answer to this query can be computed by taking a conjunction of a tuple from b and a tuple from c, testing its satisfiability and, if satisfiable, presenting it in the required canonical form. As with the constraint selection, we can use filtering to reduce the cost of satisfiability tests. The filtering step discards those pairs of tuples that have disjoint ranges on a common attribute. A refinement step then performs a full test for satisfiability for the remaining pairs. Note that the regular join does not involve constraints and hence does not require the refinement step. In this paper, we associate the notion of join only with the filtering step, and treat the full test for satisfiability as a separate operation.

We would like to use the ideas developed for regular joins for the filtering in the constraint join. The indexed join (that is, for each tuple of one relation finding all corresponding tuples of the second using an index) for constraint relations differs from the indexed join for regular relations only in the different index structures that can be used. However, an analogy for the sort join (sorting both relations on common attributes and then finding all matching tuples in one merge) is not clear, since there is no appropriate total ordering on multidimensional intervals. In Section 8 we adapt work in computational geometry to give an analog to the sort join.

Finally, consider the two major approaches to query optimization for regular databases. One is based on algebraic simplification of a query and compile-time heuristics. The other is based on cost estimation of different strategies. Neither of these is adequate for constraint database systems. The heuristics of the algebraic approach, such as performing selections as early as possible, are based on the assumption that selection conditions are readily available. In contrast, extracting such conditions from the constraints of a query involves linear programming techniques which are in general expensive. For the cost estimation approach, we have a similar problem of extracting explicit constraints which are needed for the estimation. Even if these constraints were readily available, there is a second problem: it is typically necessary to make assumptions about distribution of the data (like uniformity within, and independence of, columns) in the database, and these appear unlikely to hold in constraint databases.

6. Algorithm for Constraint Selection and Projection

Here the considered queries are of the form

CONSTRUCT	$a(\overline{Y})$
FROM	$b(\overline{Z})$
WHERE	$cons(\overline{W})$

We proceed by presenting an evaluation scheme which represents many evaluation plans. Evaluation schemes and plans are not intended to represent the decision-making process, but only to represent the decisions that need to be made, and the work that needs to be done. We then discuss the trial evaluation, which is necessary for estimating costs, and some heuristics which can be used to order evaluation plans. The generic gambling algorithm, described in the next section, uses this information to choose which plans receive a trial evaluation and, ultimately, to choose an evaluation plan.

We propose the following evaluation scheme for this query.

0. If $\overline{Z} \cap \overline{W}$ is empty then no selection is involved. Project b onto $\overline{Y}$, eliminating duplicates, and conjoin the constraint in each generalized tuple with the projection of $cons(\overline{W})$ onto $\overline{Y}$.

1. Choose a non-empty subset T of the common attributes $\overline{Z} \cap \overline{W}$. For each $X \in T$, extract from $cons$ a range on X. Let S be the set of all attributes in $\overline{Z} \cup \overline{W}$ for which there are non-trivial range constraints (including those attributes from T).

2. Pick an index maintained on b whose selection condition can be explicitly checked by the range constraints on attributes in S. Using this index, select all tuples from b satisfying the constraints.

3. From these tuples, filter out those which do not satisfy simply checkable constraints from $cons$ and the extracted range constraints.

4. Project out all regular attributes of b that do not appear elsewhere, eliminating duplicates.

5. For each remaining tuple t, check the satisfiability of the conjunction of t and $cons$. If it is satisfiable, put it in canonical form. If it is not, discard it.

This scheme leaves open the specific choice of a subset T of variables, and an index. Fixing a choice gives rise to a particular *evaluation plan*.

The cost of an evaluation plan depends strongly on the ranges extracted in Step 1. Therefore, the *estimation* of such cost requires, in addition to statistical sampling, some amount of *actual* evaluation. Call this process of sampling/evaluation a *trial evaluation* of the plan. Now, even trial evaluation can be expensive and therefore it is unrealistic to estimate the cost of all evaluation plans. In fact the cost of estimation may exceed the cost of a naive evaluation.

In the next section, we provide our *gambling algorithm* that balances these two costs by considering evaluations plans one at a time and limiting the cost of the estimation of a plan to a portion of the cost of the best plan according to the estimation so far. For the remainder of this section, we detail the trial evaluation and provide heuristics on the order in which the plans are to be considered for estimation.

The trial evaluation for a given plan is described by steps (a) – (e) below. These steps comprise the sub-procedure DO-TRIAL-EVAL-OF of the gambling algorithm for the case of selection-projection queries. (We provide different steps for other kinds of queries later.)

(a) Perform Step 1 above.

(b) Take a random sample of b. The number of tuples, say n, in the sample is a compile-time parameter.

(c) Select the tuples in the sample satisfying the selection condition of the index chosen in Step 2. Let n_1 denote the number of tuples selected in Step 2.

(d) Perform filtering (Step 3) and projection (Step 4) on these n_1 selected tuples. Measure the average cost per tuple, say a_1. Let n_2 denote the number of tuples selected in Step 3.

(e) Perform the satisfiability test (Step 4) on these n_2 selected tuples. Measure the average cost per tuple, say a_2.

Note that the Step (b) of the trial evaluation is done only once for all plans. The cost of the entire evaluation of the plan, except Step 1, can now be estimated as follows. (It is referred to as FIND Estimated-cost in the gambling algorithm.) First we estimate the number N_1 of the tuples selected from b using the chosen index in Step 2 by $(N/n) * n_1$ where N is the number of tuples in b. Then, we estimate the number N_2 of the tuples selected in Step 3 by $(N/n) * n_2$. The cost of Step 2 is estimated by $f(N, N_1)$, where f is a given cost function[2] for the index chosen. The costs of Step 3 and Step 4 are estimated by $N_1 * a_1$ and $N_2 * a_2$ respectively. Finally, in addition to the estimations of the costs above, we also compute the confidence intervals for the cost using standard statistical methods.

We conclude this section with two suggested heuristics on how to order the evaluation plans for the gambling algorithm, which can be used in conjunction with other heuristics. We propose to consider plans earlier when they:

1. require fewer additional range extractions in Step 1, and thus have potentially cheaper trial evaluation. In particular, we start with a plan that requires no extraction.

2. have a "stronger" index in Step 2. Indices on values are considered stronger than indices on intervals. Indices with an equality selection condition are stronger that those with range condition; the latter are stronger than those with one inequality condition. In particular, those plans having any index are stronger than the others.

7. The Gambling Optimization Algorithm

The input is $(e_1, \ldots, e_m)$, the list of evaluation plans to be considered in this order, induced by heuristics for a specific class of queries. The output is an evaluation plan e that is "recommended as the best". The basic idea of the algorithm is to perform trials of evaluation plans, one at a time, "gambling" some work required for estimation of the plan in an attempt to discover a better plan. The bound for the gambling cost depends on the best estimated cost so far. The algorithm consists of application of two major parts:

1. CHOOSE-SMALL-SET-OF-BEST-PLANS

2. CHOOSE-BEST-PLAN

The idea behind this split into two parts is as follows. When we are considering each of the plans in turn, we need to use statistical sampling in order to estimate the costs. In general, this estimation is expensive, especially for the more complex types of queries. If we take large samples for greater accuracy of the estimation, we might spend most of the gambling cost just on sampling, giving up consideration of many potential plans. On the other hand, taking small samples may lead, because of the lack of accuracy, to recommend a plan that is significantly worse than the real best plan. Our two-phase algorithm provides a balance. In the first phase, we use samples that are relatively small, so that we can spend the gambling time on considering many potential plans. However, instead of keeping just the best estimated plan we keep a small set of the best plans. Then, in the second phase we concentrate on a more accurate sampling, spending the remaining amount of the gambling time to try to find the best plan.

The algorithm has several parameters, including the degrees of confidence used in statistical tests, some number constants (such as the maximum number of "best" plans that will be output), and some fractional constants (such as the proportion ε that represents a significant difference in cost).

The CHOOSE-SMALL-SET-OF-BEST-PLANS procedure appears in Figure 3. It is almost self-explanatory[3]; roughly speaking, it iterates over evaluation plans until the total time spent is expected to exceed Max-Trials-Cost, to select the best-seeming plans. Here we just clarify some important points. The pair of lower and upper Bounds-of-estimated-cost of an evaluation plan is derived from the statistical confidence intervals. Incremental-spent-cost is the cost spent by the algorithm after the most recent improvement of the Best-total-cost is made. Max-Trials-Cost is used to bound the gambling time. To COMPUTE Max-trials-cost, which is redone after each improvement of Best-total-cost, we suggest the use of

set e_{best} *to the first evaluation plan to be considered;*
set Best-eval-plans *to* $\{e_{best}\}$*;*
DO-TRIAL-EVAL-OF e_{best} *and* FIND
                    Estimated--cost.e_{best} *and the pair* Bounds-of-estimated-cost.e_{best}*;*
set Total-spent-cost *and* Incremental-spent-cost *to the work done so far;*
set Best-total-cost *to* Estimated-cost.e_{best} + Total-spent-cost*;*
set the pair Bounds-of-best-total-cost *to the sum of*
                    Total-spent-cost *and the pair* Bounds-of-estimated-cost.e_{best}*;*
COMPUTE Max-trials-cost *as a function*
                    of Best-total-cost *and* Bounds-of-best-total-cost*;*

let e be the next plan to be considered;

$$\textbf{while}\ \left(\begin{array}{c}\textit{there is an evaluation plan e to consider}\\ \textbf{and}\\ \text{ESTIMATED-COST-OF-DO-TRIAL-EVAL-OF } e \leq\\ \texttt{Max-trials-cost} - \texttt{Incremental-spent-cost}\end{array}\right)\ \textbf{do begin}$$

    DO-TRIAL-EVAL-OF e *and* FIND
                Estimated-cost.e *and* Bounds-of-estimated-cost.e*;*
    update Incremental-spent-cost *and* Total-spent-cost *to include the work above;*
    if *size of* Best-eval-plans < MAX-EVAL-PLANS **then**
        add e to Best-eval-plans
    else if Estimated-cost.e < Estimated-cost.e_{worst}
               for the worst plan e_{worst} *in* Best-eval-plans **then**
        discard e_{worst} *from* Best-eval-plans *and add e to it;*
    if *e has been added to* Best-eval-plans **then begin**
        if Estimated-cost.e < Estimated-cost.e_{best} **then begin**
            set e_{best} *to e;*
            set Old-best-total-cost *to* Best-total-cost*;*
            set Best-total-cost *to* Estimated-cost.e_{best} + Total-spent-cost*;*
            set the pair Bounds-of-best-total-cost *to the sum of*
                Total-spent-cost *and the pair* Bounds-of-estimated-cost.e_{best}*;*
        end*;*
        if Best-total-cost < Old-best-total-cost **then begin**
            COMPUTE Max-trials-cost *as a function*
                of Best-total-cost *and* Bounds-of-best-total-cost*;*
            set Incremental-spent-cost *to* 0*;*
        end
        let e be the next plan to consider (if there is one)
    end
end
return Best-eval-plans

Figure 3. Procedure CHOOSE-SMALL-SET-OF-BEST-PLANS

$$\min\{\alpha * \text{Best} - \text{total} - \text{cost},$$
$$\beta * (\textit{lower bound of } \text{Best} - \text{total} - \text{cost})\}$$

where α denotes some fraction of the entire evaluation cost we are ready to gamble. The parameter β should be a higher fraction than α and serves as a "watch dog", that is, if we overestimate the best Best-total-cost, then, in the worst case we are going to spend at most fraction β of the real cost. Finally, MAX-EVAL-PLANS is a compile-time parameter specifying the maximal number of best plans to be kept for the output.

The input to CHOOSE-BEST-PLAN is Best-eval-plans which is provided by CHOOSE-SMALL-SET-OF-BEST-PLANS; the output is the recommended plan. In each iteration of the algorithm some computational cost is paid for additional sampling to estimate more accurately the costs of the current best plan e_{best} and the plan e which is more likely than other plans to replace the current best. Also, we discard all plans for which it can be statistically verified that they are either more expensive than e_{best} or close to it up to a certain small percentage ε. This ε denotes a marginal percentage of cost, and is used to avoid useless sampling for comparing plans that have practically indistinguishable costs. The iterations end when either only one plan is left, or when we have exhausted Max-sampling-cost.

The procedure CHOOSE-BEST-PLAN appears in Figure 4. Max-trials-cost is computed as in the procedure CHOOSE-SMALL-SET-OF-BEST-PLANS, but with different coefficients, reflecting the fraction of the entire cost we are ready to gamble. One-trial-cost is the cost spent in one iteration; it depends on a compile-time parameter MAX-ITERATIONS. It is important that MAX-ITERATIONS be sufficiently large, so that Max-trials-cost will be spent fairly and many plans will have chance to compete for the first place. Note that, intuitively, there is a trend in the iterations to eventually discard e as the confidence intervals of costs for e_{best} and e get smaller, since it becomes more likely that the confidence C_e, that the cost of e will exceed the cost of e_{best}, is significant. On the other hand, MAX-ITERATIONS should not be too large, because of the overhead this can create. Finally, EVALUATE-OPTIMAL-PARTITION-OF One-trial-cost means, intuitively, maximizing the confidence of the decision which plan, e_{best} or e, is the best. This is done by minimizing the variance of the random variable Estimated-cost.e $-$ Estimated-cost.e_{best}, which is a function of the sizes of the samples for e_{best} and e, subject to the constraint that the total cost on sampling is One-trial-cost. This problem usually translates to minimizing a quadratic function in one variable and can be easily done.

8. A Constraint Sort Join Algorithm

We adapt the algorithm of [15, 50] for n-dimensional rectangle intersection to perform an analog of the sorted equijoin. It is not possible to sort directly on a constrained attribute, since each tuple allows a range of values for that attribute and tuples may overlap. Instead we sort the endpoints of the ranges in the tuples, using not only the value of the endpoint, but also the type of the boundary: whether it is a point or a lower or upper boundary, and whether the boundary was caused by a strict or nonstrict inequality. (We must assume here that, for each common attribute X of type constrained real in the relations, there is a range for X in the canonical form of each relation.)

let $e_{best} \in$ Best-eval-plans *be the plan that has the least estimated cost;*
set Spent-cost *to* 0;
while *size of* Best-eval-plans > 1 **do begin**
    for each plan e', *except* e_{best}, COMPUTE *statistical confidence* $C_{e'}$ *with which the cost of* e'
        exceeds the cost of e_{best} *minus* ε *percent; suppose* C_e *is the lowest;*
    discard all plans e' *in* Best-eval-plans *with* $C_{e'} \geq$ SIGNIFICANT_CONFIDENCE;
    COMPUTE Max-trials-cost *as a function of*
        Estimated-cost.e_{best} *and* Bounds-of-estimated-cost.e_{best};
    set One-trial-cost *to* Max-trials-cost / MAX-ITERATIONS;
    if One-trial-cost $>$ Max-trials-cost $-$ Spent-cost **then**
        discard all plans but e_{best} *from* Best-eval-plans
    else begin
        increment Spent-cost *by* One-trial-cost;
        EVALUATE-OPTIMAL-PARTITION-OF One-trial-cost *giving costs* Cost1 *and* Cost2
        of work to be spent on estimating costs of e_{best} *and* e *respectively;*
        TAKE *additional samples for estimating costs of* e_{best} *and* e *spending*
        Cost1 *and* Cost2 *respectively and re-estimate the costs of* e_{best} *and* e;
        if Estimated-cost.e_{best} $>$ Estimated-cost.e **then**
            set e_{best} *to* e;
  end
end
return e_{best}

Figure 4. Procedure CHOOSE-BEST-PLAN

The value $value(e)$ of an endpoint e may be any real number, $-\infty$ or ∞. For each endpoint e, there is a boundary type $bdry(e)$, and these are ordered as follows: *upper-strict* $<$ *lower-nonstrict* $<$ *point* $<$ *upper-nonstrict* $<$ *lower-strict*. We write $e_1 \preceq e_2$ if $value(e_1) \leq value(e_2)$, or $value(e_1) = value(e_2)$ and $bdry(e_1) \leq bdry(e_2)$.

To simplify the exposition, we assume initially that there is only one common attribute which is not regular in both relations. For each relation P, let p be the relation on the common attributes which is the projection of P except that there are, in general, two elements of p corresponding to each tuple, one for each endpoint[4]. (In practice it is not necessary to construct p explicitly.) We say that p is $\preceq$-sorted if it is sorted according to the lexicographic combination of the order on the regular attributes and $\preceq$. We write $tuple(p_i)$ to denote the tuple of P that produced the i'th element of p. We say $p_i \preceq q_j$ if p_i and q_j agree on values for the regular attributes and the value of p_i on the remaining attribute $\preceq$ the value of q_j on that attribute.

The algorithm (Figure 5) first $\preceq$-sorts p and q corresponding to the input relations P and Q. It then applies the plane-sweep technique [15], traversing the endpoints in order from least to greatest. At each stage of the sweep, Active-set-for-p (Active-set-for-q) holds the set of generalized tuples of P (Q) which would contain the current endpoint if their constraints were replaced by *true*. If the current endpoint e comes from p then $tuple(e) \bowtie$ Active-set-for-q must be contained in $P \bowtie Q$, and similarly if e comes from q. We record this information at lower endpoints only, since upper endpoints only duplicate the information. Note that, in performing the joins we must perform a satisfiability

construct p and q from input relations P and Q;
⪯-sort p and q;
initialize Output *to ∅;*
initialize Active-set-for-p *to ∅;*
initialize Active-set-for-q *to ∅;*
initialize i and j to 1;
repeat
   if $p_i \preceq q_j$ **then begin**
     if p_i *is a point* **then**
       add $tuple(p_i)$ ⋈ Active-set-for-q *to* Output;
     if p_i *is a lower boundary* **then begin**
       add $tuple(p_i)$ *to* Active-set-for-p;
       add $tuple(p_i)$ ⋈ Active-set-for-q *to* Output
     end;
     if p_i *is an upper boundary* **then**
       remove $tuple(p_i)$ *from* Active-set-for-p;
     increment i;
     end
   else
     We perform the same steps as in the then clause,
     with the roles of p and q, and i and j swapped;
until *p or q has been exhausted;*
return Output

Figure 5. A sort join algorithm

test on each generalized tuple and place each constraint in canonical form. The remainder of the algorithm updates Active-set-for-p and Active-set-for-q.

When we have only one dimension (that is, only one constrained attribute) then Active-set-for-p and Active-set-for-q can be simple set data structures. For two dimensions, we want to filter out from Active-set-for-q those tuples which fail to intersect the current tuple due to the ranges on the second constrained attribute. The appropriate data structure is the interval tree [15] which allows us to do this filtering efficiently. In general, for d dimensions we use a combination of range and interval trees [15, 50]. This gives the algorithm for a d-dimensional sorted join a worst-case time of $O(N \log N + M \log M + \log^{d-2} N + \log^{d-2} M + K)$, and a worst-case space cost of $O(M \log^{d-1} M + N \log^{d-1} N)$, where P has M tuples, Q has N tuples and the output relation has K tuples.

We refer to the regular attributes and the first constrained attribute as *scanned* attributes and the remaining attributes, those for which filtering is done inside the active sets, are called *active* attributes.

9. Constraint Multi-Join

The worst case complexity of the regular or constraint join of n relations is exponential in n, since an intermediate relation may contain an exponential number of tuples. However, it is often desirable to perform a sequence of (constraint) joins $R1 \bowtie R2 \bowtie \ldots \bowtie Rn$, which involve relatively many relations, but on a small overall number d of attributes. Superimposing (joining) many layers of a two- or three-dimensional geographic map is an example.

For regular (non-constraint) equi-join, the size of the intermediate relation has the worst case bound N^d, where N is the bound on the number of distinct constants for each x_i, $i = 1, \ldots, d$, since N^d is the maximal number of tuples that can be created over d domains each having at most N elements. In contrast, generally for the constraint join no polynomial bound exists. In this section we propose a multi-join algorithm that has, for range-constraint relations, a similar bound on the size of intermediate relations, thus yielding a similar polynomial worst case complexity on the join $R_1, \ldots, R_n$. The algorithm is, however, exponential in d, and thus suitable only for relatively small d's. This algorithm provides a bound on the size of the relations produced by filtering with range constraints on the multi-join.

We assume here, as in the previous section, that, for each x_j of the type constrained real, the range of x is precomputed. Further we assume that the join is performed in two phases: first, using just the range constraints, as a filtering phase; second, the actual combination of constraint tuples is tested for satisfiability, as a final phase. Thus, the algorithms presented in this section only deal with the join of range-constraint relations.

A naive extension of the non-constraint analysis to range constraints is not completely satisfactory. Let N be an upper bound on the number of all boundaries of ranges that appear appearing anywhere in the relations. Hence there are at most $N(N - 1)/2 + N$ (that is, $O(N^2)$) possible ranges (including point ranges of the form $[a, a]$) that can be composed for x_j. (Note we only create new ranges in the join by intersecting ranges, thus no new boundaries are created.) Thus, the bound on the range-constraint relation over $x_1, \ldots, x_d$ is $O(N^{2d}) = O((N^d)^2)$, polynomial, but much larger than the "non-constraint" bound $O(N^d)$.

The key idea in reducing this cost is to work with relations that are in what we call *range-disjoint form*, for which we can guarantee a tighter bound. We say that a range-constraint relation R is in the *range-disjoint form* if the following holds: for every constrained real $x_j, j = 1, \ldots, d$, and every two distinct tuples t_1 and t_2 the ranges of t_1 and t_2 over x_j are either disjoint or identical.

The *range-constraint multi-join* algorithm and the algorithm for transforming relations into range-disjoint form, used in the former algorithm, are both presented below.

Range-Constraint Multi-Join Algorithm

Input: range-constraint relations $R_1, \ldots, R_n$, with attributes $x_1, \ldots, x_d$.

Output: $R_1 \bowtie R_2 \bowtie \ldots \bowtie R_n$, that is, a range-constraint relation R, that is logically equivalent to (i.e. represents the same regular relations as) $R_1 \wedge R_2 \wedge \ldots \wedge R_n$.

Begin

STEP 1: Transform each constraint relation R_i, to range disjoint form, that is, to a constraint relation R_i' which is logically equivalent to R_i (i.e. R_i and R_i' finitely represent the same regular relation) and which is in *range-disjoint* form.

STEP 2: Perform $R_1' \bowtie R_2' \bowtie \ldots \bowtie R_n'$ using the *sort join algorithm*. (Note that intermediate relations will be in range-disjoint form.)

End

The algorithm used in Step 1 of the multi-join filtering algorithm is given below.

Range-Disjoint Form Algorithm

Input: range constraint relation R, and a subset of attributes $x_1, \ldots, x_e$, which are of type constrained real (this is a subset of $x_1, \ldots, x_d$)

Output: Range-disjoint form of R, i.e. a constraint relation R' which is logically equivalent to R, and which is in range-disjoint form.

Begin

STEP 1: Scan R and, for each x_j, $j = 1, \ldots, e$, construct a sorted list $a_{j1}, \ldots, a_{jk}$ of, and an index (say B-tree) on all range boundaries of x_j. we call a range between two adjacent boundaries an *elementary* range.

STEP 2: Intialize R' to the empty (range-constraint) relation and initialize a (hash) index for tuples to be inserted to R', to detect duplicates. Associated with each tuple in R' is an auxiliary structure that may contain information from many of the original tuples in R.

STEP 3 For each tuple t in R do:

- For each x_j, $j = 1, \ldots, e$, use the maintained B-tree index to partition the range of x_j in t into a set of elementary ranges of x_j

- For each combination of elementary ranges for $x_1, \ldots, x_e$, construct a tuple t' with these ranges and a reference to all other attributes and constraints from the tuple t. Insert t' to R' while employing the hash index to detect duplicates. If t' duplicates an existing tuple s in R', the reference to the remaining attributes/constraints is added to the auxiliary structure of s.

End

We have the following simple claim:

CLAIM 1 *If N is the bound on the number of boundaries used for ranges of each variable x_i for $1 \leq i \leq d$, then the size of a range-constraint relation in range-disjoint form over $x_1, \ldots, x_d$ is bounded by $O(N^d)$.*

The claim is established quite simply. Given N boundaries on a variable x_i, namely $b_1, b_2, \ldots, b_N$, there are $2N + 1$ intervals on x_i that may appear in a tuple in the relation. N of these are point-intervals $[b_i, b_i]$, $N - 1$ are intervals $[b_i, b_{i+1}]$, and two are semi-infinite intervals. Since there are d variables involved, there may be up to $(2N + 1)^d$ distinct tuples on these variables, which is $O(N^d)$ if d is bounded.

When the range-disjoint relation has been constructed from an original relation R, associated with each tuple is a collection of (generalized) tuples containing values for other variables in the relation and constraints on all the variables. Accessing this collection introduces a factor of $O(M)$, where M is the number of tuples in the original relation. Thus the number of range constraint tuples in the transformed relation is $O(N^d)$, but the space occupied is $O(N^d * M)$.

Overall complexity of the multi-join filtering algorithm is the complexity of constraint sort join applied $n - 1$ times, where the size of the intermediate relation is bounded by $O(N^d)$. We use here the straightforward fact that binary equi-join on range constraint relations preserves the *range-disjoint-form* property. This gives the multi-join filtering algorithm a worst-case time of

$$O(n(N^d \log N^d + \log^{d-2} N^d)) = O(n(dN^d \log N + d^{d-2} \log^{d-2} N))$$

which is $O(nN^d \log N)$ if d is bounded by a constant.

10.   Optimization for Constraint Select-Project-Join Queries

In this section we show how to use the gambling algorithm to evaluate constraint join-select-project queries. We consider queries having up to two relations, that is, of the form

CONSTRUCT $a(\overline{X})$
            FROM $b(\overline{Y})$,
                     $c(\overline{Z})$
            WHERE $cons(\overline{W})$

where b and c are constraint relations and $cons(\overline{W})$ is a set of linear constraints. We propose the following evaluation scheme:

1. Decide on whether to use a regular join, or a constraint sort join or constraint indexed join algorithm.

2. For a constraint sort join choose *scanned* attributes that should include all regular (in both relations) common attributes, in addition to one selected constrained common attribute. Choose also a set of *active* common attributes. If the set of scanned attributes is already ordered, decide on whether selections are to be done on this relation (in the process probably destroying the ordering).

3. For an index join, decide which of the relations is to be scanned, and choose an index on common attribute(s) for the other relation. The selections before the join will be done only on the scanned relation.

4. Choose a subset T of attributes from $cons(\overline{W})$ and for each attribute $V \in T$ extract from $cons$ the range on V. Only useful attributes should be chosen in T, that is, those that appear in at least one of the relations on which selection is to be done. Let S denote the set of all attributes for which there are non-trivial range constraint.

5. For each relation r on which selection is to be done,

   (A) Pick an index whose selection condition can be explicitly checked by the range constraints on attributes in S.

   (B) Using this index, select all tuples from r which satisfy the range constraints.

   (C) From these tuples filter out those which do not satisfy simply checkable constraints w.r.t r in $cons$ and the extracted range constraints.

   (D) Project out all regular attributes in r that do not appear elsewhere in the query, eliminating duplicates.[5]

6. Perform the chosen join algorithm on the resulting relations.

7. Filter out all tuples in the new relation that do not satisfy constraints in $cons$ that are simply checkable w.r.t. the new relation, or do not satisfy the extracted range constraints.

8. Project out all regular attributes in the new relation that do not appear in $cons$ nor in the answer relation a, eliminating duplicates.

9. For each remaining tuple t, filter out those for which the conjunction of t and $cons$ is unsatisfiable.

10. From the remaining tuples project out regular attributes that do not appear in a, eliminate duplicates and put the resulting tuples into the required for a canonical form;

Each series of choices in the evaluation scheme gives rise to a possible evaluation plan. We discuss only briefly the trial evaluation of a particular plan e, and estimating its cost, referred in the gambling algorithm as "DO-TRIAL-EVAL-OF e" and "FIND Estimated-cost.e." First we extract ranges from $cons$ for variables in T in Step 4. Then, we take a sample of tuples from the relations on which selection is to be done. Exactly as in the case of select-project query in Section 6, we estimate the number of tuples satisfying the selecting condition of the index, and the number of tuples after the additional filtering and projection in Step 5(b,c). Using this information, we estimate the cost of the index and the filtering.

Estimation of the cost of the join in Step 6 depends on the join method. For indexed join, we use the sample from the scanned relation. This sample is likely to have been taken already for estimation of selection cost. Then we actually join each tuple in the sample with the second relation using the chosen index. This is done in order to measure the average cost per tuple and to estimate the number of tuples in the result of the join in Step 6. For sort-join, we take sample of pairs of tuples from the relations b and c. Note that in order to get sufficient accuracy of the estimation the size of the sample should be significantly larger than that of indexed join. We use this sample to estimate the average number of tuples in b that can be joined with one tuple in c in the sort join and vice versa, and then to substitute these numbers in the formula for the sort-join cost. The cost estimation of the remaining steps is done by actually performing this steps on the result of the "simulated cost" and then normalizing the costs, analogically to what is done in the estimation for select-project queries. Here too we use statistical tests to compute Bounds-of-best-total-cost of e with significant statistical confidence.

The only non-trivial part of the estimation of trial evaluation cost, referred in the gambling algorithm as "ESTIMATED-COST-OF-DO-TRIAL-EVAL-OF e" is estimating range extraction costs. This is done exactly as in the case for select-project queries.

Some of the work that is done in estimating the cost of one plan can be re-used for other plans. This includes the sampling of relations, the extraction of ranges, and the testing of the satisfiability of some conjunctions of constraints. Thus, after one plan has been evaluated the cost of estimating other plans might change.

The number of evaluation plans is quite large, too large to investigate all of them. It is necessary to focus on a well-chosen few. We provide some heuristics on the order in which evaluation plans are to be considered in the gambling algorithm. We propose to consider plans earlier when they:

1. require fewer additional range extractions.

2. among the plans with indexed join, use a "stronger" index, where "stronger" is defined as for select-project queries. For the plans with sort join consider as follows. If there is at least one attribute to be active, consider first the plans with smaller number of active attributes. Among those, consider first those with active attribute that is regular in one relation[6].

3. have stronger indices for selection.

4. use an indexed join when picking a plan to be the first.

Among plans that are not distinguished by the previous criteria, pick any one, preserving fairness (for example pick one at random).

11. Conclusions and Future Research

The introduction of linear constraints to relations and queries substantially extends the expressiveness of relational databases. However, it also makes the problem of query optimization more difficult, since some of the assumptions underlying conventional query optimization no longer apply.

One assumption of conventional approaches to query optimization is that the data and operations to be performed are explicit. This assumption no longer holds in constraint databases, since the constraints in a query might only implicitly specify selection or join conditions.

A second assumption of conventional approaches is on the distribution of data and/or the cost of operations. Cost estimation approaches typically make uniformity and independence assumptions about the data; it is not even clear what these concepts mean in the context of constraint data. In all cost models of query evaluation, selection is assumed to be a low cost operation but when constraints are involved even a selection can be expensive (depending on the chosen form for constraints). Thus conventional approaches to query optimization for relational data are not appropriate for constraint databases.

Furthermore, to compare different evaluation plans it is necessary to perform constraint manipulation operations (for example, to determine what a selection condition is, and whether it can exploit an index). It may happen that the cost of estimating one evaluation plan is greater than the cost of executing another. Thus the cost of choosing an evaluation plan must be considered a potentially significant part of the cost of the overall query evaluation.

This has led us to devise a generic algorithm that balances the cost of estimating an evaluation plan against the current estimated cost for query evaluation. The algorithm is prepared to "gamble" some time in estimating a new evaluation plan in the hope of discovering a better plan, but will risk only a proportion of the estimated cost for query evaluation. While query evaluation appears expensive, many plans may be considered, but if an inexpensive plan is discovered, few further plans will be evaluated.

In addition to the issue of query planning, we must also consider the representation of the data, and the operations involved in query evaluation. Constraint information can be presented in many mathematically-equivalent ways, but use of a canonical form is computationally advantageous. We have outlined the possibilities, and chosen a flexible approach that allows us to avoid, or at least defer, some computationally expensive operations (such as quantifier elimination) and to perform some indexing.

Thus far, there are no indexing schemes capable of efficiently accessing tuples through their constrained attributes when there are arbitrary linear constraints on the attributes. Consequently, we must represent range information explicitly in the constraints and use established data structures on ranges to perform indexing. Such indexes are not exact (in the sense that the collection of ranges on constrained variables in a tuple only approximates the values represented by the tuple) but can be used to perform filtering for selections and indexed joins on constrained attributes. We have presented an analog of a sort join based on ranges using techniques from computational geometry. Similarly, we have shown how the cost of filtering a multi-join using ranges can be bounded.

This work provides a framework in which linear constraint databases can be implemented. However, considerable empirical investigation is necessary to evaluate the framework. The gambling algorithm receives as input a sequence of evaluation plans. To produce evaluation plans and evaluate them, we must have (1) a paradigm to express evaluation plans that are powerful enough to "encode" efficient algorithms, (2) a set of meaningful transformation rules that can be used to enumerate promising evaluation plans, and (3) a system that is able to evaluate the evaluation plans. Achieving these three objectives is a formidable task in itself and, in fact, this is the aim of the CCUBE project [9]. Currently, variations of algorithms suggested in this paper are being implemented on top of the CCUBE system in the framework of global optimization. The CCUBE data manipulation language, *Constraint Comprehension Calculus* (C^3), is an integration of a constraint calculus for extensible constraint domains within monoid comprehensions, which serves as an optimization-level language for queries (see [9] for details).

Acknowledgements

The work was supported in part by NSF RIA grant No. 92-122, Office of Naval Research under prime grant No. N00014-94-1-1153, and by Australian Research Council grant No. A49700519.

Notes

1. In [28], existential quantifiers are not allowed.
2. Typically, $f(m, k) = O(\log m + k)$.
3. Subprocedures requiring additional explanation appear in the algorithm in SMALL CAPITALS.
4. If a range is, in fact, a point then p contains only one element for that tuple.
5. Two tuples are duplicate if they are identical including the canonical form of the constraints.
6. Recall that since we always put regular common attributes to be scanned, an active attribute cannot be regular in both relations.

References

1. M.M. Astrahan, et al.(1976). System R: A Relational Approach to Database Management. *ACM Trans. on Database Systems* 1:97–137.
2. F. Afrati, S. Cosmadakis, S. Grumbach & G. Kuper.(1994). Linear versus polynomial constraints in database query languages. In A. Borning, editor, *Proc. 2nd International Workshop on Principles and Practice of Constraint Programming*, volume 874 of *Lecture Notes in Conmputer Science*, pages 181–192, Springer Verlag, Rosario, WA..
3. P.A. Bernstein& N. Goodman.(1981). The Power of Natural Semijoins. *SIAM Journal on Computing* 10:751–771.
4. A. Brodsky, J. Jaffar, & M.J. Maher.(1993). Toward Practical Constraint Databases. *Proc. 19th International Conference on Very Large Data Bases*, Dublin, Ireland.
5. A. Brodsky., C. Lassez, J.-L Lassez & M.J. Maher.(1995). Separability of Polyhedra for Optimal Filtering of Spatial and Constraint Data. *Proc. ACM SIGACT-SIGMOD-SIGART Symposium on Principles of Database Systems*, ACM Press.
6. A. Brodsky & Y. Kornatzky.(1995). The LyriC language: Quering constraint objects. In Carey and Schneider, editors, *Proc. ACM SIGMOD International Conference on Management of Data*, San Jose, CA.
7. M. Baudinet, M. Niezette & P. Wolper.(1991). On the representation of infinite temporal data and queries. In *Proc. ACM SIGACT-SIGART-SIGMOD Symp. on Principles of Database Systems*.
8. A. Brodsky& Y. Sagiv.(1989). Inference of monotonicity constraints in datalog programs. *Proc. ACM SIGACT-SIGART-SIGMOD Symp. on Principles of Database Systems*, pages 190–199. Philadelphia, PA.
9. A. Brodsky, J. Chen, V. E. Segal & P.A. Exarkhopoulo.(1997). The CCUBE Constraint Object-Oriented Database System. *Constraints*, this issue. Preliminary version in: Constraint Databases and Applications, Proc. Second International Workshop on Constraint Databases Systems (CDB97), Lecture Notes in Computer Science, pages 134–159, Springer.
10. A. Brodsky & X.S. Wang.(1995). On approximation-based query evaluation, expensive predicates and constraint objects. In *Proc. ILPS95 Workshop on Constraints, Databases and Logic Programming*, Portland, OR.

11. J. Chomicki & T. Imielinski.(1989). Relational Specifications of Infinite Query Answers. *Proc. ACM SIG-MOD*, pages 174-183.

12. V.S. Chakravarthy& J. Minker.(1986). Multiple Query Processing in Deductive Databases using Query Graphs. *Proc. VLDB*, pages 384–391.

13. D.D. Chamberlin, et al.(1981). Support for Repetitive Transactions and Adhoc Queries in System R. *ACM Trans. on Database Systems* 6:70–94.

14. D. Daniels, et al.(1982). An Introduction to Distributed Query Compilation in R*. IBM Research Report RJ3497.

15. H. Edelsbrunner.(1983). A new approach to rectangle intersections, Part II, *International Journal of Computer Mathematics* 13:221–229.

16. P.P. Griffiths, et al.(1979). Access Path Selection in a Relational Database Management System. *Proc. SIGMOD*, pages 23–34.

17. A. Guttman.(1984). R-trees: A dynamic index structure for spatial searching. *Proc. ACM SIGMOD*, pages 47–57.

18. D.Q. Goldin & P.C. Kanellakis.(1996). Constraint query algebras. *Constraints* 1:45–83.

19. S. Grumbach & J. Su.(1995). Dense-order constraint databases. In *Proc. ACM SIGACT-SIGMOD-SIGART Symp. on Principles of Database Systems.*

20. P.A.V. Hall.(1976). Optimization of a Single Relational Expression in a Relational Database. *IBM Journal of Research and Development* 20:244–257.

21. M.R. Hansen, B.S. Hansen., P. Lucas & P. van Emde Boas.(1989). Integrating Relational Databases and Constraint Languages. *Computer Languages* 14:63–82.

22. R. Helm., K. Marriott, & M. Odersky.(1991). Constraint-based Query Optimization for Spatial Databases. *Proc. 10th PODS*, pages 181–191.

23. J. Jaffar & M. J. Maher.(1994). Constraint Logic Programming: A Survey. *Journal of Logic Programming* 19&20:503–581.

24. J. Jaffar, S. Michaylov, P. Stuckey & R. Yap.(1992). The CLP($\mathcal{R}$) Language and System. *ACM Transactions on Programming Languages* 14:339-395.

25. J. Jaffar & J.-L. Lassez.(1987). Constraint Logic Programming. *Proc. Conf. on Principles of Programming Languages*, pages 111–119.

26. J. Jaffar, M.J. Maher, P. Stuckey & R. Yap.(1993). Projecting CLP($\mathfrak{R}$) Constraints. *New Generation Computing* 11:449–469.

27. A. Klug.(1988). On Conjunctive Queries Containing Inequalities. *JACM* 35:146–160.

28. P. Kanellakis, G. Kuper & P. Revesz.(1990). Constraint Query Languages, *Journal of Computer and System Sciences*(forthcoming). (A preliminary version appeared in *Proc. 9th PODS*, pages 299–313.)

29. G.M. Kuper.(1993). Aggregation in constraint databases. In *Proc. Workshop on Principles and Practice of Constraint Programming.*

30. D. Kemp & P. Stuckey.(1993). Bottom Up Constraint Logic Programming Without Constraint Solving. Technical Report, Dept. of Computer Science, University of Melbourne.

31. D. Kemp , K. Ramamohanarao, I. Balbin & K. Meenakshi.(1989). Propagating Constraints in Recursive Deductive Databases. *Proc. North American Conference on Logic Programming, pages* 981–998.

32. P. Kanellakis, S. Ramaswamy, D.E. Vengroff & J.S. Vitter.(1993). Indexing for Data Models with Constraints and Classes. *Proc. PODS.*

33. F. Kabanza, J.-M. Stevenne & P. Wolper.(1990). Handling infinite temporal data. In *Proc. ACM SIGACT-SIGMOD-SIGART Symp. on Principles of Database Systems.*

34. J.-L. Lassez.(1990). Querying Constraints. *Proc. 9th PODS,* pages 288–298.

35. J.-L. Lassez, T. Huynh & K. McAloon.(1989). Simplification and Elimination of Redundant Linear Arithmetic Constraints. In *Proc. North American Conference on Logic Programming*, Cleveland, pages 35–51.

36. A. Levy & Y. Sagiv.(1992). Constraints and Redundancy in Datalog. *Proc. 11-th PODS,* pages 67-80.

37. M.J.Maher.(1989). A Transformation System for Deductive Database Modules with Perfect Model Semantics. *Proc. 9th Conf. on Foundations of Software Technology and Theoretical Computer Science,* Bangalore, India, LNCS 405, pages 89–98. Also in: *Theoretical Computer Science* 110:377–403.

38. E.M. McCreight.(1985). Priority Search Trees. *SIAM Journal of Computing* 14:257-276.

39. L.F. Mackert & G.M. Lohman.(1986). R* Optimizer Validation and Performance Evaluation for Local Queries. *Proc. SIGMOD*, pages 84–95.

40. J. Minker.(1978). Search Strategy and Selection Function for an Inferential Relational System. *ACM Trans. on Database Systems* 3:1–31.

41. I.S. Mumick, S.J. Finkelstein, H. Pirahesh & R. Ramakrishnan.(1990). Magic Conditions. *Proc. 9th PODS*, pages 314–330.

42. M. Niezette & J.-M. Stevenne.(1992). An efficient symbolic representation of periodic time. In *Proc. of First International Conference on Information and Knowledge management.*

43. F.P. Palermo.(1974). A Database Search Problem. in: *Information Systems COINS IV*, J.T. Tou (Ed), Plenum Press.

44. R.M. Pecherer.(1975). Efficient Evaluation of Expressions in a Relational Algebra. *Proc. ACM Pacific Conf.*, pages 44–49.

45. J. Paredaens, J. Van den Bussche & D. Van Gucht.(1994). Towards a theory of spatial database queries. In *Proc. ACM SIGACT-SIGMOD-SIGART Symp. on Principles of Database Systems.*

46. R. Ramakrishnan.(1991). Magic Templates: A Spellbinding Approach to Logic Programs. *Journal of Logic Programming*, 11:189-216.

47. P.Z. Revesz.(1993). A closed form for datalog queries with integer order. *Theoretical Computer Science* 116:pp.

48. P.Z. Revesz.(1995). Datalog queries of set constraint databases. In *Proc. International Conference on Database Theory.*

49. N. Roussopoulos & D. Leifker.(1985). Direct spatial search on pictorial databases using packed R-trees. *Proc. ACM SIGMOD*, pages 17–31.

50. H.W. Six & D. Wood.(1982). Counting and reporting intersections of d-ranges. *IEEE Trans. Computing* C-31:181–187.

51. C.Tollu, S. Grumbach & J. Su.(1995). Linear constraint databases. In *Proc. LCC; To appear in LNCS Springer-Verlag volume.*

52. J.M. Smith & P.Y.Chang.(1975). Optimizing the Performance of a Relational Algebra Database Interface. *Communications of the ACM* 18:568–579.

53. T. Sellis, N. Roussopoulos & C. Faloutsus.(1987). The R^+-tree: A dynamic index for multidimensional objects. *Proc. 13th Int. Conf. Very Large Data Bases*, pages 507–518.

54. D. Srivastava.(1992). Subsumption and Indexing in Constraint Query Languages with Linear Arithmetic Constraints. *Annals of Mathematics and Artificial Intelligence*, to appear.

55. D. Srivastava & R. Ramakrishnan.(1992). Pushing Constraint Selections. *Proc. 11th PODS*, pages 301–315.

56. D. Srivastava, R. Ramakrishnan & P. Revesz.(1994). Constraint objects. In *Proc. 2nd Workshop on the Principles and Practice of Constraint Programming*, Orcas Island, WA.

57. L. Vandeurzen, M. Gyssens & D. Van Gucht.(1995). On the desirability and limitations of linear spatial query languages. In M. J. Egenhofer and J. R. Herring, editors, *Proc. 4th Symposium on Advances in Spatial Databases*, volume 951 of *Lecture Notes in Computer Science*, pages 14–28. Springer Verlag.

58. K.-Y. Whang & R. Krishnamurthy.(1990). Query Optimization in a Memory-Resident Domain Relational Calculus Database System. *ACM Trans. on Database Systems* 15: 67–95.

59. E. Wong & K. Youssefi.(1976). Decomposition – A Strategy for Query Processing. *ACM Trans. on Database Systems* 1:223–241.

60. M. Yannakakis (1981). Algorithms for Acyclic Database Schemes. *Proc. VLDB*, pages 82–94.

Constraints: An International Journal, 2, 305–335 (1997)

A Decompositional Approach for Computing Least Fixed-Points of Datalog Programs with $\mathcal{Z}$-Counters

LAURENT FRIBOURG   fribourg@lsv.ens-cachan.fr
Ecole Normale Supérieure Cachan & CNRS, 61 av. Président Wilson, 94235 Cachan - France

HANS OLSÉN   hanol@ida.liu.se
IDA, Linköping University, S-58183 Linköping - Sweden

Abstract. We present a method for characterizing the least fixed-points of a certain class of Datalog programs in Presburger arithmetic. The method consists in applying a set of rules that transform general computation paths into "canonical" ones. We use the method for treating the problem of reachability in the field of Petri nets, thus relating some unconnected results and extending them in several directions.

Keywords: decomposition, linear arithmetic, least fixed-point, Petri nets, reachability set

1. Introduction

The problem of computing fixpoints for arithmetical programs has been investigated from the seventies in an imperative framework. A typical application was to check whether or not array bounds were violated. A pioneering work in this field is the work by Cousot-Halbwachs [9]. The subject has known a renewal of interest with the development of logic programming and deductive databases with arithmetical constraints. Several new applications were then possible in these frameworks: proof of termination of logic programs [15, 31, 36] compilation of recursive queries in temporal databases [2, 21] verification of safety properties of concurrent systems [17]. However almost all these works are interested in finding not the *least* fixpoint but rather an approximation of it using some techniques of Abstract Interpretation (convex hull, widening, ...). A notable exception is the work of [33] and of [6] whose procedures allow to compute least fixpoints, but for very restrictive classes of programs, viz. programs with no or at most one incremental argument. In this paper we are interested in finding the *least* fixed points for Datalog programs having *all* their arguments incremented by the recursive clauses. The arguments of the programs can be seen as *counters*. By applying a clause from-right-to left (in a forward/bottom-up manner), one increments all the arguments providing that the constraints of the clause body are satisfied. The problem of computing least fixed-points for such programs is closely related, as will be explained, to the problem of characterizing the set of the reachable markings ("reachability set") of Petri nets. The main difference is that the variables of our programs take their values on $\mathcal{Z}$ instead of $\mathcal{N}$ as in the case of Petri nets. We will see however that some transformation rules by "decomposition" defined for Petri nets, such as Berthelot's post-fusion rule [3], still apply to our programs with $\mathcal{Z}$-counters. The fact that we manipulate variables taking their values on $\mathcal{Z}$ rather than on $\mathcal{N}$ will allow us to encode in a simple way the important extension of Petri nets with *inhibitors*. As an example, we will see how

67

to prove the mutual exclusion property of a Petri net modelling a system of readers and writers where the number of processes is parametric. We also show how our method allows us to treat the reachability problem for a special class of Petri nets, called BPP-nets, thus generalizing a result of [10]).

The plan of this paper is as follows. In Section 2 we give some preliminaries. Section 3 recalls some basic facts about Petri nets. Section 4 gives the basic rules of our decompositional method. Section 5 compares our approach with relevant work. Section 6 shows that our method allows us to solve the reachability problem for the special class of Basic Parallel Process nets. Section 7 gives a further generalized form of our basic decomposition rule. Section 8 briefly discusses the compilation into an arithmetic formula and our implementation. We conclude in Section 9.

2. Preliminaries

Our aim in this paper is to express the least fixed-point of a certain class of logic programs as a linear integer arithmetic expression (a Presburger formula). We consider programs of the form:

$$
\begin{aligned}
& p(x_1,\ldots,x_m) && \leftarrow B(x_1,\ldots,x_m). \\
r_1: \quad & p(x_1+k_{1,1},\ldots,x_m+k_{1,m}) && \leftarrow x_{i_{1,1}} > a_{1,1},\ldots,x_{i_{1,m_1}} > a_{1,m_1}, \\
& && \quad p(x_1,\ldots,x_m). \\
& \vdots \\
r_n: \quad & p(x_1+k_{n,1},\ldots,x_m+k_{n,m}) && \leftarrow x_{i_{n,1}} > a_{n,1},\ldots,x_{i_{n,m_n}} > a_{n,m_n}, \\
& && \quad p(x_1,\ldots,x_m).
\end{aligned}
$$

where $B(x_1,\ldots,x_m)$ is a linear integer relation, $k_{i,j}, a_{i,l} \in \mathcal{Z}$ are integer constants and r_j is simply the name of the j:th recursive clause. We will usually denote by $\overline{x}$ the vector $\langle x_1,\ldots,x_m\rangle$, by $\overline{k}_{r_j}$ the vector $\langle k_{j,1},\ldots,k_{j,m}\rangle$ and by $\vartheta_{r_j}(\overline{x})$ the constraint $x_{i_{j,1}} > a_{j,1},\ldots,x_{i_{j,m_j}} > a_{j,m_j}$. Usually the constants $a_{i,l}$ are equal to zero.

One can see these programs as classical programs with counters expressed under a logic programming or Datalog form. These programs have thus the power of expressivity of Turing machines. In the following we will refer to this class of programs as *(Datalog) programs with $\mathcal{Z}$-counters*. The motivation for studying this class is mainly because syntactically it is restricted enough to allow simple decomposition rules to be formulated and since there are no terms other than integers one can work within an arithmetic context. At the same time these programs are expressive enough to be interesting.

We introduce a convenient description of the execution of programs with $\mathcal{Z}$-counters in a bottom-up manner. Let $\Sigma = \{r_1,\ldots,r_n\}$. A string $w \in \Sigma^*$ is called a *path*, and is interpreted as a sequence of applications of the clauses in a bottom-up manner. Given some point $\overline{x}$, the point reached by applying the path w is denoted $\overline{x}w$. Formally: $\overline{x}w = \overline{x} + \overline{k}_w$, where $\overline{k}_w$ is defined by:

$$\bar{k}_\varepsilon = \bar{0}$$
$$\bar{k}_{r_j w} = \bar{k}_{r_j} + \bar{k}_w$$

Note that the expression $\bar{x}w$ does not take the constraints in the bodies of the clauses into account. We say that a path w is *applicable* at a point $\bar{x}$, if all constraints along the path are satisfied, and we write $\vartheta_w(\bar{x})$. Formally:

$$\vartheta_\varepsilon(\bar{x}) \quad \Leftrightarrow \quad \text{true}$$
$$\vartheta_{r_j w}(\bar{x}) \quad \Leftrightarrow \quad \vartheta_{r_j}(\bar{x}) \wedge \vartheta_w(\bar{x}r_j)$$

The expression $\vartheta_w(\bar{x})$ is said to be the *constraint* associated to path w at point $\bar{x}$. It is easily seen that $\vartheta_w(\bar{x})$ can be put under the form $x_{i_1} > a'_1, \ldots, x_{i_{m'}} > a'_{m'}$. As an example, consider the two clauses (borrowed from an example given later on):

$$r_3 : \quad p(x_2 + 1, x_3 - 1, x_4, x_5 + 1, x_6, x_7) \quad \leftarrow \quad x_3 > 0, \ p(x_2, \ldots, x_7).$$
$$r_5 : \quad p(x_2, x_3, x_4, x_5 - 1, x_6 + 1, x_7) \quad \leftarrow \quad x_5 > 0, \ p(x_2, \ldots, x_7).$$

The constraint $\vartheta_{r_3 r_5}(\bar{x})$ associated with $r_3 r_5$ is $\vartheta_{r_3}(\bar{x}) \wedge \vartheta_{r_5}(\bar{x}r_3)$, that is $x_3 > 0 \wedge x_5 + 1 > 0$, i.e.: $x_3 > 0 \wedge x_5 > -1$.

A point $\bar{x}'$ is *reachable* from a point $\bar{x}$ by a path w if $\bar{x}w = \bar{x}'$ and w is applicable at $\bar{x}$:

$$\bar{x} \xrightarrow{w} \bar{x}' \quad \Leftrightarrow \quad \bar{x}w = \bar{x}' \wedge \vartheta_w(\bar{x})$$

A point $\bar{x}'$ is reachable from a point $\bar{x}$ by a language $L \subseteq \Sigma^*$ if there exists a path $w \in L$ such that $\bar{x}'$ is reachable from $\bar{x}$ by w:

$$\bar{x} \xrightarrow{L} \bar{x}' \quad \Leftrightarrow \quad \exists w \in L : \bar{x} \xrightarrow{w} \bar{x}'$$

We usually write $\bar{x} \xrightarrow{L_1} \bar{x}'' \xrightarrow{L_2} \bar{x}'$, instead of $\bar{x} \xrightarrow{L_1} \bar{x}'' \wedge \bar{x}'' \xrightarrow{L_2} \bar{x}'$. From the definitions above, we immediately get:

PROPOSITION 1 *For any path $w \in \Sigma^*$ and any languages $L_1, L_2 \subseteq \Sigma^*$. We have:*

1. $\bar{x} \xrightarrow{L_1 + L_2} \bar{x}' \Leftrightarrow \bar{x} \xrightarrow{L_1} \bar{x}' \vee \bar{x} \xrightarrow{L_2} \bar{x}'$

2. $\bar{x} \xrightarrow{L_1 L_2} \bar{x}' \Leftrightarrow \exists \bar{x}'' : \bar{x} \xrightarrow{L_1} \bar{x}'' \xrightarrow{L_2} \bar{x}'$

3. $\bar{x} \xrightarrow{w^*} \bar{x}' \Leftrightarrow \exists n \geq 0 : \bar{x}' = \bar{x} + n \cdot \bar{k}_w \wedge \forall 0 \leq n' < n : \vartheta_w(\bar{x} + n' \cdot \bar{k}_w)$

In part 3 of the proposition, when $n = 0$, we have $\bar{x} = \bar{x}'$, and the expression $\forall 0 \leq n' < n : \vartheta_w(\bar{x} + n' \cdot \bar{k}_w)$ is vacuously true. Actually, the universally quantified variable n' can always be eliminated from this expression. This is because the constraints $\vartheta_w(\bar{x})$ are necessarily of the form $\bar{x} \geq \bar{a}_w$, where $\bar{x} \geq \bar{a}_w$ denotes a conjunction of the form $x_{i_1} > a'_{1,w}, \ldots, x_{i_{m'}} > a'_{m',w}$. Thus, $\vartheta_w(\bar{x} + n' \cdot \bar{k}_w)$ is $\bar{x} + n' \cdot \bar{k}_w \geq \bar{a}_w$. It is easy to see that, for $n > 0$, the universally quantified expression $\forall 0 \leq n' < n : \bar{x} + n' \cdot \bar{k}_w > \bar{a}_w$ is equivalent to $\bar{x} + (n-1) \cdot \bar{k}_w^- > \bar{a}_w$ where $\bar{k}_w^-$ is the vector obtained from $\bar{k}_w$ by letting all nonnegative components be set to zero. For example if $\vartheta_w(\overline{x})$ is $x_1 > 0 \wedge x_2 > 0$, and k_w is $\langle 2, -3 \rangle$, then $\forall 0 \le n' < n : \overline{x} + n' \cdot \overline{k}_w > \overline{a}_w$ is

$$
\begin{aligned}
& \forall 0 \le n' < n : x_1 + n' \cdot 2 > 0 \ \wedge \ x_2 + n' \cdot (-3) > 0 \\
\Leftrightarrow \quad & x_1 + (n-1) \cdot 0 > 0 \ \wedge \ x_2 + (n-1) \cdot (-3) > 0 \\
\Leftrightarrow \quad & x_1 > 0 \ \wedge \ x_2 - 3n + 3 > 0.
\end{aligned}
$$

As a consequence, from part 3 of the proposition, it follows that, given a finite sequence of transitions w, the relation $\overline{x} \xrightarrow{w^*} \overline{x}'$ is actually an *existentially* quantified formula of Presburger arithmetic having $\overline{x}$ and $\overline{x}'$ as free variables. More generally suppose that L is a language of the form $L_1...L_s$ where L_i is either a finite language or a language of the form w_i^*, then, by proposition 1, it follows that the relation $\overline{x} \xrightarrow{L} \overline{x}'$ can be expressed as an existentially quantified formula of Presburger arithmetic having $\overline{x}$ and $\overline{x}'$ as free variables. We call such a language L a *flat* language (because Kleene's star operator '*' applies only to strings w).

Given a program with $B(\overline{x})$ as a base case and recursive clauses labelled by Σ, the least fixed-point of its immediate consequence operator (see [20, 22], which is also the least $\mathcal{Z}$-model of the program, may be expressed as:

$$
\mathrm{lfp} = \{ \ \overline{x}' \mid \exists \overline{x} : \ B(\overline{x}) \wedge \overline{x} \xrightarrow{\Sigma^*} \overline{x}' \ \}
$$

Our aim is to characterize the membership relation $\overline{y} \in \mathrm{lfp}$ as an arithmetic formula having $\overline{y}$ as a free variable. For solving this problem, it suffices actually to characterize the relation $\overline{x} \xrightarrow{\Sigma^*} \overline{x}'$ as an arithmetic formula having $\overline{x}$ and $\overline{x}'$ as free variables. In order to achieve this, our approach here is to find a flat language $L \subseteq \Sigma^*$, such that the following equivalence holds: $\overline{x} \xrightarrow{\Sigma^*} \overline{x}' \Leftrightarrow \overline{x} \xrightarrow{L} \overline{x}'$. This gives us an arithmetic characterization of the least fixed-point. The language L is constructed by making use of decomposition rules on paths. Such rules state that, if a path v links a point $\overline{x}$ to a point $\overline{x}'$ via Σ^*, then v can be reordered as a path w of the form $w = w_1 w_2 \cdots w_s$ such that $w_1, w_2, \cdots, w_s$ belong to some restricted languages. Such a "decompositional approach" is well known in Petri-net theory (see, e.g., [38]). The rest of the paper is mainly devoted to describe the decomposition rules that we use and their applications for solving the reachability problem with Petri nets and some of their extensions.

3. The Reachability Problem for Petri Nets

3.1. Petri nets as programs with $\mathcal{Z}$-counters

There is a close connection between the class of programs with $\mathcal{Z}$-counters and Petri nets, and more precisely, between the computation of the least fixed-point of programs with $\mathcal{Z}$-counters and the "reachability problem" for Petri nets. Let us first give an informal explanation of what a Petri net is. (This is inspired from [11].) A Petri net is characterized by a set of places (drawn as circles), a set of transitions (drawn as bars), and for each transition

τ, a set of weighted input-arcs going from a subset of places ("input-places") to τ, and a set of weighted output-arcs going from τ to a subset of places ("output-places"). A *marking* is a mapping of the set of places to the set $\mathcal{N}$ of nonnegative integers. The number assigned to a place represents the number of tokens contained by this place. A marking *enables* a transition τ if it assigns all the input places of τ with a number greater than or equal to the weight of the corresponding input-arc. If the transition is enabled, then it can be *fired*, and its firing leads to the successor marking, which is defined for every place as follows: the number of tokens specified by the weight of the corresponding input-arc is removed from each input place of the transition, and the number of tokens specified by the weight of the corresponding output place is added to each output place. (If a place is both an input and an output place, then its number of tokens is changed by the difference of weights between the corresponding output and input arcs.)

The reachability problem for a Petri net consists in characterizing the set of all the markings that are "reachable" from a given initial marking, that is the set of markings that can be produced by iteratively firing all the possible enabled transitions. Let us explain how the reachability problem of a Petri net with n transitions and m places can be encoded as a Datalog program with $\mathcal{Z}$-counters. Each place π_i of the Petri net is represented by a variable x_i, and its value encodes the number of tokens at that place. As a base case relation $B(\overline{x})$, one take the equation $\overline{x} = \overline{a}^0$ where $\overline{a}^0$ denotes the initial marking; each transition τ_j in the net is represented by a recursive clause r_j of the program as follows:

head constants: For each place π_i, the constant $k_{j,i}$ is equal to the weight of the output-arc going from τ_j to π_i, minus the weight of the input arc going from π_i to τ_j.

body constraints: For each input place π_i of transition τ_j, there is a constraint in the clause r_j of the form $x_i > a_{j,i} - 1$ where $a_{j,i}$ is equal to the weight of the input arc going out from π_i to τ_j. (No other constraints occur in the clause.)

Each clause of the program encodes the enabling condition of the corresponding Petri net transition. The above program therefore encodes the reachability problem for the considered Petri net: a tuple $\overline{y}$ belongs to the least fixed-point of the program iff it corresponds to a marking reachable from the initial one via the firing of a certain sequence of Petri net transitions. In other words the least fixed-point of the recursive program coincides with the set of the reachable markings ("reachability set") of the Petri net.

Note that the class of Datalog programs with $\mathcal{Z}$-counters is more general than the class of above programs encoding the reachability problem for Petri nets. From a syntactical point of view, the difference is that, with programs encoding the reachability problem, all the variables take their values on the domain $\mathcal{N}$ of non-negative integers while the domain for programs with $\mathcal{Z}$-counters is $\mathcal{Z}$. From a theoretical point of view, programs with $\mathcal{Z}$-counters have the power of Turing machines while (programs coding for the reachability problem of) Petri nets have not. We will come back to this issue in the forthcoming subsection.

3.2. 0-tests

There are many extensions to the Petri-net formalism, one of which allows *inhibitors* or 0-tests. In such extensions, the transitions may be conditioned by the fact that some input place contains 0 token. This test is materialized by the existence of an "inhibitor-arc" (represented as circle-headed arcs) from the place to the transition. Petri-nets with inhibitors are naturally encoded as Datalog programs with $\mathcal{Z}$-counters by adding a constraint $x_i = 0$ in the body of clause r_j whenever there is an inhibitor arc from place i to transition j. When the input place is known to be bounded (i.e., the place can never contain more than a fixed number of tokens during the evolution of the Petri net configuration), it is well-known that one can simulate such a 0-test using conventional Petri nets. For example, if the bound of the inhibitor place is known to be 1, it is easy to add a "complementary place" to the net whose value is 0 (resp. 1) when the inhibitor place is 1 (resp. 0). Instead of testing the inhibitor place to 0, it is equivalent to test if the complementary place contains (at least) one token. Such a simulation is not possible when the place is unbounded. Actually Petri nets with inhibitor places can simulate Turing machines, so there is no hope to simulate such an extension while keeping inside the class of Petri nets.

On the other hand, within our framework where the variables of the program can take *negative* values, it is easy to simulate 0-tests. We encode inhibitor arcs by replacing a constraint $x_j = 0$ by $x'_j > 0$ where x'_j is a newly introduced variable. This new variable x'_j is to be equal to $1 - x_j$. The variable x'_j is introduced as a new argument into p. Its initial value a'^0_j is set to $1 - a^0_j$, where a^0_j denotes the initial value of x_j. Within each recursive clause r_i of the program, the new argument x'_j is incremented by $-k_{i,j}$ (where $k_{i,j}$ denotes the value the variable x_j is incremented by r_i). Formally, if we denote the newly defined predicate by p', we have in the least $\mathcal{Z}$-model of the union of the programs defining p and p': $p(\overline{x}) \Leftrightarrow \exists x'_j\, p'(\overline{x}, x'_j)$.

3.3. Parametric initial markings

Recall that the least fixed-point of the encoding program (i.e., the reachability set of the corresponding Petri net) can be expressed as follows:

$$\mathrm{lfp} = \{\, \overline{x}' \mid \exists \overline{x} : B(\overline{x}) \wedge \overline{x} \xrightarrow{\Sigma^*} \overline{x}' \,\}$$

Here $B(\overline{x})$ is $\overline{x} = \overline{a}^0$ where $\overline{a}^0$ denotes the initial marking of the Petri net, that is *a priori* a tuple of nonnegative constants. Our aim is to characterize the relation $\overline{y} \in \mathrm{lfp}$ as an arithmetical formula having $\overline{y}$ as a free variable. It is however often interesting to reason more generically with some *parametric initial markings*, i.e., initial markings where certain places are assigned parameters instead of constant values. This defines a family of Petri nets, which are obtained by replacing successively the parameters with all the possible positive or null values.

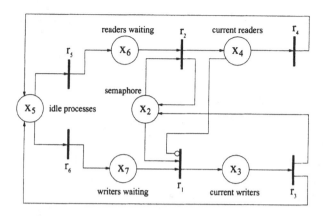

Figure 1. A readers-writers protocol.

One can easily encode the reachability relation for a Petri net with a parametric initial marking via a program with $\mathcal{Z}$-counter by adding the initial marking parameters as extra arguments of the encoding predicate. For the sake of notation simplicity however, we will not make such extra predicate arguments appear explicitly in the following. (The parameters will just appear in the base clause associated with the initial marking.) In the case of a Petri net with an initial marking containing a tuple of parameters, say $\bar{q}$, our aim will be to characterize the relation $\bar{y} \in$ lfp as an arithmetical formula having $\bar{y}$ and $\bar{q}$ as free variables.

3.4. Example

We illustrate the encoding of Petri-nets with inhibitors and parametric initial markings by an example.

Example: We consider here a Petri net implementing a simple readers-writers protocol. (This is inspired from (Ajmone, 95), p.17.) This Petri net has six places encoded by the variables $x_2, x_3, x_4, x_5, x_6,$ x_7 and six transitions encoded by the recursive clauses $r_1, r_2, r_3, r_4, r_5, r_6$. (It will be clear later on why the enumeration of places x_i starts with $i = 2$.) Place x_5 represents the number of idle processes. Place x_6 (resp. x_7) the number of candidates for reading (resp. writing). Place x_4 (resp. x_3) represents the number of current readers (resp. writers). Place x_2 is a semaphore for guaranteeing mutual exclusion of readers and writers. Only one inhibitor arc exists in the net, connecting x_4 to r_1. The Petri net is represented on figure 1. (The weights of the arcs are always equal to 1, and do not appear explicitly on the figure.) Only two places are initially marked: x_2 and x_5. The latter contains a parametric number of tokens, defined by the parameter q, while the former contains one token. The program P encoding this Petri-net is the following:

$$p(x_2, x_3, x_4, x_5, x_6, x_7) \quad\quad\quad \leftarrow x_2 = 1, x_3 = 0, x_4 = 0, x_5 = q,$$
$$q \geq 0, x_6 = 0, x_7 = 0.$$

$r_1:$ $p(x_2 - 1, x_3 + 1, x_4, x_5, x_6, x_7 - 1) \leftarrow x_2 > 0, x_7 > 0, x_4 = 0,$
                                             $p(x_2, \ldots, x_7).$

$r_2:$ $p(x_2, x_3, x_4 + 1, x_5, x_6 - 1, x_7) \quad\leftarrow x_2 > 0, x_6 > 0,$
                                             $p(x_2, \ldots, x_7).$

$r_3:$ $p(x_2 + 1, x_3 - 1, x_4, x_5 + 1, x_6, x_7) \leftarrow x_3 > 0,$
                                             $p(x_2, \ldots, x_7).$

$r_4:$ $p(x_2, x_3, x_4 - 1, x_5 + 1, x_6, x_7) \quad\leftarrow x_4 > 0,$
                                             $p(x_2, \ldots, x_7).$

$r_5:$ $p(x_2, x_3, x_4, x_5 - 1, x_6 + 1, x_7) \quad\leftarrow x_5 > 0,$
                                             $p(x_2, \ldots, x_7).$

$r_6:$ $p(x_2, x_3, x_4, x_5 - 1, x_6, x_7 + 1) \quad\leftarrow x_5 > 0,$
                                             $p(x_2, \ldots, x_7).$

To replace the constraint $x_4 = 0$, we introduce the new variable x_1 and construct a new program P' defined in such a way that $x_1 = 1 - x_4$, holds in the least model of P', and replace $x_4 = 0$ by $x_1 > 0$ in clause r_1. We get:

$$p'(x_1, x_2, x_3, x_4, x_5, x_6, x_7) \quad\quad \leftarrow x_1 = 1 - x_4, x_2 = 1,$$
$$x_3 = 0, x_4 = 0, x_5 = q,$$
$$q \geq 0, x_6 = 0, x_7 = 0.$$

$r_1:$ $p'(x_1, x_2 - 1, x_3 + 1, x_4, x_5, x_6, x_7 - 1) \leftarrow x_2 > 0, x_7 > 0, x_1 > 0,$
                                             $p'(x_1, \ldots, x_7).$

$r_2:$ $p'(x_1 - 1, x_2, x_3, x_4 + 1, x_5, x_6 - 1, x_7) \leftarrow x_2 > 0, x_6 > 0,$
                                             $p'(x_1, \ldots, x_7).$

$r_3:$ $p'(x_1, x_2 + 1, x_3 - 1, x_4, x_5 + 1, x_6, x_7) \leftarrow x_3 > 0,$
                                             $p'(x_1, \ldots, x_7).$

$r_4:$ $p'(x_1 + 1, x_2, x_3, x_4 - 1, x_5 + 1, x_6, x_7) \leftarrow x_4 > 0,$
                                             $p'(x_1, \ldots, x_7).$

$r_5:$ $p'(x_1, x_2, x_3, x_4, x_5 - 1, x_6 + 1, x_7) \leftarrow x_5 > 0,$
                                             $p'(x_1, \ldots, x_7).$

$r_6:$ $p'(x_1, x_2, x_3, x_4, x_5 - 1, x_6, x_7 + 1) \leftarrow x_5 > 0,$
                                             $p'(x_1, \ldots, x_7).$

We have the following equivalence:

$$p(x_2, x_3, x_4, x_5, x_6, x_7) \Leftrightarrow \exists x_1 : p'(x_1, x_2, x_3, x_4, x_5, x_6, x_7)$$

We would like to prove that, for this protocol, there is always at most one current writer (i.e. $x_3 = 0 \vee x_3 = 1$), and that reading and writing can never occur at the same time (i.e.: $x_3 = 0 \vee x_4 = 0$). Formally, we must prove:

$$p'(x_1, x_2, x_3, x_4, x_5, x_6, x_7) \Rightarrow (x_3 = 0 \vee x_3 = 1)$$

$$p'(x_1, x_2, x_3, x_4, x_5, x_6, x_7) \Rightarrow (x_3 = 0 \lor x_4 = 0)$$

The classical methods of verification of Petri nets by invariants (see, e.g., [?, 30]) are able to prove the first implication: by analysing the transitions without taking into account the guards, they generate a set of linear combinations $\Sigma_{i=1}^{7} \lambda_i x_i$ of $x_1, ..., x_7$, which are left invariant by any transition r_j ($1 \le j \le 6$).[1] Among the generated invariants, there is the formula $x_2 + x_3 = 1$. Since the variables x_2 and x_3 take only positive or null values, it follows immediately that x_3 must be 0 or 1. The second property of "mutual exclusion" ($x_3 = 0 \lor x_4 = 0$) is more difficult to establish. (See however [27]) for a recent method extending the classical methods with invariants for dealing with such mutual exclusion properties.) We will see in this paper how our method of construction of least fixed-points allows us to solve this problem (see section 8). □

4. Construction of Least Fixed-points

The transformations we are going to present, only concern the recursive clauses. Since these clauses all have the same form (i.e. no reordering or sharing of variables, and all recursive calls are exactly the same) we will represent a program by an "incrementation matrix" whose j:th row is the vector $\bar{k}_j$ of coefficients of the j:th recursive clause of the program, and the constraints and the name of the clause are written to the right of the corresponding row of the matrix.

Example: The program P' of Section 3.4 is represented by:

0	-1	1	0	0	0	-1	$x_2 > 0, x_7 > 0, x_1 > 0$	$: r_1$
-1	0	0	1	0	-1	0	$x_2 > 0, x_6 > 0$	$: r_2$
0	1	-1	0	1	0	0	$x_3 > 0$	$: r_3$
1	0	0	-1	1	0	0	$x_4 > 0$	$: r_4$
0	0	0	0	-1	1	0	$x_5 > 0$	$: r_5$
0	0	0	0	-1	0	1	$x_5 > 0$	$: r_6$
x_1	x_2	x_3	x_4	x_5	x_6	x_7		

□

Without loss of understanding, we will also call "program" the set Σ of the labels $r_1, .., r_n$ of the recursive clauses.

4.1. Decomposition rules

As explained before, the method we use to compute the reachability set consists in showing that any path can be reordered into some specific "simpler" form. In this paper we present in detail only two transformation rules. (The definition of some other rules is given besides in appendix A.) The rules are stated in the form: $\bar{x} \xrightarrow{\Sigma^*} \bar{x}' \Leftrightarrow \bar{x} \xrightarrow{L_1 L_2 \cdots L_s} \bar{x}'$. We say that Σ^* *decomposes as* $L_1 L_2 \cdots L_s$. Each languages L_i ($1 \le i \le s$) denotes here either a finite language or a language of the form Σ_i^* where Σ_i is a label for a new "simpler" program.

Programs Σ_i are "simpler" than the original program (labeled by Σ) by either containing a fewer number of recursive clauses, or by letting more variables invariant. (From a syntactic point of view, a variable is invariant when the corresponding column in the incrementation matrix is null.)

Formally, we define the *dimension* of a program with $\mathcal{Z}$-counters as a couple (m, n) where n is the number of clauses of the program, and m is the number of *non invariant* variables of the program (i.e. the number of non null columns in the corresponding incrementation matrix). We also define an order on these dimensions as follows: The dimension (m_1, n_1) is lower than (m_2, n_2) iff $m_1 < m_2$, or $m_1 = m_2$ and $n_1 < n_2$. Each transformation rule thus decomposes the original language Σ^* into either finite languages (for which the reachability problem is solvable in the existential fragment of Presburger arithmetic, see section 2) or into languages associated with programs of lower dimension. There are two kinds of "elementary" programs with a *basic* dimension. The first kind consists in programs of dimension $(1, n)$, i.e. programs made of n clauses, $r_1, \ldots, r_n$ with all but one column being null. As will be seen later on (see section 4.2, remark 3), the reachability problem for such programs can be easily solved and expressed in the existential fragment of Presburger arithmetic. The second kind of elementary programs are programs of dimension $(m, 1)$, i.e., programs made of a single clause, say r_1. In this case the expression $\overline{x} \xrightarrow{\Sigma^*} \overline{x}'$ reduces to $\overline{x} \xrightarrow{r_1^*} \overline{x}'$, which can be also expressed in the existential fragment of Presburger arithmetic (see section 2). Therefore the decomposition process must eventually terminate either successfully, thus leading to a characterization of the reachability relation in Presburger arithmetic, or it terminates with failure because no decomposition rule can be applied.

In keeping with a former approach [12], we will consider two types of decomposition rules: *monotonic* and *cyclic* rules. The monotonic decompositions are based on the fact that some clauses of a program may be applied all at once at some point during a computation, while the cyclic decompositions exploit that there is some fixed sequences of clause firings that can be repeated. We first present one monotonic decomposition rule, then one cyclic rule.

4.2. Monotonic decomposition rule

The first decomposition rule is called *monotonic clause*. This decomposition applies when there is a clause whose coefficients in the head are all nonegative or nonpositive. Thus, the monotonic clause is stated in two versions: one *increasing*, and one *decreasing*. For the purposes of this paper, we only state the increasing version (the decreasing one being symmetric). This rule applies to a program whose matrix is of the form:

$$
\begin{array}{ccc}
\vdots & & \vartheta_{r_{...}} \quad : r_{...} \\
+ \quad \cdots \quad + & & \vartheta_{r_l} \quad : r_l \\
\vdots & & \vartheta_{r_{...}} \quad : r_{...} \\
x_1 & x_m &
\end{array}
$$

This means that, in the program, we have $\forall j : k_{l,j} \geq 0$. In such a case, clause r_l can be "prioritized" before all the rest of the clauses: given a path w starting at a point $\overline{x}$ where $\vartheta_{r_l}(\overline{x})$ holds, one can always reorder w so that all the clauses r_l are applied first. Formally we have:

PROPOSITION 2 *Let $r_l \in \Sigma$ be a clause such that $\forall j : k_{l,j} \geq 0$. Then:*

$$\overline{x} \xrightarrow{\Sigma^*} \overline{x}' \iff \overline{x} \xrightarrow{(\Sigma-\{r_l\})^* r_l^* (\Sigma-\{r_l\})^*} \overline{x}'$$

Proof: Since $\overline{k}_{r_l}$ is a vector made of nonnegative coefficients $k_{l,j}$, we have: $\vartheta_{r_j}(\overline{x}) \Rightarrow \vartheta_{r_j}(\overline{x} + \overline{k}_{r_l})$, i.e. $\vartheta_{r_j}(\overline{x}) \Rightarrow \vartheta_{r_j}(\overline{x}r_l)$, for all $r_j \in \Sigma$. The constraint ϑ_{r_j} is thus invariant under the application of r_l. Therefore, if $\overline{x}'$ is reachable from $\overline{x}$ by some path $w = w_1 r_l w_2$, and $\vartheta_{r_l}(\overline{x})$ holds, then also the path $w' = r_l w_1 w_2$ is applicable, so all the applications of r_l can be pushed to the beginning, and thus $\overline{x}'$ must be reachable from $\overline{x}$ by some path $w'' = r_l \cdots r_l w_3$ where $w_3 \in (\Sigma - \{r_l\})^*$.

Clearly, if $\overline{x}'$ is reachable from $\overline{x}$ by any path $w \in \Sigma^*$ containing r_l, then r_l must occur somewhere for the first time. At that point ϑ_{r_l} must hold, so, by the above, $\overline{x}'$ is reachable by some path $w' \in (\Sigma - \{r_l\})^* r_l^* (\Sigma - \{r_l\})^*$. ∎

Remark 1

As seen in the proof, the requirement that all the coefficients $k_{l,j}$ should be nonnegative is unnecessarily strong. It is enough that $\vartheta_{r_j}(\overline{x}) \Rightarrow \vartheta_{r_j}(\overline{x}r_l)$ holds for every clause $r_j \in \Sigma$, which means that r_l preserves all the constraints of Σ.

Remark 2

It is clear that the languages involved in the right-part of the equivalence in proposition 2, viz. $(\Sigma - \{r_l\})^*$ and r_l^*, are of lower dimension than Σ provided that Σ contains more than one clause. (If Σ contains only one clause, say r_1, then the program is elementary and, as already pointed out, the relation $\overline{x} \xrightarrow{r_1^*} \overline{x}'$ is characterizable as an existentially quantified Presburger formula.)

Remark 3

Consider an elementary program Σ of dimension $(1, n)$. It means that all the columns of its incrementation matrix are null except one, say the h-th column. So the l-th row is monotonic (increasing if $k_{l,h} \geq 0$, or decreasing if $k_{l,h} \leq 0$), for any $1 \leq l \leq n$. Therefore one can apply the monotonic rule, thus decomposing program Σ into $\{r_l\}$ and $\Sigma - \{r_l\}$. For the same reasons, the monotonic rule applies again to the latter program $\Sigma - \{r_l\}$. By iteratively applying the rule, one can thus decompose the reachability problem via Σ^* into reachability problems via $r_1^*, r_2^*, ..., r_n^*$. It follows that one can characterize the reachability problem via Σ^* in the existential fragment of Presburger arithmetic.

Other monotonic decomposition rules are given in appendix A.

4.3. Cyclic decomposition rule

The cyclic decomposition rule that we consider applies to matrices of the general form (after possible reordering among clauses $r_1, ..., r_n$):

$$
\left.
\begin{array}{l}
\bullet \; ... \; \bullet \; + \; \bullet \; ... \; \bullet \qquad \cdots \quad : r_1 \\
\qquad\qquad \vdots \\
\bullet \; ... \; \bullet \; + \; \bullet \; ... \; \bullet \qquad \cdots \quad : r_l \\
+ \; ... \; + \; -1 \; + \; ... \; + \quad x_j > 0 \; : r_{l+1} \\
\qquad\qquad \vdots \\
+ \; ... \; + \; -1 \; + \; ... \; + \quad x_j > 0 \; : r_n \\
\qquad\qquad x_j
\end{array}
\right.
$$

where R and R' are sets of rules such that $\Sigma = R \uplus R'$, the constraints of all the clauses in R are exactly $x_j > 0$ and x_j does not occur in the constraints of any rule in R'. Formally this means

1. $\forall r_i \in R : k_{i,h} \geq 0$ for $h \neq j$
1'. $\forall r_i \in R' : x_j$ does not occur in $\vartheta_{r_i}(\bar{x})$
2. $\forall r_i \in R' : k_{i,j} \geq 0$
3. $\forall r_i \in R : k_{i,j} = -1$
4. $\forall r_i \in R : \vartheta_{r_i}(\bar{x}) \equiv x_j > 0$

Under conditions $1, 1', 2, 3, 4$, given a path w starting at a point where x_j is greater than 0, one can reorder w so that all the R-clauses are applied first (similarly to the situation of the monotonic transformation), but now such a priority of application for the R-clauses must end at some point: this is because, here, the coefficients $k_{i,j}$ ($l+1 \leq i \leq n$) are not positive or null, but equal to -1. So the value of x_j decreases at each application of an R-clause until x_j becomes null. At this stage, no R-clause is applicable, and an R'-clause r_i ($1 \leq i \leq l$) must be applied. The j-th coordinate of the newly generated tuple is then equal to $k_{i,j}$. If $k_{i,j}$ is strictly positive, then any of the "highest priority" R-clauses can be applied again a number of times equal to $k_{i,j}$ until x_j becomes null again. This shows that any path w of Σ^* can be reordered into a path whose core is made of repeated "cyclic sequences" of the form $r_i w$ with $w \in R^{k_{i,j}}$. (As usual, the expression R^k denotes the set of paths in R^* of length k.) Note that these "cyclic sequences" let x_j invariant, and are applied when $x_j = 0$. To summarize, the strategy of application of the clauses here is to apply R-clauses in priority, whenever they are applicable (i.e., when $x_j > 0$), until x_j becomes null.

Remark 4

Actually, requirements 1 and 1' that all the coefficients $k_{i,h}$ should be nonnegative (for $h \neq j$), and x_j should not occur in the R'-constraints, are unnecessarily strong. It is enough that, under condition $x_j > 0$, rules of R "commute" with those of R' in the following sense: $x_j > 0 \wedge \bar{x} \xrightarrow{R'R} \bar{x}' \Rightarrow \bar{x} \xrightarrow{RR'} \bar{x}'$.

Remark 5

Requirement 4 can be also relaxed: a similar decomposition holds when the constraints of the R-clauses are not atomic (i.e., not equal to $x_j > 0$) but contain other guards (i.e., when $\vartheta_{r_i}(\overline{x}) \Rightarrow x_j > 0$).

Before stating formally the cyclic decomposition rule, we introduce and briefly comment on some notation used in the formal statement of the rule. The expression $r_i R^k$ denotes the set $\{r_i w \mid w \in R^k\}$. The expression $R^{0<*<k}$ denotes the set of paths w in R^* of length greater than 0 and less than k. If $r_i R^k$ represents a set of cyclic sequences, the expression $r_i R^{0<*<k}$ thus represents the set of *prefixes* of such sequences. (The prefix reduced to r_i is discarded by the notation, and appears in the rule statement as an element of R'.) The language $(\bigcup_{r_i \in R'} r_i R^{k_{i,j}})^*$ also appears in the rule statement. The program associated with this language is made of recursive clauses of the form: $p(\overline{x} + \overline{k}_{r_i w}) \leftarrow \vartheta_{r_i w}(\overline{x}), p(\overline{x}).$, where w is in $R^{k_{i,j}}$.

The dimension of such a program is less than the dimension of Σ because it lets one more variable, viz. x_j, invariant (The x_j column in the corresponding incrementation matrix is null.)

PROPOSITION 3 *Let* $R, R' \subseteq \Sigma$ *be sets of (labels of) clauses such that* $\Sigma = R \uplus R'$, *and let* x_j *be a variable such that:*

1. $x_j > 0 \wedge \overline{x} \xrightarrow{R'R} \overline{x}' \Rightarrow \overline{x} \xrightarrow{RR'} \overline{x}'$

2. $\forall r_i \in R' : k_{i,j} \geq 0$

3. $\forall r_i \in R : k_{i,j} = -1$

4. $\forall r_i \in R : \vartheta_{r_i}(\overline{x}) \Rightarrow x_j > 0$

Then we have

A

$$x_j \geq 0 \wedge \overline{x} \xrightarrow{\Sigma^*} \overline{x}' \Rightarrow$$

$$\overline{x} \xrightarrow{R^* R'^*} \overline{x}'$$

$$\vee$$

$$\exists \overline{x}'' : \overline{x} \xrightarrow{R^*} \overline{x}'' \xrightarrow{\Sigma^*} \overline{x}' \wedge x_j'' = 0$$

B

$$x_j = 0 \wedge \overline{x} \xrightarrow{\Sigma^*} \overline{x}' \Rightarrow$$

$$\overline{x} \xrightarrow{\left(\bigcup_{r_i \in R'} r_i R^{k_{i,j}}\right)^* \left(\varepsilon + \bigcup_{r_i \in R'} r_i R^{0<*<k_{i,j}}\right) R'^*} \overline{x}'$$

where x_j *is let invariant by all the paths in* $\left(\bigcup_{r_i \in R'} r_i R^{k_{i,j}}\right)^*$.

C

$$\overline{x} \xrightarrow{\Sigma^*} \overline{x}' \Leftrightarrow$$

$$\overline{x} \xrightarrow{R'^* R^* R'^*} \overline{x}'$$

$$\vee$$

$$\exists \overline{x}'' : \overline{x} \xrightarrow{R'^* R^*} \overline{x}'' \xrightarrow{\left(\bigcup_{r_i \in R'} r_i R^{k_{i,j}}\right)^* \left(\varepsilon + \bigcup_{r_i \in R'} r_i R^{0 < * < k_{i,j}}\right) R'^*} \overline{x}' \wedge$$
$$x_j'' = 0$$

where x_j is let invariant by all the paths in $\left(\bigcup_{r_i \in R'} r_i R^{k_{i,j}}\right)^*$.

Before proving this proposition, let us stress that part **C** of the proposition provides us with a decomposition rule that reduces the reachability problem via Σ^* to several reachability problems via languages which are of lower dimensions. The sublanguages are R'^*, R^*, $(\varepsilon + \bigcup_{r_i \subset R'} r_i R^{0 < * < k_{i,j}})$ and $(\bigcup_{r_i \in R'} r_i R^{k_{i,j}})^*$. Languages R'^* and R^* have fewer clauses than Σ^* (and at least as many variables kept invariant), so they are of lower dimension. The language $(\varepsilon + \bigcup_{r_i \in R'} r_i R^{0 < * < k_{i,j}})$ is finite. As already pointed out, the language $(\bigcup_{r_i \in R'} r_i R^{k_{i,j}})^*$ is of lower dimension than Σ^* because it leaves a new variable (viz., x_j) invariant.

Proof: The first statement, **A**, of the proposition states that any point $\overline{x}'$ reachable from a point $\overline{x}$ such that $x_j \geq 0$, is reachable either by a path consisting of a sequence of applications of clauses of R only followed by a sequence of applications of clauses of R' only, or $\overline{x}'$ is reachable via a point $\overline{x}''$ (with $x_j'' = 0$), which is itself reachable from $\overline{x}$ by a sequence of applications of clauses of R only. We prove this by induction on the length n of the paths. The case when $n = 0$ is trivial. The induction hypothesis is the following implication: For all $v \in \Sigma^*$ such that $|v| < n$, $(x_j \geq 0 \wedge \overline{x} \xrightarrow{v} \overline{x}' \Rightarrow (\overline{x} \xrightarrow{v'} \overline{x}' \vee \exists \overline{x}'' : \overline{x} \xrightarrow{v''} \overline{x}'' \xrightarrow{v'''} \overline{x}' \wedge x_j'' = 0))$, for some $v' \in R^* R'^*$, $v'' \in R^*$, $v''' \in \Sigma^*$ such that $|v'| = |v''v'''| = |v|$. Suppose now that $x_j \geq 0 \wedge \overline{x} \xrightarrow{w} \overline{x}'$ hold for some $\overline{x}, \overline{x}'$ and $w \in \Sigma^*$ such that $|w| = n$, and let us prove **D**: $(\overline{x} \xrightarrow{w'} \overline{x}' \vee \exists \overline{x}''' : \overline{x} \xrightarrow{w''} \overline{x}''' \xrightarrow{w'''} \overline{x}' \wedge x_j'' = 0)$ for some $w' \in R^* R'^*$, $w'' \in R^*$ and $w''' \in \Sigma^*$ such that $|w'| = |w''w'''| = |w|$. If no R-clause appears in w, then $w \in R'^*$ so clearly $w \in R^* R'^*$, and **D** follows by choosing w' as w. Otherwise some clause of R must occur in w for the first time. Then $w = w_1 r_i w_2$ for some $w_1 \in R'^*$, $r_i \in R$ and $w_2 \in \Sigma^*$. If $x_j = 0$ we choose $\overline{x}''' = \overline{x}$, $w'' = \varepsilon$ and $w''' = w_1 r_i w_2$, which again proves **D**. Therefore assume $x_j > 0$. By precondition 2, all the clauses of R' make x_j increase, so $x_j > 0$ is invariant for all the paths in R'^*. By repeated use of precondition 1, $w_1 r_i$ may then be replaced by some $r_i' w_1'$ such that $r_i' \in R$, $w_1' \in R'^*$ and $|w_1'| = |w_1|$, so $\overline{x} \xrightarrow{r_i'} \overline{x}'' \xrightarrow{w_1' w_2} \overline{x}'$ holds for some $\overline{x}''$. By precondition 3, all the clauses in R decrease x_j by one, so either $x_j'' = 0$, in which case we choose w'' as r_i' and w''' as $w_1' w_2$ for proving **D**, or $x_j'' > 0$ still holds. Since $|w_1' w_2| < |w|$, by the induction hypothesis, $\overline{x} \xrightarrow{v'} \overline{x}' \vee \exists \overline{x}''' : \overline{x}'' \xrightarrow{v''} \overline{x}''' \xrightarrow{v'''} \overline{x}' \wedge x_j'' = 0$, holds for some $v' \in R^* R'^*$, $v'' \in R^*$, $v''' \in \Sigma^*$ and $|v'| = |v''v'''| = |w_1' w_2|$, and therefore $\overline{x} \xrightarrow{r_i' v'} \overline{x}' \vee \exists \overline{x}''' : \overline{x} \xrightarrow{r_i' v''} \overline{x}''' \xrightarrow{v'''} \overline{x}' \wedge x_j'' = 0$. Thus **D** holds, since

$r_i'v' \in R^*R'^*$, $r_iv'' \in R^*$ and $|r_iv'| = |r_iv''v'''| = |w|$. The slightly stronger result that $|w'| = |w''w'''| = |w|$, will be used below.

The second statement, **B**, says that if $\overline{x}'$ is reachable from some point $\overline{x}$ such that $x_j = 0$, then $\overline{x}'$ is reachable by a sequence of repeated cycles $r_iR^{k_{i,j}}$, where $r_i \in R'$, possibly followed by a prefix $r_iR^{0<*<k_{i,j}}$ of a cycle and finally by a sequence of applications of clauses of R' only. It is obvious that the paths $r_iR^{k_{i,j}}$ keep $x_j = 0$ invariant since r_i increases x_j by $k_{i,j}$, and all clauses of R decreases x_j by one, so r_i followed by $k_{i,j}$ applications of R-clauses sums up to zero. The statement is proved by induction. Again the base case when $n = 0$ is trivial. The induction hypothesis is the following implication: for all $v \in \Sigma^*$ such that $|v| < n$, $x_j = 0 \wedge \overline{x} \xrightarrow{v} \overline{x}' \Rightarrow \overline{x} \xrightarrow{LR'^*} \overline{x}'$, where $L = \left(\bigcup_{r_i \in R'} r_iR^{k_{i,j}}\right)^* \left(\varepsilon + \bigcup_{r_i \in R'} r_iR^{0<*<k_{i,j}}\right)$. Suppose that $x_j = 0 \wedge \overline{x} \xrightarrow{w} \overline{x}'$ hold for some $\overline{x}$, $\overline{x}'$ and $w \in \Sigma^*$ such that $|w| = n$, and let us prove $\overline{x} \xrightarrow{LR'^*} \overline{x}'$. Since $x_j = 0$, by precondition 4, no clause of R can be applied, so the first clause application must be some $r_i \in R'$, and therefore $w = r_iw_1$ for some $w_1 \in \Sigma^*$. Thus $x_j = 0 \wedge \overline{x} \xrightarrow{r_i} \overline{x}'' \xrightarrow{w_1} \overline{x}'$ holds for some $\overline{x}''$. If $k_{i,j} = 0$, then $x_j'' = 0$. Since $|w_1| < |w|$, by the induction hypothesis, $\overline{x}'' \xrightarrow{LR'^*} \overline{x}'$ holds, so $\overline{x} \xrightarrow{r_iLR'^*} \overline{x}'$. This proves $\overline{x} \xrightarrow{LR'^*} \overline{x}'$, since $r_iL \subseteq L$. Therefore assume $k_{i,j} > 0$, in which case $x_j'' > 0$ must hold. But by the proof of case **A** of the proposition, if $x_j'' > 0 \wedge \overline{x}'' \xrightarrow{w_1} \overline{x}'$ holds, then either **E1**: $\overline{x}'' \xrightarrow{w_1'} \overline{x}'$ or **E2**: $\exists \overline{x}''' : \overline{x}'' \xrightarrow{w_1''} \overline{x}''' \xrightarrow{w_1'''} \overline{x}' \wedge x_j''' = 0$ must hold for some $w_1' \in R^*R'^*$, $w_1'' \in R^*$ and $w_1''' \in \Sigma^*$ such that $|w_1'| = |w_1''w_1'''| = |w_1|$. Assume that **E2** holds. Then $|w_1''| = k_{i,j}$ must hold and, since $|w_1'''| < |w|$, by the induction hypothesis, $\overline{x}''' \xrightarrow{LR'^*} \overline{x}'$, so $\overline{x} \xrightarrow{r_iw_1''LR'^*} \overline{x}'$, which proves $\overline{x} \xrightarrow{LR'^*} \overline{x}'$, since $r_iw_1''L \subseteq L$. Suppose now that **E2** does *not* hold. By **E1**, $w_1' = uu'$ for some $u \in R^*$ and $u' \in R'^*$. Furthermore, $|u| < k_{i,j}$ must hold, since otherwise w_1'' could be chosen as u, and **E2** would hold. Therefore $r_iuu' \in \left(\varepsilon + \bigcup_{r_i \in R'} r_iR^{0<*<k_{i,j}}\right) R'^* \subseteq LR'^*$, and again, $\overline{x} \xrightarrow{LR'^*} \overline{x}'$ holds.

The third statement, **C**, follows by simply combining **A** and **B**, and by noting that if $x_j < 0$, by precondition 4, only R'-clauses can be applied. Either we reach the end point, or we reach some point where $x_j \geq 0$, and then cases **A** and **B** of the proposition apply. ∎

Remark 6:
In the special case where the constraints of R-clauses are atomic (i.e., all equal to $x_j > 0$), it is easy to show that the application of R-clauses is commutative. Therefore, we have for all r_i in R'

$$\overline{x}'' \xrightarrow{r_iR^k} \overline{x}''' \Rightarrow \overline{x}'' \xrightarrow{r_i\bigcup_{m_1+m_2+\ldots+m_{n-l}=k} r_{l+1}^{m_1}r_{l+2}^{m_2}\ldots r_n^{m_{n-l}}} \overline{x}'''$$

Hence we need not consider all the paths of r_iR^k, but only those of the form $r_ir_{l+1}^{m_1}r_{l+2}^{m_2} \cdots r_n^{m_{n-l}}$, where $m_1 + m_2 + \ldots + m_{n-l} = k$. (Actually, the ordering on $r_{l+1}, r_{l+2}, \ldots r_n$ is arbitrary.)

Remark 7:

In the special case where the constraints of R-clauses are atomic (i.e., all equal to $x_j > 0$), let us also notice that, for all clause $w \in r_i R^k$, the associated constraint $\vartheta_w(\overline{x}'')$ is equal to $\vartheta_{r_i}(\overline{x}'')$: This is trivial if $k = 0$; in the case where $k > 0$, constraint $\vartheta_w(\overline{x}'')$ is equal to $\vartheta_{r_i}(\overline{x}'') \wedge x_j'' + k > 0 \wedge \ldots \wedge x_j'' + 1 > 0$, and reduces to ϑ_{r_i} because x_j'' is equal to 0 (see statement C of proposition 3). In other words, one can always drop the constraints relevant to x_j within clauses of $r_i R^k$. One can see that x_j-constraints can be dropped also in the general case where constraints of R-clauses are not atomic.

Example: Consider the matrix in the example representing the program for the protocol of Section 3.4. Let us in proposition 3 choose $R = \{r_5, r_6\}$ and $R' = \{r_1, r_2, r_3, r_4\}$, and let $x_j = x_5$. We see that this matrix conforms to the special case discussed above where the decomposition of proposition 3 is applicable. We have: $k_{1,5} = 0$, $k_{2,5} = 0$, $k_{3,5} = 1$ and $k_{4,5} = 1$. Thus, $r_1 R^{k_{1,5}} = r_1$, $r_2 R^{k_{2,5}} = r_2$, $r_3 R^{k_{3,5}} = r_3 r_5 + r_3 r_6$ and $r_4 R^{k_{4,5}} = r_4 r_5 + r_4 r_6$. Furthermore: $\varepsilon + \bigcup_{r_i \in R'} r_i R^{0<*<k_{i,5}} = \varepsilon + r_1 R^{0<*<0} + r_2 R^{0<*<0} + r_3 R^{0<*<1} + r_4 R^{0<*<1} = \varepsilon$. By proposition 3.C, we have:

$$\overline{x} \xrightarrow{(r_1+r_2+r_3+r_4+r_5+r_6)^*} \overline{x}' \iff$$

$$\overline{x} \xrightarrow{(r_1+r_2+r_3+r_4)^*(r_5+r_6)^*(r_1+r_2+r_3+r_4)^*} \overline{x}'$$

$$\vee$$

$$\exists \overline{x}'' : \overline{x} \xrightarrow{(r_1+r_2+r_3+r_4)^*(r_5+r_6)^*} \overline{x}'' \wedge$$

$$\overline{x}'' \xrightarrow{(r_1+r_2+r_3 r_5+r_3 r_6+r_4 r_5+r_4 r_6)^*(r_1+r_2+r_3+r_4)^*} \overline{x}' \wedge x_5'' = 0$$

and all the paths in $(r_1+r_2+r_3 r_5+r_3 r_6+r_4 r_5+r_4 r_6)^*$ keep $x_5 = 0$ invariant. The matrix M' of the program corresponding to the set of clauses $\{r_1, r_2, r_3 r_5, r_3 r_6, r_4 r_5, r_4 r_6\}$ is shown below:

0	−1	1	0	0	0	−1	$x_2 > 0, x_7 > 0, x_1 > 0$	$: r_1$
−1	0	0	1	0	−1	0	$x_2 > 0, x_6 > 0$	$: r_2$
0	1	−1	0	0	1	0	$x_3 > 0, x_5 > -1$	$: r_3 r_5$
0	1	−1	0	0	0	1	$x_3 > 0, x_5 > -1$	$: r_3 r_6$
1	0	0	−1	0	1	0	$x_4 > 0, x_5 > -1$	$: r_4 r_5$
1	0	0	−1	0	0	1	$x_4 > 0, x_5 > -1$	$: r_4 r_6$
x_1	x_2	x_3	x_4	x_5	x_6	x_7		

Thus, $(r_1+r_2+r_3+r_4)^*$ and $(r_5+r_6)^*$ involves fewer clauses than the original program, while $(r_1+r_2+r_3 r_5+r_3 r_6+r_4 r_5+r_4 r_6)^*$ involves the same number of clauses but lets one more variable, viz. x_5, invariant. (The corresponding column in the incrementation matrix is null.)

$\square$

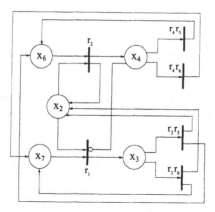

Figure 2. Readers-writers protocol with fused transitions.

5. Comparison with Related Work

5.1. Comparison with Berthelot's work

As can be seen in the example, in the matrix M' corresponding to the set of cyclic sequences, the constraint $x_5 > -1$ is systematically satisfied since it is applied, by proposition 3, to a point of coordinate $x_5 = 0$ and x_5 is kept invariant. So an obvious optimization, for the treatment of the matrix, will be to remove the null column as well as the guard $x_5 > -1$ (*cf.* Remark 7). In terms of Petri nets, this corresponds to remove the place x_5 and to perform the "fusion" of transitions r_2, r_3, r_4 (which have x_5 as an output place) and transitions r_5, r_6 (which have x_5 as an input place). The resulting Petri net is represented in Figure 2. This kind of optimization can be done generally, under the preconditions of proposition 3. An analogous transformation of Petri nets is called *post-fusion* transformation in [3]. Our version of the cyclic decomposition can thus be seen as a variant of Berthelot's post-fusion rule. Berthelot also defined some other transformations like *pre-fusion*. It is possible to give in our framework a counterpart also for this transformation (see appendix A). The point that should be stressed here is that our cyclic decomposition rules are more general than Berthelot's rules because they apply to general programs with $\mathcal{Z}$-counters where variables take their values on $\mathcal{Z}$ (instead of $\mathcal{N}$ as in the case of Petri nets). This allows us in particular to encode 0-tests as already seen. In Section 7 we will see that our cyclic decomposition rule can also, under certain conditions, be generalized one step further by allowing R-transitions to pick up more than one token from place x_j. (For rules $r_i \in R$, coefficients $k_{i,j}$ will be allowed to be less than -1.)

5.2.   Comparison with related work in constraint databases

Our decomposition can be seen as a means of eliminating redundant paths (proof derivations) leading from a fact to another fact. This issue of eliminating redundancy during
bottom-up execution of Datalog or logic programs (with constraints) has given rise to two
different kind of methods: static methods and dynamic ones. In the static approach, basic
rules of transformation are applied to the program itself in order to narrow its bottom-up tree
of derivations. This is applicable when the program satisfies certain properties for which
sufficient syntactic criteria exist: e.g., boundedness [28], commutatitivity [32], splittability
[29, 23]. In the dynamic approach, redundant derivations are eliminated during the execution of the program. For example, [37] discusses the run-time detection and elimination of
redundant subgoals and redundant parts of SLD-derivation trees. In [18] redundant derivations are removed during bottom-up execution by, first, unfolding the original program (see
[35]) according to a strategy defined by a control language, then eliminating redundant
unfolded clauses. In the dynamic approach, the detection of redundancy basically relies on
various enhancements of the classical notion of "subsumption" (*cf.* [24, 25]). Our work
here belongs to the static approach. One of the decomposition rules of our system (see the
rule of "stratification", proposition 5, appendix A) is thus a commutativity rule in the sense
of [32]. The main originality of our system lies in the subset of cyclic rules, which do not
simply rearrange clauses of the original program, but create new clauses by "fusion" of old
ones. This fusion can be interpreted as a restricted form of unfolding as in the work of [18],
but here, the strategy of unfolding is fixed by the rule, and its correctness always guaranteed
without need for dynamic tests of subsumption. Let us finally mention that dynamic tests
of subsumption can still be easily integrated within our method. For example, we will see
in Section 8 how tests of invariance (analogous to the subsumption tests used in bottom-up
evaluation of constraint databases [26]) are added to the basic decomposition procedure in
order to optimize the construction of the least fixed-point.

6.   Application to BPP-Nets

Since programs with $\mathcal{Z}$-counters are Turing equivalent it is clear that the decomposition
process cannot always succeed. Even for Petri nets it is known that nets with more than
four places, in general do not have a a reachability set expressible in linear arithmetic [19].
In this section we consider a subclass of Petri nets for which the decomposition process is
guaranteed to succeed in generating a flat language.

Recently an interesting subset of Petri nets has been introduced and investigated: BPP-
nets. A Petri net is a BPP-net if every transition has at most [2] one input place and removes
exactly one token from that one place. BPP stands for Basic Parallel Process: this is a class
of CSS process defined in [7]; the reachability problem for BPP-nets is NP-complete [11].
When one encodes the reachability problem for BPP-nets, using the method of section 3,
one obtains a program such that, for any clause $r_i \in \Sigma$, all the coefficients of the head are
nonnegative except (maybe) one, which is equal to -1. For all clause r_i, if such a negative
coefficient, say $k_{i,h}$, exists, then the constraint of r_i is atomic and equal to $x_h > 0$. We call

such a clause r_i a *BPP-clause*. Let us assume given a BPP-net Σ (i.e., a set of BPP-clauses), and consider the following property

Prop(Σ): Σ^* can be decomposed into a sequence $L_1...L_s$ such that, for all $1 \leq i \leq s$, the language L_i is either finite, or of the form w_i^* for some path w_i, or of the form Σ_i^* for some BPP-net Σ_i.

By iterative application of this proposition, one generates eventually a *flat* decomposition of the given BPP-net Σ. (The process terminates because all our rules of decomposition transform a program into programs of lower dimension.) Let us now prove Prop(Σ).

Proof: If there exists a clause r_i in Σ such that all the coefficients of its head are nonnegative, the monotonic (increasing) decomposition rule is applied, and Σ^* is decomposed into $(\Sigma - \{r_i\})^* r_i^* (\Sigma - \{r_i\})^*$. If there are still such clauses in $\Sigma - \{r_i\}$, we apply again the monotonic rule, and so on until one gets a sequence made only of expressions of the form r_j^* and expressions of the form Σ'^*, where Σ' denotes the subset of clauses of Σ having at least one negative coefficient. By assumption, every clause of Σ' must then contain *exactly one* negative coefficient (equal to -1) and its constraint must be atomic. In order to prove Prop(Σ), it then suffices to prove Prop(Σ'). Assume that Σ' is nonempty (otherwise, the property is trivial), and let us show that the cyclic decomposition rule applies to Σ'. We have to determine which sets of rules to take as for R, R' and which variable to take as for x_j in order to apply proposition 3. As for x_j we choose a variable such that column j of the matrix contains an element equal to -1 (which must exist). As R we take all the clauses r_i such that $k_{i,j} = -1$, and as R' we take $\Sigma' - R$.

Let us show that R can be decomposed under a flat form. Since all the clauses $r_i \in R$ have the same atomic constraint $x_j > 0$ and all the coefficients $k_{i,j}$ are equal (to -1), one easily sees that all the rules in R commute as required for the stratification decomposition of proposition 5 (see appendix A). So by repeatedly applying this decomposition, R^* can be flattened. (Actually, if R is made of l clauses $r_{i_1}, .., r_{i_l}$, R^* can be decomposed into the flat form $r_{i_1}^* ... r_{i_l}^*$.)

If R' is empty, then Σ' is R, and can thus be put under a flat form. Assume therefore that R' is nonempty. Thus, for every $r_i \in R'$ we have $k_{i,j} \geq 0$, and therefore conditions $1, 1', 2, 3, 4$ of the specialized case of Section 4.3 are satisfied, so the cyclic decomposition applies. By equivalence **C** of proposition 3, reachability by Σ'^* is reduced to reachability as:

$$\overline{x} \xrightarrow{\Sigma'^*} \overline{x}' \iff$$

$$\overline{x} \xrightarrow{R'^* R^* R'^*} \overline{x}'$$

$$\vee$$

$$\exists \overline{x}'' : \overline{x} \xrightarrow{R'^* R^*} \overline{x}'' \xrightarrow{\left(\bigcup_{r_i \in R'} r_i R^{k_{i,j}} \right)^* \left(\varepsilon + \bigcup_{r_i \in R'} r_i R^{0<*<k_{i,j}} \right) R'^*} \overline{x}' \wedge$$
$$x_j'' = 0$$

where x_j is let invariant by all the paths in $\left(\bigcup_{r_i \in R'} r_i R^{k_{i,j}}\right)^*$.

Clearly R' is still of the form corresponding to a BPP-net. Besides R^* can be put under a flat form, and $\varepsilon + \bigcup_{r_i \in R'} r_i R^{0<*<k_{i,j}}$ is finite. In order to achieve the proof of $\text{Prop}(\Sigma')$, it then suffices to show that $\bigcup_{r_i \in R'} r_i R^{k_{i,j}}$ corresponds to a BPP-net, that is: for any clause $w \in \bigcup_{r_i \in R'} r_i R^{k_{i,j}}$, all the coefficients $k_{w,j}$ are nonnegative except (maybe) one, which is equal to -1; besides, if such a negative coefficient, say $k_{w,h}$, exists, the constraint of w is atomic and equal to $x_h > 0$. Let us consider those rows of matrix Σ' which are involved in $\bigcup_{r_i \in R'} r_i R^{k_{i,j}}$:

$$
\left.
\begin{array}{l}
+ \ \ldots \ + \ k_{i,h} \ + \ \ldots \ + \ k_{i,j} \ + \ \ldots \ + \quad \vartheta_{r_i} \ : r_i \in R' \\[4pt]
+ \ \ldots \ + \ \ \ + \ \ \ + \ \ldots \ + \ -1 \ + \ \ldots \ + \quad x_j > 0 \\[4pt]
\hspace{4cm} \vdots \\[4pt]
+ \ \ldots \ + \ \ \ + \ \ \ + \ \ldots \ + \ -1 \ + \ \ldots \ + \quad x_j > 0
\end{array}
\right\} R
$$

$$
\underset{x_h}{} \hspace{3cm} \underset{x_j}{}
$$

By composition of these rows, any clause w in $\bigcup_{r_i \in R'} r_i R^{k_{i,j}}$, has a vector of coefficients $\bar{k}_w$ of the form: $\quad \langle +, \ldots, +, l_h, +, \ldots, +, 0, +, \ldots, + \rangle \quad$ with $l_h \geq k_{i,h}$, and a constraint $\vartheta_w(\bar{x})$ equal to $\vartheta_{r_i}(\bar{x})$ (see remark 7). If $k_{i,h}$ is nonnegative, then all the coefficients of w are non negative (since $l_h \geq k_{i,h}$). If $k_{i,h} = -1$, then ϑ_{r_i} is of the form $x_h > 0$, and so is ϑ_w (since $\vartheta_w = \vartheta_{r_i}$); besides all the coefficients of w are nonnegative (except perhaps, l_h, which may be equal to -1). In any case, clause w is a BPP-clause, and $\bigcup_{r_i \in R'} r_i R^{k_{i,j}}$ corresponds to a BPP-net. This completes the proof of $\text{Prop}(\Sigma')$, hence of $\text{Prop}(\Sigma)$. ∎

Thus, for BPP-nets, the decomposition process is guaranteed to terminate successfully and one obtains an existentially quantified Presburger arithmetic formula having $\bar{y}$ as a free variable for characterizing the fact that $\bar{y}$ belongs to the reachability set. This yields a new proof of the fact that the reachability set for BPP-nets is a semilinear set [11]. Note that Esparza's proof makes use of the notion of "siphon", and is completely different from our method. Note also that our result is actually more general since our decomposition succeeds for BPP-nets without any assumption on the initial markings: our decomposition process shows that the relation $\bar{x} \xrightarrow{\Sigma^*} \bar{x}'$ is an existentially quantified Presburger formula having $\bar{x}$ and $\bar{x}'$ as free variables (that is, $\{\langle \bar{x}, \bar{x}' \rangle \mid \bar{x} \xrightarrow{\Sigma^*} \bar{x}'\}$ is a semilinear set (see (Ginsburg, 66)) while the result of Esparza states that $\{\bar{x}' \mid \bar{a}^0 \xrightarrow{\Sigma^*} \bar{x}'\}$ is a semilinear set, for any tuple of constants $\bar{a}^0$).

Remark 8:

The requirement that, in a BPP-clause r_i, the constraint should be *atomic* (equal to $x_h > 0$) in case there is a negative coefficient $k_{i,h}$, is essential here to our proof of semi-linearity of the reachability set. Otherwise, it is not possible to apply the postfusion rule (because r_i does not commute in general with R-clauses). Actually, the result of semi-linearity does not extend to programs with non atomic constraints: (Hopcroft, 79) gives a vector addition system (VAS) corresponding to a Datalog program with

$\mathcal{Z}$-counters made of 5 clauses having nonnegative coefficients (except one equal to -1) and *non* atomic constraints, for which the reachability set is *not* semi-linear.

7. A Generalized Form of the Decomposition Cyclic Rule

The cyclic decomposition rule presented above, can be given a more general formulation, which makes it applicable even when the coefficient $k_{i,j}$ of R-rule r_i is less than -1. We illustrate this general formulation by considering a 3-clauses program of a typical form and vizualizing its associated least fixpoint. The program is defined by the base case vector $\langle 30, 19, -57 \rangle$ and the incrementation matrix:

$$
\begin{array}{rrr}
-2 & -1 & 3 \\
-1 & -2 & 4 \\
4 & 3 & -7 \\
x_1 & x_2 & x_3
\end{array}
\quad
\begin{array}{l}
x_1 > 0 \ : r_1 \\
x_2 > 0 \ : r_2 \\
x_3 > 0 \ : r_3
\end{array}
$$

Its least fixpoint is represented in Figure 3, under the form of the set of all its applicable paths. All horizontal (resp. vertical, transversal) segment of a path corresponds to the application of the first (resp. second,third) recursive rule. The orientation of the figures in terms of r_1, r_2 and r_3 is:

Let us choose x_j to be x_3, R' to be $\{r_1, r_2\}$ and R to be $\{r_3\}$. A priori, proposition 3 does not apply because $k_{3,3}$, viz. -7, is not equal to -1. We are going to explain however that an analogous decomposition applies, and that, similarly to what part **C** of proposition 3 says, we have: $\langle 30, 19, -57 \rangle \xrightarrow{(r_1+r_2+r_3)^*} \overline{x}' \ \Rightarrow \ \langle 30, 19, -57 \rangle \xrightarrow{(r_1+r_2)^* r_3^* L(r_1+r_2)^*} \overline{x}'$ where L is a counterpart of the sequences of cyclic sequences $(\bigcup r_i R^{k_i})^* (\epsilon + \bigcup r_i R^{0 < * < k_i})$.

Compare the language expression $(r_1 + r_2)^* r_3^* L(r_1 + r_2)^*$ with figure 3. The lower left part of the figure is a planar area where 2 rules only are applicable (one coordinate, viz. x_3, remains always less than or equal to zero), and is therefore included into a $\{r_1, r_2\}$-plane, which corresponds to the initial sublanguage $(r_1 + r_2)^*$. After a while, $x_3 > 0$ becomes true, and a number of transversal moves r_3 apply, which is captured by the sublanguage r_3^*. As is seen in the figure, the r_3-moves soon cease. After the last application of r_3, it must hold that $0 \geq x_3 > -7$ (since r_3 is not applicable, but was applicable immediately before, and the application of r_3 makes x_3 decreased by 7). At this point, only r_1 and r_2 can be applied. Since r_1 makes x_3 increase by 3, and r_2 by 4, we must have: $4 \geq x_3 > 0$, when x_3 becomes strictly greater than zero for the first time. Now, in keeping with the firing strategy of proposition 3, clause r_3 should be fired as soon as it is applicable. In the figure, the set of points reached by such a strategy is the "ceiling" of the cone (we move upwards as soon as we can). [3] The coordinate x_3 of a reordered path is thus led to take cyclically 11

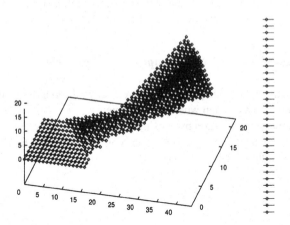

Figure 3. Graph depicting all admissible firing sequences.

values, those between 4 and -6. These values can be considered as *states* of a deterministic finite state automaton defining the language L of reordered paths. The transitions of such an automaton are completely defined by our strategy of clause firing, which gives priority to clause r_3 whenever it is applicable (i.e., when $x_3 > 0$). From any state, $4 \geq x_3 > 0$, there is only one arrow going out, labeled r_3, and the next state is $x_3 - 7$. From any state $0 \geq x_3 > -7$, there are two arrows going out, one labeled r_1 for which the next state is $x_3 + 3$, and one labeled r_2 for which the next state is $x_3 + 4$. The automaton is shown in Figure 4. The construction is identical to that of [8] for solving the linear diophantine equation:

$$3m_1 + 4m_2 - 7m_3 = 0$$

which expresses the fact that any path consisting of m_1, m_2 and m_3 applications of r_1-,r_2- and r_3-clauses, respectively, lets x_3 invariant. It is easy to see that every cycle in the automaton yields a solution to the equation above.

Let us denote by $L_{s,t}$ the language of paths leading from state s to state t. It should be clear now that one can always reorder paths as follows:

$$\langle 30, 19, -57 \rangle \xrightarrow{(r_1+r_2+r_3)^*} \overline{x}' \;\Rightarrow\; \langle 30, 19, -57 \rangle \xrightarrow{(r_1+r_2)^* r_3^* L (r_1+r_2)^*} \overline{x}'$$

where L is $\bigcup_{4 \geq s, t > -7} L_{s,t}$. This is because, first, as already seen, we use $(r_1 + r_2)^*$ paths or r_3^* until one reaches a state $4 \geq s > -7$ in the automaton (that is, $x_3 = s$). Then the clauses are fired according to the strategy defined by the automaton until no more r_3 clauses are still to be fired. From that point on one walks in the $(r_1+r_2)^*$-plane, leaving the automaton at some state $4 \geq t > -7$ (that is, $x_3 = t$ and $x_3 r_i > 4$ for $i = 1, 2$). In Figure 3 this means following the "ceiling" of the cone, and then "filling it up" with $\{r_1, r_2\}$-planes.

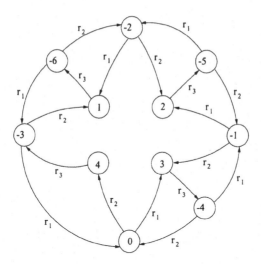

Figure 4. Automaton defining a firing strategy.

This informal explanation of the example can be turned into a formal proof of the following generalization of proposition 3.

PROPOSITION 4 *Let $R, R' \subseteq \Sigma$ be a set of clauses such that $\Sigma = R \uplus R'$, and let x_j be a variable and c some fixed constant such that:*

1. $x_j > c \wedge \overline{x} \xrightarrow{R'R} \overline{x}' \Rightarrow \overline{x} \xrightarrow{RR'} \overline{x}'$

2. $\forall r_i \in R' : k_{i,j} \geq 0$

3. $\forall r_i \in R : k_{i,j} < 0$

4. $\forall r_i \in R : \vartheta_{r_i}(\overline{x}) \Rightarrow x_j > c$

Then there exists a finite set of languages $L_{s,t}$, with $b \geq s, t > a$, where $a = \min\{k_{i,j} + c \mid r_i \in R\}$ and $b = \max\{k_{i,j} + c \mid r_i \in R'\}$, such that:

A

$$x_j > c \wedge \overline{x} \xrightarrow{\Sigma^*} \overline{x}' \Rightarrow$$

$$\overline{x} \xrightarrow{R^* R'^*} \overline{x}'$$
$$\vee$$
$$\exists \overline{x}'' : x_j > c \wedge \overline{x} \xrightarrow{R^*} \overline{x}'' \xrightarrow{\Sigma^*} \overline{x}' \wedge b \geq x_j'' > c$$

B

$$\forall b \geq s > a : \left(\begin{array}{c} x_j = s \wedge \overline{x} \xrightarrow{\Sigma^*} \overline{x}' \Rightarrow \\[2mm] \overline{x} \xrightarrow{\left(\bigcup_{b \geq t > a} L_{s,t}\right) R'^*} \overline{x}' \end{array} \right)$$

C

$$\overline{x} \xrightarrow{\Sigma^*} \overline{x}' \Leftrightarrow$$

$$\overline{x} \xrightarrow{R'^* R^* \left(\bigcup_{b \geq s, t > a} L_{s,t}\right) R'^*} \overline{x}'$$

As can be seen in Figure 4, the languages $L_{s,t}$ are in general not of the form $L_1 L_2 \cdots L_u$ where L_i is either finite or of the form Σ_i^* (with Σ_i finite), but may contain nested '*'. For example the expression $(r_1 r_3 (r_1 r_2 r_3)^* r_2)^*$ is a subset of the language $L_{0,0}$, while $(r_1 r_3 r_2 + r_1 r_2 r_3)^*$ is not. This means that proposition 4 may not in general be applied iteratively. However, by applying other decompositions such as monotonic rules, one can sometimes retrieve a language that can be expressed under such a "flat" form (without nesting of '*'). For a program with 3 recursive clauses and atomic constraints, as the one above, whose matrix has the general form:

$$
\begin{array}{ccc}
\bullet & \bullet & + \qquad x_1 > 0 \; : r_1 \\
\bullet & \bullet & + \qquad x_2 > 0 \; : r_2 \\
+ & + & - \qquad x_3 > 0 \; : r_3 \\
x_1 & x_2 & x_3
\end{array}
$$

we have shown that such a decomposition is *always* possible, which allows to solve the problem of the arithmetical characterization of the least fixed-point (see [13]).

We can look back at the results stated in proposition 3, and interpret them as a special case of the above automaton-based construction. Under the conditions of proposition 3, the constant $a = \min\{k_{i,j} + c \mid r_i \in R\}$ is equal to -1. So the states of the automaton range here from 0 to b. For each nonnull state, there is one outgoing R-arc and some entering R'-arcs. For the null state $s = 0$, there is one entering R-arc and some outgoing R'-arcs. The reordered paths, as defined by part **C** of proposition 3, can now be constructed, using this specialized automaton, as illustrated on Figure 5. Figure 6 gives a geometrical interpretation of the fact all the cycles closely follow the hyper plane $x_j = 0$.

8. Compilation into Arithmetic

We have an experimental implementation in SICSTUS-PROLOG currently containing seven decomposition rules, two of which are cyclic (*cf.* appendix A). Besides the decomposition module, it contains a theorem prover for Presburger arithmetic based on the decision procedure of (Boudet, 96). The system outputs a regular expression defining a flat language (if

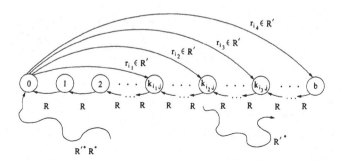

Figure 5. Firing strategy of proposition 4.

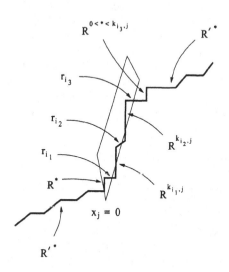

Figure 6. Paths tracking hyperplane.

the decomposition is successful) and constructs a graph representation of the corresponding Presburger formula (see [4]). For the readers-writers protocol of figure 1, our system finds a flat language $L \subseteq \Sigma^*$ such that $\overline{x} \xrightarrow{\Sigma^*} \overline{x}' \Leftrightarrow \overline{x} \xrightarrow{L} \overline{x}'$, which is:

$$
\begin{aligned}
L = \ & r_5^* r_6^* r_2^* r_1^* r_2^* r_4^* (r_2 r_4)^* r_5^* (r_2 r_4)^* r_5^* r_6^* r_2^* r_1^* r_2^* r_3^* (r_1 r_3)^* r_2^* r_4^* (r_1 r_3)^* (r_2 r_4)^* \\
& (r_1 r_3)^* r_2^* r_5^* r_6^* (r_1 r_3 r_5)^* r_2^* (r_4 r_6)^* (r_4 r_5)^* (r_1 r_3 r_5)^* (r_2 r_4 r_6)^* (r_1 r_3 r_5)^* \\
& (r_1 r_3)^* r_2^* r_4^* (r_1 r_3)^* (r_2 r_4)^* (r_1 r_3)^* r_5^* r_6^* r_2^* r_1^* r_2^* r_4^* (r_2 r_4)^* r_5^* (r_2 r_4)^* r_5^* r_6^* \\
& r_2^* r_1^* r_2^*
\end{aligned}
$$

The expression consists of 51 factors and was computed in 0.43 seconds on a SPARC-10 machine. The decomposition was achieved by using 7 applications of the cyclic post-fusion rule presented above, 10 applications of the stratification rule and 1 application of monotonic guard (see appendix A).

Let us denote the above language L as $w_1^* w_2^* \cdots w_{51}^*$. When computing the least fixed-point of a program, we are interested in the set lfp : $\{\overline{x}' | \exists \overline{x} : B(\overline{x}) \wedge \overline{x} \xrightarrow{w_1^* w_2^* \cdots w_{51}^*} \overline{x}'\}$. We are thus led to construct a sequence $\{\xi_i(\overline{x})\}_{i=0,\dots,51}$ of relations defined by:

$$
\begin{aligned}
\xi_0(\overline{x}) \ & \Leftrightarrow \ B(\overline{x}) \\
\xi_{i+1}(\overline{x}) \ & \Leftrightarrow \ \exists \overline{x}'' : \xi_i(\overline{x}'') \wedge \overline{x}'' \xrightarrow{w_{i+1}^*} \overline{x}
\end{aligned}
$$

We have: $\overline{x} \in \text{lfp} \Leftrightarrow \xi_{51}(\overline{x})$. The decision procedure for Presburger arithmetic is invoked to construct the sequence of ξ_is. Actually, a dynamic test of "invariance" is added during the compilation process into arithmetic in order to check whether the lfp has already been generated. That is, for each i ($0 \leq i \leq 50$), one checks whether

$$\forall r \in \{r_1, \dots, r_6\} : \xi_i(\overline{x}) \wedge \vartheta_r(\overline{x}) \Rightarrow \xi_i(\overline{x}r).$$

If this is true, there is no need to continue, and this may significantly reduce the size of the final expression. This corresponds to the test of *subsumption*, as used in constraint databases or bottom-up Constraint Logic Programming (see, e.g.,[26]). In the present case of the 51 strings long expression, the least fixed-point is thus reached after only 4 steps, and is thus given by

$$\text{lfp} = \{\overline{x}' | \exists \overline{x} : B(\overline{x}) \wedge \overline{x} \xrightarrow{r_5^* r_6^* r_2^* r_1^*} \overline{x}'\}$$

The corresponding arithmetical expression is (see appendix B):

$$
\begin{aligned}
\text{lfp} \equiv \xi_4(\overline{x}) \Leftrightarrow \ & x_1 = 1 - x_4 \ \wedge \\
& ((x_2 = 1 \wedge x_3 = 0 \wedge x_4 \geq 0) \vee \\
& (x_2 = 0 \wedge x_3 = 1 \wedge x_4 = 0)) \ \wedge \\
& x_5 \geq 0 \wedge x_6 \geq 0 \wedge x_7 \geq 0 \wedge \\
& x_3 + x_4 + x_5 + x_6 + x_7 = q
\end{aligned}
$$

It is easy to see that the mutual exclusion property, $x_3 = 0 \vee x_4 = 0$, holds. Our program constructs the arithmetical form of the least fixed-point in 1.1 second, and proves the property in 0.5 second.

Details on our integration of Boudet-Comon decision procedure for linear arithmetic (coupled with bottom-up evaluation with subsumption) into the basic decomposition process can be found in [14].

9. Conclusion

We have developed a decompositional approach for computing the least fixed-points of Datalog programs with $\mathcal{Z}$-counters. As an application we have focused on the computation of reachability sets for Petri nets. We have thus related some unconnected topics such as Berthelot's transformation rules and Esparza's semilinearity result for the reachability set of BPP-nets. We have also shown how these results can be extended in several directions (BPP-nets with parametric initial markings, post-fusion rule for Petri nets with input arcs picking up more than one token). Our system implementation gives already promising results, as illustrated here on the readers-writers protocol. Other experimental results in the field of parametrized protocols and manufacturing systems are presented in [14].

Acknowledgments

Special thanks are due to Alain Finkel for providing us with many useful informations on Petri nets. We thank also the referees for their helpful suggestions.

Appendix A

We present here some other decomposition rules used in our system in addition to the rules of monotonic clause and cyclic postfusion. The first rule is called *stratification*. Exploiting some commutativity property (*cf.* [32]), it states that some clauses can be applied before all the others.

PROPOSITION 5 *Let $R, R' \subset \Sigma$ be sets of clauses such that $\Sigma = R \uplus R'$, and such that $\overline{x} \xrightarrow{R'R} \overline{x}' \Rightarrow \overline{x} \xrightarrow{RR'} \overline{x}'$. Then we have: $\overline{x} \xrightarrow{\Sigma^*} \overline{x}' \Leftrightarrow \overline{x} \xrightarrow{R^*R'^*} \overline{x}'$*

Note that the condition $\overline{x} \xrightarrow{R'R} \overline{x}' \Rightarrow \overline{x} \xrightarrow{RR'} \overline{x}'$ reduces to check a finite set of inequalities among constants. The second decomposition rule is called *monotonic guard* and comes in two versions: *increasing* and *decreasing*. It is essentially "constraint pushing" [34] and applies when there is a single-signed column. We present here only the decreasing version.

PROPOSITION 6 *Let $R \subseteq \Sigma$ be a set of clauses and let x_j be a variable such that:*

1. $\forall r_i \in \Sigma : k_{i,j} \leq 0$

2. $\forall r_i \in R : \vartheta_{r_i}(\overline{x}) \Rightarrow x_j > c$ *for some fixed constant c.*

Then: $\overline{x} \xrightarrow{\Sigma^*} \overline{x}' \Leftrightarrow (\overline{x} \xrightarrow{(\Sigma-R)^*} \overline{x}' \vee \exists \overline{x}'' : \overline{x} \xrightarrow{\Sigma'^*} \overline{x}'' \xrightarrow{\Sigma(\Sigma-R)^*} \overline{x}' \wedge x_j'' > c)$ where Σ' is obtained from Σ by removing all constraints of the form $x_j > c$ from every clause in R.

decomposition rule is *pre-fusion*. In the post-fusion decomposition the
into the sets R and R'. Intuitively, R "consumes" a resource while R'
he idea of the post-fusion strategy was to "consume" as soon as possible:
fired as soon as their constraints were satisfied, thus having high priority.
ea of pre-fusion is to focus on R'-clauses and to "delay" their firing as
For post-fusion it was not necessary to distinguish the rules $r_i \in R'$ that
he variable x_j, from those that let x_j invariant (that is, distinguish $k_{i,j} > 0$
For pre-fusion, instead of R' we consider two sets R' and R'' where R'
es that strictly increase the variable and R'' are those that let it invariant.
ents $k_{i,j}$ of clauses $r_i \in R'$ must be equal to $+1$, which is a restriction
) We wish to "delay" the application of R'-rules until immediately before
an R-rule. For this to be possible, R'-rules must be permutable with
occur between an R'-rule and an R-rule. This requirement is expressed
dition of proposition 7 below. Condition 4 essentially says that R''-rules
variant. The rest of the preconditions are the same as for post-fusion.

Let $R, R', R'' \subseteq \Sigma$ be disjoint sets of rules such that $\Sigma = R \uplus R' \uplus R''$,
riable such that:

$$\Rightarrow \overline{x} \xrightarrow{R''R'} \overline{x}'$$

$$\xrightarrow{R'R} \overline{x}' \Rightarrow \overline{x} \xrightarrow{RR'} \overline{x}'$$

$$_{,j} = 1$$

$$_{i,j} = 0$$

$$_j = -1$$

$$_i(\overline{x}) \Rightarrow x_j > 0$$

$$) \wedge \overline{x} \xrightarrow{\Sigma^*} \overline{x}' \Rightarrow$$

$$\xrightarrow{(R''+R)^* R'^*} \overline{x}'$$

$$\vee$$

$$\overline{x}'' : \overline{x} \xrightarrow{(R''+R)^*} \overline{x}'' \xrightarrow{\Sigma^*} \overline{x}' \wedge x_j'' = 0$$

$$) \wedge \overline{x} \xrightarrow{\Sigma^*} \overline{x}' \Rightarrow$$

$$\xrightarrow{(R'R+R'')^* R'^*} \overline{x}'$$

et invariant by all the paths in $(R'R + R'')^*$.

C

$$\overline{x} \xrightarrow{\Sigma^*} \overline{x}' \Leftrightarrow$$

$$\overline{x} \xrightarrow{(R''+R)^*R'^*} \overline{x}'$$

$$\vee$$

$$\exists \overline{x}'' : \overline{x} \xrightarrow{R''^*R'^*+(R''+R)^*} \overline{x}'' \xrightarrow{(R'R+R'')^*R'^*} \overline{x}' \wedge$$
$$x''_j = 0$$

where x_j is let invariant by all the paths in $(R'R + R'')^*$.

Appendix B

Let us compute the fixed-point of the program P' of Example 3.4 from the language $L = r_5^* r_6^* r_2^* r_1^* \ldots$ of section 8, generated by our program. We get the sequence (making arithmetic simplifications at each step):

$$\xi_0(\overline{x}) \Leftrightarrow B(\overline{x}) \qquad \Leftrightarrow x_1 = 1 - x_4 \wedge x_2 = 1 \wedge x_3 = 0 \wedge$$
$$x_4 = 0 \wedge x_5 = q \wedge q \geq 0 \wedge$$
$$x_6 = 0 \wedge x_7 = 0$$

$$\xi_1(\overline{x}) \Leftrightarrow \exists \overline{x}'' : \xi_0(\overline{x}'') \wedge \overline{x}'' \xrightarrow{r_5^*} \overline{x} \Leftrightarrow x_1 = 1 - x_4 \wedge x_2 = 1 \wedge x_3 = 0 \wedge$$
$$x_4 = 0 \wedge x_5 \geq 0 \wedge x_6 \geq 0 \wedge$$
$$x_7 = 0 \wedge x_5 + x_6 = q$$

$$\xi_2(\overline{x}) \Leftrightarrow \exists \overline{x}'' : \xi_1(\overline{x}'') \wedge \overline{x}'' \xrightarrow{r_6^*} \overline{x} \Leftrightarrow x_1 = 1 - x_4 \wedge x_2 = 1 \wedge x_3 = 0 \wedge$$
$$x_4 = 0 \wedge x_5 \geq 0 \wedge x_6 \geq 0 \wedge$$
$$x_7 \geq 0 \wedge x_5 + x_6 + x_7 = q$$

$$\xi_3(\overline{x}) \Leftrightarrow \exists \overline{x}'' : \xi_2(\overline{x}'') \wedge \overline{x}'' \xrightarrow{r_2^*} \overline{x} \Leftrightarrow x_1 = 1 - x_4 \wedge x_2 = 1 \wedge x_3 = 0 \wedge$$
$$x_4 \geq 0 \wedge x_5 \geq 0 \wedge x_6 \geq 0 \wedge$$
$$x_7 \geq 0 \wedge x_4 + x_5 + x_6 + x_7 = q$$

$$\xi_4(\overline{x}) \Leftrightarrow \exists \overline{x}'' : \xi_3(\overline{x}'') \wedge \overline{x}'' \xrightarrow{r_1^*} \overline{x} \Leftrightarrow x_1 = 1 - x_4 \wedge$$
$$((x_2 = 1 \wedge x_3 = 0 \wedge x_4 \geq 0) \vee$$
$$(x_2 = 0 \wedge x_3 = 1 \wedge x_4 = 0)) \wedge$$
$$x_5 \geq 0 \wedge x_6 \geq 0 \wedge x_7 \geq 0 \wedge$$
$$x_3 + x_4 + x_5 + x_6 + x_7 = q$$

One may easily check that $\forall r_i \in \{r_1, \ldots, r_6\} : \vartheta_{r_i}(\overline{x}) \wedge \xi_4(\overline{x}) \Rightarrow \xi_4(\overline{x} r_i)$. This means that the fixed-point has been reached.

Notes

1. Coefficients λ_i are found by solving the system $\langle \lambda_1, \ldots, \lambda_7 \rangle . M = \langle 0, \ldots, 0 \rangle$, where M is a matrix whose j-th column ($1 \leq j \leq 6$) is vector $\overline{k}_{r_j}$.

2. The original definition states that every transition has *exactly* one input place, but it is convenient here to relax it somewhat.

3. This incidentally shows that the set of points in the "ceiling" of the figure must satisfy $4 \geq x_3 > -7$.

References

1. M. Ajmone Marsan, G. Balbo, G. Conte, S. Donatelli & G. Franceschinis. (1995). *Modelling with Generalized Stochastic Petri Nets*. John Wiley & Sons, Chichester.

2. M. Baudinet, M. Niezette & P. Wolper. (1991). On the Representation of Infinite Temporal Data Queries. *Proc. 10th ACM Symp. on Principles of Database Systems*, pages 280-290.

3. G. Berthelot. (1986). Transformations and Decompositions of Nets.*Advances in Petri Nets*, LNCS 254, pages 359-376, Springer-Verlag.

4. A. Boudet & H. Comon. (1996). Diophantine Equations, Presburger Arithmetic and Finite Automata. *Proc. 21st Intl. Colloquium on Trees in Algebra and Programming*, LNCS 1059, pages 30-43, Springer-Verlag.

5. G.W. Brams. (1983). *Réseaux de Petri: Théorie et Pratique*. Masson, Paris.

6. J. Chomicki & T. Imielinski. (1988). Temporal Deductive Databases and Infinite Objects. *Proc. 7th ACM Symp. on Principles of Database Systems*, Austin, pages 61-81.

7. S. Christensen. (1993). *Decidability and Decompositionin Process Algebras*. Ph.D. Thesis,University of Edinburgh, CST-105-93.

8. M. Clausen & A. Fortenbacher. (1989). Efficient Solution of Linear Diophantine Equations. *J. Symbolic Computation* 8:201-216.

9. P. Cousot & N. Halbwachs. (1978). Automatic Discovery of Linear Restraints among Variables of a Program. *Conference Record 5th ACM Symp. on Principles of Programming Languages*, Tucson, pages 84-96.

10. J. Esparza & M. Nielsen. (1994). Decidability Issues for Petri Nets. *Bulletin of the EATCS*, Number 52.

11. J. Esparza. (1995). Petri Nets, Commutative Context-Free Grammars, and Basic Parallel Processes. *Proc. of Fundamentals of Computer Theory '95*, LNCS 965, pages 221-232, Springer-Verlag.

12. L. Fribourg & M. Veloso Peixoto. (1994). Bottom-up Evaluation of Datalog Programs with Incremental Arguments and Linear Arithmetic Constraints. *Proc. Post-ILPS'94 Workshop on Constraints and Databases*, Ithaca, N.Y., pages 109-125.

13. L. Fribourg & H. Olsén. (1995). *Datalog Programs with Arithmetical Constraints: Hierarchic, Periodic an Spiralling Least Fixpoints*. Technical Report LIENS-95-26, Ecole Normale Supérieure, Paris.

14. L. Fribourg & H. Olsén. (1997). Proving Safety Properties of Infinite State Systems by Compilation into Presburger Arithmetic. *Proc. 8th Intl. Conf. on Concurrency Theory*, Warsaw, Poland, LNCS, Springer-Verlag.

15. A. Van Gelder. (1990). Deriving Constraints among Argument Sizes in Logic Programs. *Proc. 9th ACM Symp. on Principles of Database Systems*, Nashville, pages 47-60.

16. S. Ginsburg & E.H. Spanier. (1966). Semigroups, Presburger formulas and languages. *Pacific Journal of Mathematics* 16:285-296.

17. N. Halbwachs. (1993). Delay Analysis in Synchronous Programs. *Proc. Computer Aided Verification*, LNCS 697, pages 333-346, Springer-Verlag.

18. A.R. Helm. (1989). On the Detection and Elimination of Redundant Derivations during Bottom-up Execution. *Proc. North American Conference on Logic Programming*, Cleveland, Ohio, pages 945-961.

19. J. Hopcroft & J.-J. Pansiot. (1979). On the Reachability Problem for 5-dimensional Vector Addition Systems. *Theoretical Computer Science* 8:135-159.

20. J. Jaffar & J.L. Lassez. (1987). Constraint Logic Programming. *Proc.14th ACM Symp. on Principles of Programming Languages*, pages 111-119.

21. F. Kabanza, J.M. Stevenne & P. Wolper. (1990). Handling Infinite Temporal Data. *Proc. 9th ACM Symp. on Principles of Database Systems*, Nashville, pages 392-403.

22. P. Kanellakis, G. Kuper & P. Revesz. (1990). Constraint Query Languages. Internal Report. (Short version in *Proc. 9th ACM Symp. on Principles of Database Systems*, Nashville, pages 299-313).

23. J.-L. Lassez & M.J. Maher. (1983). The Denotational Semantics of Horn Clauses As a Production System. *Proc. AAAI-83*, Washington D.C., pages 229-231.

24. D.W. Loveland. (1978). *Automated Theorem Proving: A Logical Basis*. North-Holland, Amsterdam.

25. M.J. Maher. (1988). Equivalences of Logic Programs. In J. Minker, editor, *Foundations of Deductive Databases and of Logic Programming*, pages 627-658. Morgan Kaufmann Publishers.

26. M.J. Maher. (1993). A Logic Programming View of CLP.*Proc. 10th Intl. Conf. on Logic Programming*, Budapest, pages 737-753.

27. S. Melzer & J. Esparza. (1995). Checking System Properties via Integer Programming. SFB-Bericht 342/13/95A, Technische Universitaet Muenchen. (See also: proceedings of ESOP '96).

28. J.F. Naughton & Y. Sagiv. (1987). A Decidable Class of Bounded Recursions. *Proc. 6th ACM Symp. on Principles of Database Systems,*San Diego, pages 171-180.

29. N.J. Nilsson. (1982). *Principles of Artificial Intelligence*. Springer-Verlag.

30. J.L. Peterson. (1981). *Petri Net Theory and the Modeling of Systems*. Prentice-Hall.

31. L. Plümer. (1990) Termination Proofs for Logic Programs based on Predicate Inequalities. *Proc. 7th Intl. Conf. on Logic Programming*, Jerusalem, pages 634-648.

32. R. Ramakrishnan, Y. Sagiv, J.D. Ulmann & M.Y. Vardi. (1989). Proof-Tree Transformation Theorems and their Applications. *Proc. 8th ACM Symp. on Principles of Database Systems*, Philadelphia, pages 172-181.

33. P. Revesz. (1990). A Closed Form for Datalog Queries with Integer Order. *Proc. 3rd International Conference on Database Theory*, Paris, pages 187-201.

34. D. Srivastava & R. Ramakrishnan. (1992). Pushing Constraints Selections. *Proc. 11th ACM Symp. on Principles of Database Systems*, San Diego, pages 301-315.

35. H. Tamaki & T. Sato. (1984). Unfold/fold Transformations of Logic Programs. *Proc. 2nd Intl. Conf. on Logic Programming*, Uppsala, pages 127-138.

36. K. Verschaetse & D. De Schreye. (1991). Deriving Termination Proofs for Logic Programs using Abstract Procedures. *Proc. 8th Intl. Conf. on Logic Programming*, Paris, pages 301-315.

37. L. Vieille. (1989). Recursive Query Processing: The Power of Logic. *Theoretical Computer Science* 69:1-53.

38. H.-C. Yen. (1996). On the Regularity of Petri Net Languages. *Information and Computation* 124:168-181.

Constraints: An International Journal, 2, 337–359 (1997)

Memoing Evaluation for Constraint Extensions of Datalog *

DAVID TOMAN   david@cs.toronto.edu
Department of Computer Science, University of Toronto

Abstract. This paper proposes an efficient method for evaluation of deductive queries over constraint databases. The method is based on a combination of the top-down resolution with memoing and the closed form bottom-up evaluation. In this way the top-down evaluation is guaranteed to terminate for all queries for which the bottom-up evaluation terminates. The main advantage of the proposed method is the direct use of the information present in partially instantiated queries without the need for rewriting of the original program. The evaluation algorithm automatically propagates the necessary constraints during the computation. In addition, the top-down evaluation potentially allows the use of compilation techniques, developed for compilers of logic programming languages, which can make the query evaluation very efficient.

Keywords: Datalog, constraint class, top-down evaluation, memoing evaluation of logic programs, SLG.

1. Introduction

We propose a new method for evaluating deductive queries over constraint databases [10]. The evaluation of queries over such databases is different from the one used in standard database systems. The constraints are used as the actual representation of data stored in the database rather than mere restrictions of the contents of otherwise ground relations. Algorithms for query evaluation over constraint databases have to satisfy the following criteria:

1. the evaluation algorithm has to terminate for all input queries,

2. the algorithm should be able to encompass various classes of constraints over wide range of domains, and

3. partially instantiated queries have to be evaluated efficiently.

The first requirement is especially difficult to achieve in the case of constraint databases: the extents of constraint relations are often infinite. There are two main approaches to satisfy the above requirements in the case of Datalog. However, neither of them seems to address all three of the requirements.

The first approach is based on a fixpoint, bottom-up evaluation of the rules. Here the first condition is usually met, e.g., for Datalog [31], Datalog with dense order constraints [10], Datalog with integer constraints [19, 30], and sets [23]. However, the evaluation process is not *goal-oriented* and thus the evaluation of partially instantiated queries is fairly inefficient. Application of standard program transformation techniques, e.g., the Magic Rewriting, does not completely solve the problem (cf. Section 4).

---

* A preliminary report on this work appeared in Proc. 1995 ILPS, Portland, OR, [28].

The second approach is based on a top-down, resolution-based method. Here the second and third conditions are usually met. However, the termination guarantees are often sacrificed [31] in order to improve the expressiveness and efficiency; an exception is [26] where no constraints are allowed. On the other hand these methods can take full advantage of compilation techniques developed for other logic programming languages, e.g., [5, 25, 32]. This greatly improves the practical efficiency of query evaluation in the case of Datalog [26]. We show that similar results can be achieved for constraint extensions of Datalog.

In this paper we try to combine the advantages of the above two approaches. We propose an evaluation method, *Constraint Memoing*, applicable to constraint-based extensions of Datalog (Datalog^C), that has the following features:

- Integrated Constraint Representation. Constraint Memoing integrates the constraints as *first-class* data into the evaluation procedure. This approach is different from most CLP systems, where constraints are handled by a separate *constraint solver* [8]. We propose much tighter integration of constraints into the query evaluation: they are handled very similarly to standard ground tuples (or terms in the CLP systems). This is achieved by defining several *constraint operations* over the representation of the constraints that are used by the query evaluation algorithm (cf. Definition 2). Moreover, the same operations are also needed for the bottom-up evaluation [10] and thus we can reuse results obtained in [10, 19, 23, 30].

- Termination. Constraint Memoing guarantees termination of queries for all classes of constraints that have a terminating closed-form bottom-up evaluation procedure. Also, the complexity bounds of the bottom-up procedure are preserved.

- The expressiveness of the language can be easily extended to accommodate various classes of constraints as long as every class of constraints is equipped with several elementary operations on the underlying representation of the constraints. This step is quite subtle if termination of queries is to be preserved. In contrast to bottom-up methods, it is also possible to extend the query language to classes of constraints, where termination is not guaranteed. Even in those cases the algorithm reduces the possibility of non-termination [21].

- The use of a top-down method allows a fully goal-oriented query evaluation: the information present in partially instantiated queries is used to prune the search space of queries. The efficiency achieved by this method is better than the efficiency of comparable bottom-up methods including program rewriting techniques (e.g., Magic Set Transformation).

- The top-down evaluation strategy allows a direct use of the results obtained in the area of compilation techniques for logic programming languages [7, 25, 32]. Handling the constraints as first-class data allows us to use these techniques for query evaluation in constraint databases.

In [31] the bottom-up approach (equipped with a query transformation phase) is shown to be no worse than the top-down approach for restricted classes of Datalog programs over ground relations. We show that the top-down approach is no worse than the bottom-up approach in the worst case, and in many empirical examples the top-down evaluation is much faster than bottom-up evaluation of the same query.

The rest of the paper is organized as follows: Section 2 introduces the constraint representation, the abstract constraint operations, and a closed form bottom-up evaluation procedure for Datalog^C in terms of these operations. Section 3 describes the proposed evaluation method, Constraint Memoing, includes the soundness, completeness, and termination proofs, and discusses possible optimization techniques specific to the proposed method. Section 4 introduces a general Magic Templates transformation (MT^C) for Datalog^C for comparison purposes. Section 5 studies both the analytical complexity of query evaluation using Constraint Memoing and gives results that provide empirical evidence of the practicality of the proposed evaluation method. Section 6 concludes the presentation with a brief discussion of the related work and with possibilities of further improvements and directions for research.

2. Preliminaries

This section introduces the basic building blocks in terms of which the evaluation of Datalog^C queries is defined. Also, for reference, the standard bottom-up query evaluation procedure is introduced in terms of these building blocks.

DEFINITION 1 *Let C_0 be a set of satisfiable atomic constraints. We define C to be the least set of constraints closed under the following rules:*

1. *true $\in C$.*

2. *$C_0 \subseteq C$.*

3. *if $C_1, C_2 \in C$ and $C_1 \wedge C_2$ is satisfiable then $C_1 \wedge C_2 \in C$.*

4. *if $C \in C$ and $x \in FV(C)$ then there exists a quantifier free formula $C_1 \vee \ldots \vee C_k$ (in DNF) equivalent to $\exists x.C$ such that $C_i \in C$ for every satisfiable C_i where $0 < i \leq k$.*

5. *if $C \in C$ and θ is a renaming of variables then $C\theta \in C$.*

$FV(C)$ denotes the set of free variables in C.

This definition is similar to the definition of Constraint Domain [8]. However, C contains only satisfiable constraints. The elements of C are used as a finite representation of the (possibly infinite) relations stored in a constraint database. The query evaluation over such a representation is based on the following operations:

DEFINITION 2 (CONSTRAINT CLASS) *Let V be a set of variables. A Constraint class is a set of constraints C from Definition 1 equipped with the following (computable) operations:*

Constraint Conjunction $\wedge^C : C \times C \rightarrow C \cup \{\perp\}$ *that for every pair of constraints C_1, C_2 computes the* conjunction $C_1 \wedge C_2$ *if the conjunction is satisfiable; otherwise it fails (returns $\perp$).*

Constraint Projection $\exists^{\mathcal{C}} : \mathcal{P}_{\text{fin}}(\mathcal{V}) \times \mathcal{C} \to \mathcal{P}_{\text{fin}}(\mathcal{C})$ *that for every constraint C and every finite set of variables V computes the set $\{C_i\}$ that satisfies the condition*

$$\left(\bigvee_{C_i \in \exists^{\mathcal{C}}(V,C)} C_i \right) \equiv \exists x_1. \cdots \exists x_l. C$$

where $x_j \in V$ for $0 < j \leq l$. Note that by Definition 1 the function is well defined and always returns a finite subset of $\mathcal{C}$.

Constraint Subsumption $\leq^{\mathcal{C}} : \mathcal{C} \times \mathcal{C} \to$ bool *that satisfies following condition:*

$$C_1 \leq^{\mathcal{C}} C_2 \text{ implies } C_1 \supset C_2$$

The first two operations are, in the world of constraints, the equivalents of relational algebra join and projection operations. However, while in the case of ground tuples the projection returns always only one tuple (constraint), in the case of more general constraints the constraint projection may return a set containing more than one constraint representing a disjunction [30, 33].

EXAMPLE: In [30] we considered the following example: Assume that we want to eliminate quantifier $\exists y$ from the constraint:

$$(\exists y)(x + c_1 < y \wedge y + c_2 < z \wedge y \equiv_k d)$$

Clearly we cannot replace it simply by $x + c_1 + c_2 + 1 < z$ as in the case of gap-order constraints: we need to take into account the periodicity constraint $y \equiv_k d$, i.e., we need to make sure that there is at least one integer of the form $\{d + nk\}$ between $x + c_1$ and $z - c_2$. Thus, the equivalent quantifier-free formula is

$$(x + c_1 + 1) \equiv_k d \ \wedge \ x + c_1 + c_2 + 1 < z \ \vee$$
$$(x + c_1 + 2) \equiv_k d \ \wedge \ x + c_1 + c_2 + 2 < z \ \vee$$
$$\vdots$$
$$(x + c_1 + k) \equiv_k d \ \wedge \ x + c_1 + c_2 + k < z$$

It is easy to see that the variable y was successfully eliminated and the resulting constraint is a disjunction of conjunctions of periodicity and gap-order constraints.   □

The last operation, the constraint subsumption, replaces the duplicate elimination for ground tuples. Note that the $\not\leq^{\mathcal{C}}$ is not unique by definition and does not have to imply $\not\supset$. However, a *better approximation* of $\supset$ relation by the $\leq^{\mathcal{C}}$ operation reduces the number of possible duplicate answers and improves the efficiency of the evaluation methods. In the following text we omit the superscripts $^{\mathcal{C}}$. We also use a *strict* ($\bot$-preserving) version of $\wedge^{\mathcal{C}}$.

The following definition states a fundamental property of constraint classes on which the termination proofs of bottom-up query evaluation procedures are implicitly based [19, 23, 30, 31].

DEFINITION 3 (CONSTRAINT-COMPACT CLASS OF CONSTRAINTS) *Let C be a constraint class. If for every finite set of variables V and for every set $\mathcal{D} \subseteq C$ such that $\forall C \in \mathcal{D}.FV(C) \subseteq V$ there is a finite subset $\mathcal{D}_{\text{fin}} \subseteq \mathcal{D}$ such that $\forall C \in \mathcal{D}.\exists C' \in \mathcal{D}_{\text{fin}}.C \leq^C C'$ (i.e., $\mathcal{D}_{\text{fin}}$ covers $\mathcal{D}$ with respect to $\leq^C$) then C is* constraint-compact.

This property plays a central role in the termination proofs of both the bottom-up based query evaluation procedures (cf. Section 2.1) and the top-down query evaluation procedure developed in Section 3. In general, the above condition could be weakened to require only that every infinite set of constraints contains a finite cover (where every constraint is covered by possibly several elements of the cover). However, the use of the weaker definition may require much more expensive subsumption checks [22]. The two definitions are equivalent for constraint classes that satisfy the *single subsumption property* [16].

Example 4 (Common Constraint Classes) Standard Datalog can be defined using the class of constraints generated from the set $\{x = a : a \in A\}$ where A is the set of all constants in the Datalog program (the *active domain* [1]).

Allowing general equality may cause problems to the standard evaluation strategies (rules may not be range-restricted). However, in our case we simply generate the appropriate class of constraints from the set $\{x = a : a \in A\} \cup \{x = y\}$. The evaluation remains otherwise unchanged as we use more general evaluation mechanism.

Incorporation of more interesting constraints, e.g., constraints over integers (Z) is also easy: the *gap-order* constraints [19] are generated from the set $C_{<Z} = \{x < u : u \in A\} \cup \{u < x : u \in A\} \cup \{x + c < y : c \in Z^+\}$. Similarly the *periodicity* constraints are generated from $C_{\equiv Z} = \{x \equiv_k c : c \in A\}$. In [30] a closed form bottom-up evaluation procedure for $C_{\equiv,<Z} = C_{<Z} \cup C_{\equiv Z}$ was developed including the constraint operations from Definition 2. The *dense order* constraints over Q can be incorporated by a slight modification of constraint operations defined in [10].

All the above constraint classes are constraint-compact. However, there are also constraint classes where all the constraint operations are defined, but which are *not* constraint-compact, e.g., the class generated from the set $\{x + c < y : c \in Z\}$ (gap-order constraints with possibly negative size of the gap [19]) or the linear arithmetic constraints [10].

DEFINITION 5 (DATALOG^C PROGRAM) *Let C be a class of constraints. A* atom *is a predicate symbol with distinct variables as its arguments. A* Datalog^C *is a set of clauses of the form*

$$A \leftarrow D, B_1, \ldots, B_k$$

where A and B_i are atoms and $D \in C$.

We assume that the extensional database (EDB) is represented by a set of unit clauses $A \leftarrow D$ as a part of the Datalog^C program. A query over such database is a tuple containing an atom and a constraint the returned tuples have to satisfy.

DEFINITION 6 (QUERY) *Let P be a Datalog^C program, G an atom, and $C \in C$. We call the tuple (G, C, P) a* query. *The* answer *to the query (G, C, P) is a set of valuations θ such that $P \models (G \wedge C)\theta$. A* query evaluation procedure *is an algorithm that computes an answer to the query. A query is* partially instantiated *if the constraint C is nontrivial (i.e., $C \neq$ true).*

2.1. Closed-form Bottom-up Evaluation

The usual approach to query evaluation for Datalog^C is a variation on the bottom-up evaluation algorithm [31]. In its simplest form a bottom-up evaluation algorithm is defined as follows:

DEFINITION 7 (INTERPRETATION) *Let $R(x_1, \ldots, x_k)$ be an atom and $C \in \mathcal{C}$ a constraint such that $FV(C) \subseteq FV(R)$. A pair (R, C) is a constraint atom. A (C-)interpretation is a set of constraint atoms.*

Constraint atoms play the role of ground atoms (tuples) stored in a standard relational system. The definition of the TP operator is now similar to the definition of the corresponding operator on ground atoms. However, in this case all the operations in the definition of TP are defined with respect to the chosen class of constraints $\mathcal{C}$ (see Definition 2).

DEFINITION 8 (IMMEDIATE CONSEQUENCE OPERATOR) *Let P be a Datalog^C program and I a C-interpretation. We define*

$$\text{TP}_{\mathcal{C}}(I) = \{(A, C') : A \leftarrow D, B_1, \ldots, B_k \subset P,$$
$$(B_i, C_i) \in I \text{ for all } 0 < i \leq k, D \in \mathcal{C},$$
$$C = D \wedge C_1 \wedge \ldots \wedge C_k \text{ exists, } C' \in \exists_A.C,$$
$$\text{and if } C' \leq C'' \text{ for some } (A, C'') \in I \text{ then } C' = C''\}$$

where $\exists_A$ is a shorthand for $\lambda x.\exists^{\mathcal{C}}(FV(x) - FV(A), x)$. The variables in the constraints are renamed using the variable names in the associated atoms of the clause.

The bottom-up evaluation algorithm remains unchanged: all the modifications needed for the evaluation of *constraint* queries are encapsulated in the definition of the $\text{TP}_{\mathcal{C}}$ operator.

Algorithm 9 (Naive Bottom-up Evaluation) *Let (G, C, P) be a query. The following algorithm computes the answer to this query.*

> $I := \emptyset$
> *repeat*
> $\quad J, I := I, \text{TP}_{\mathcal{C}}(I)$
> *while* $J \neq I$
> *return* $\{C \wedge D : (G, D) \in I\}$

This arrangement also shows how other TP-based evaluation procedures can be utilized for constraint query evaluation, e.g., the semi-naive bottom-up evaluation [31]. Algorithm 9 was shown to be sound and complete for Datalog [31], Datalog$^{<Q}$, and Datalog$^{<,\equiv_Z}$ [19, 30]. A simple generalization of the proofs in [30] shows soundness and completeness of Algorithm 9 for a general class $\mathcal{C}$:

Notation 10 *Let $S \subseteq \mathcal{C}$. Then $\|S\|$ is the set of valuations θ such that $\theta \models C$ for some $C \in S$. For a constraint interpretation I we define $\|I\| = \{A\theta : (A, C) \in I, \theta \models C\}$.*

Theorem 11 (Soundness and Completeness) *Let P be a Datalog^C program. Then*

$$\| \text{TP}_{\mathcal{C}}^{\omega}(\emptyset) \| = \text{TP}^{\omega}(\emptyset).$$

Proof: *By simultaneous induction on stages of* TP *and* TP_C. *The base case holds vacuously. Let* $i > 0$. $G\vartheta \in \mathrm{TP}^i(\emptyset)$. *Then there is* θ *an extension of* ϑ *and a clause* $G \leftarrow D, B_1, \ldots, B_k$ *in P such that* $\theta \models D$ *and* $B_i\theta \in \mathrm{TP}^{i-1}(\emptyset)$. *Then by the induction hypothesis* $B_j\theta \in \parallel \mathrm{TP}_C^{i-1}(\emptyset)\parallel$. *Thus for each* B_j *there is a constraint* C_j *such that* $(B_j, C_j) \in \mathrm{TP}_C^{i-1}(\emptyset)$ *and* $\theta \models D \wedge C_1 \wedge \ldots \wedge C_k$. *By definition of* TP_C *there is* $A \in \exists_G.D \wedge C_1 \wedge \ldots \wedge C_k$ *such that* $\vartheta \models A$. *Therefore* $\vartheta \in \parallel \mathrm{TP}_C^i(\emptyset)\parallel$. *The other direction is similar.* ∎

Theorem 12 (Termination) *Let* C *be a constraint-compact class of constraints. Then Algorithm 9 terminates for every* $Datalog^C$ *query.*

Proof: *Immediate from Definitions 3 and 8. Assume, that Algorithm 9 does not terminate. Then in every iteration it generates a constraint atom that is not subsumed by any previously generated constraint atom. As there are only finitely many different predicate symbols in every* $Datalog^C$ *program, there must be at least one symbol, that occurs infinitely often among the generated atoms. However, this is an infinite set of constraints over a fixed finite set of variables and thus it must contain a finite constraint cover by Definition 3; a contradiction.* ∎

All the constraint classes in Example 4 have a closed-form terminating bottom-up evaluation procedure (based on Definitions 8 and 9).

2.2.   Goal-oriented Evaluation Strategies

There are several standard improvements to the naive bottom-up evaluation algorithm, e.g., the semi-naive algorithm [31]. However, these strategies fail to take into account the information contained in a partially instantiated query: they are not goal-oriented. There are two major approaches to solving this problem in the case of standard (ground) Datalog:

1. Rewrite the original program using the Magic Templates (MT) transformation technique [2, 17] and subsequently evaluate the transformed program bottom-up, or

2. Adopt a variant of a top-down evaluation strategy [4] based on the resolution principle [15].

In this paper we consider mainly the top-down, resolution-based methods. However, the MT optimization for constraint deductive query languages is also be introduced for comparison purposes. It is well known that the standard top-down strategies, e.g., the SLD-resolution [4], despite their efficiency, have a major drawback as query evaluation procedures: they lead to nonterminating computations even in the situations, where the bottom-up algorithms are guaranteed to terminate. Note also that breadth-first traversal of a SLD-tree does not guarantee termination in general.

The drawback is caused by occurrences of infinite paths in SLD search trees. This has been observed in several papers, e.g., [3, 27] and an alternative to SLD-resolution was proposed (under various names). The main idea lies in *remembering* answers for already resolved subgoals. This approach guarantees termination in the case of function-free logic programs [26]. We extend this method to *constraint* deductive queries while preserving the termination and complexity bounds of the bottom-up evaluation algorithms.

3. Top-down evaluation for Datalog$^{\mathcal{C}}$

In the last section the bottom-up evaluation of Datalog$^{\mathcal{C}}$ was defined in terms of elementary operations over a given constraint class. This section shows how a top-down query evaluation procedure (SLG-resolution [3]) can be refined using the same operations to handle constraint queries. This approach allows us to build an efficient top-down evaluation procedure for every class of constraints that has a closed form bottom-up evaluation procedure. Moreover, the termination and complexity bounds of the bottom-up algorithm are preserved.

The modification of the (positive fragment of the) SLG resolution for Constraint Memoing (SLG$^{\mathcal{C}}$ resolution) is defined by the following set of rewriting rules:

DEFINITION 13 (SLG$^{\mathcal{C}}$ REWRITING RULES) *Let C be a constraint class and*

$$\mathrm{root}(G; C), \mathrm{body}(G; B_1, \ldots, B_k; C), \mathrm{goal}(G; B, C'; B_2, \ldots, B_k; C), \text{ and } \mathrm{ans}(G, A)$$

where G is an atom, $B_1, \ldots, B_k$ are literals, and C, C', A are constraints in C, be nodes from which we build SLG-trees using the following rules:

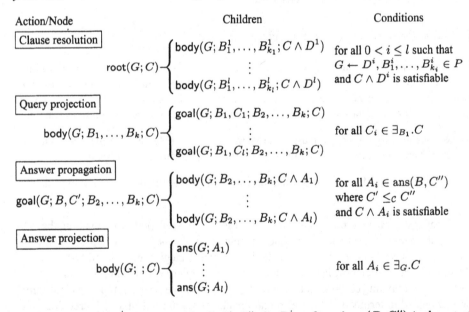

Action/Node	Children	Conditions

Clause resolution

$$\mathrm{root}(G; C) - \begin{cases} \mathrm{body}(G; B_1^1, \ldots, B_{k_1}^1; C \wedge D^1) \\ \quad\vdots \\ \mathrm{body}(G; B_1^l, \ldots, B_{k_l}^l; C \wedge D^l) \end{cases}$$

for all $0 < i \leq l$ such that $G \leftarrow D^i, B_1^i, \ldots, B_{k_i}^i \in P$ and $C \wedge D^i$ is satisfiable

Query projection

$$\mathrm{body}(G; B_1, \ldots, B_k; C) - \begin{cases} \mathrm{goal}(G; B_1, C_1; B_2, \ldots, B_k; C) \\ \quad\vdots \\ \mathrm{goal}(G; B_1, C_l; B_2, \ldots, B_k; C) \end{cases}$$

for all $C_i \in \exists_{B_1}.C$

Answer propagation

$$\mathrm{goal}(G; B, C'; B_2, \ldots, B_k; C) - \begin{cases} \mathrm{body}(G; B_2, \ldots, B_k; C \wedge A_1) \\ \quad\vdots \\ \mathrm{body}(G; B_2, \ldots, B_k; C \wedge A_l) \end{cases}$$

for all $A_i \in \mathrm{ans}(B, C'')$ where $C' \leq_c C''$ and $C \wedge A_i$ is satisfiable

Answer projection

$$\mathrm{body}(G; ; C) - \begin{cases} \mathrm{ans}(G; A_1) \\ \quad\vdots \\ \mathrm{ans}(G; A_l) \end{cases}$$

for all $A_i \in \exists_G.C$

where G, B_i, and B_i^j are atoms, $A_i, C, C', C'', C_i, D^i \in \mathcal{C}$, and $\mathrm{ans}(B, C'')$ is the set of answers collected from the leaves of the SLG-tree rooted by (B, C'') (introduced in Notation 16).

A SLG-tree is a tree built from a node $\mathrm{root}(G; C)$ by a finite application of the above rules. A SLG-forest is a set of SLG-trees.

Note that the *Answer propagation* and *Answer projection* rules have to *cooperate*: every time a new answer—an answer not subsumed by any answer in the same tree generated earlier—is produced, it is propagated to all the nodes that have already been resolved using answers from this particular tree. Also, the *Answer propagation* rule is responsible for creating new SLG-trees in the SLG-forest when no tree with a root node that subsumes the goal to be resolved can be found.

In the presented form the *Query projection* rule implements the left-to-right selection rule (common to most of the LP systems). However, any other goal selection strategy can be implemented here, e.g., selection based on specific SIPS—Sideways Information Passing Style [17].

The main difference between SLG and SLG^C is in two additional rules: the *Query Projection* and the *Answer Projection*. The *Query Projection* rule is responsible for determining what are the goals to be resolved by answer resolution (i.e., what is the goal-constraint pair to be looked for among the already computed answers). The *Answer Projection* is responsible for storing the computed answers for a given goal for subsequent lookup and propagating them to the appropriate goal nodes. Note the essential use of constraint projection which allows to determine the relevant constraint for every atom.

The SLG-resolution can handle negation using additional rules [26, 29]. However, our proposal currently allows only positive programs. Adding negation is briefly discussed in Section 6.

The SLG^C rewriting rules are used for the query evaluation as follows:

DEFINITION 14 *Let* $\mathrm{SLG}(G, C)$ *be the SLG-forest generated from the query* (G, C, P) *as follows:*

1. *create a SLG-forest containing a single tree* $\{\mathrm{root}(G; C)\}$.
2. *expand the leftmost node using the rules in Definition 13 as long as they can be applied.*
3. *return the set* $\mathrm{ans}(G, C)$ *as the answer for the query.*

Let $\mathrm{slg}(G, C)$ *be a SLG-tree rooted by the node* $\mathrm{root}(G; C)$.

We order the answers (i.e., the nodes $\mathrm{ans}(G; C)$) in the SLG-forest according to the order in time in which they were derived:

DEFINITION 15 *Let* $\mathrm{ans}(G; A)$ *and* $\mathrm{ans}(G'; A')$ *be leaves in the SLG-forest generated by the SLG-rules (cf. Definition 13). Then we say that* $\mathrm{ans}(G; A)$ *is older than* $\mathrm{ans}(G'; A')$ *if the node* $\mathrm{ans}(G; A)$ *is generated before the node* $\mathrm{ans}(G'; A')$.

We assume that the SLG-trees are ordered left-to-right in the order they were created. The choice of selection strategy does not affect the soundness/completeness of the algorithm [15]. However, the selection strategy may influence the efficiency of the system (cf. Section 6).

Notation 16 *Let* $\mathrm{ans}(G, C)$ *be the set of all* A *such that* $\mathrm{ans}(G; A) \in \mathrm{slg}(G, C)$ *and if an older* $\mathrm{ans}(G; A') \in \mathrm{slg}(G, C)$ *then* $A \not\subseteq A'$.

Lemma 17 *Let* $\mathrm{ans}(G; A)$ *be a leaf of the SLG-tree* $\mathrm{slg}(G, C)$. *Then for every application of the answer propagation rule along the path* $\mathrm{root}(G; C) \rightarrow \ldots \rightarrow \mathrm{ans}(G; A)$ *if* $\mathrm{ans}(G'; A')$ *was a propagated answer then* $\mathrm{ans}(G'; A')$ *is older than* $\mathrm{ans}(G; A)$.

Proof: *Immediate from the Definitions 13, 14, and 15.* ∎

Soundness and completeness of Constraint Memoing is proven by reduction to soundness and completeness of bottom-up evaluation (Algorithm 9). Note that the set $\text{ans}(G, C)$ may not be unique and depends on the order in which the nodes $\text{ans}(G; A)$ are generated. However, for our purposes it is sufficient that the set of valuations $\| \text{ans}(G, C) \|$ is unique.

Lemma 18 *Let* $\text{slg}(G, C)$ *be a SLG-tree and* ϑ *a valuation. Then* $\vartheta \in \| \text{ans}(G, C) \|$ *implies* $\vartheta \models C$.

Proof: *By induction on the height of the SLG-tree* $\text{slg}(G, C)$. ∎

To prove correctness of the algorithm we show that all the derived answers are also derived in the bottom-up computation:

Lemma 19 *Let* (G_0, C_0, P) *be a query. Then for every* $\text{slg}(G, C) \in \text{SLG}(G_0, C_0)$ *and every valuation* ϑ

$$\vartheta \subset \| \text{ans}(G, C) \| \implies G\vartheta \in \text{TP}^\omega(\emptyset).$$

Proof: *Induction on the "age" of answers: Let* $\text{ans}(G; C') \in \text{slg}(G, C)$ *such that* $\vartheta \models C'$. *Then there is a path*

$$\text{root}(G; C) \to \text{body}(G; B_1, \ldots, B_k; C_1) \to \ldots \to \text{ans}(G; C') \in \text{slg}(G, C)$$

that starts with a Clause Resolution *step using a clause* $G \leftarrow D, B_1, \ldots, B_k \in P$ *(cf. Figure 1). By Definition 13,* $C' \in \exists_G . C \wedge D \wedge A_1 \wedge \ldots \wedge A_k$ *where* A_i *is an answer propagated from the SLG-trees* $\text{slg}(B_i, C_i')$. *Thus, there exists* θ *an extension of* ϑ, *such that* $\theta \models C \wedge D \wedge A_1 \wedge \ldots \wedge A_k$. *Clearly,* $\theta \models A_i$ *for* $0 < i \leq k$. *By Lemma 17 all the answers* $\text{ans}(B_i; A_i)$ *used along this path have been computed before* $\text{ans}(G; C')$ *and thus by the induction hypothesis we have* $B_i\theta \in \text{TP}^\omega(\emptyset)$. *By definition of* TP *and the fact that* $\theta \models D$ *we have* $G\theta = G\vartheta \in \text{TP}^\omega(\emptyset)$. ∎

Thus, all answers—not only for the main query, but also for all subqueries represented by the SLG-trees in the SLG forest generated from the main query—are sound.

Lemma 20 *Let* G *be an atom and* $C_1, C_2 \in C$ *constraints. Then*

$$C_1 \leq C_2 \implies \| \text{ans}(G, C_1) \| \subseteq \| \text{ans}(G, C_2) \|.$$

Proof: *Immediate from the definition of* ans *and Lemma 18.* ∎

The next thing to show is that the algorithm computes all the answers to the given query. This is a little bit more complicated, as the algorithm does not compute all the answers to an *uninstantiated* query like the bottom-up evaluation does. However we can show:

Lemma 21 *Let* (G_0, C_0, P) *be a query. Then for every* $\text{slg}(G, C) \in \text{SLG}(G_0, C_0)$ *and every valuation* ϑ

$$G\vartheta \in \text{TP}^\omega(\emptyset) \wedge \vartheta \models C \implies \vartheta \in \| \text{ans}(G, C) \|.$$

Operation	SLG-tree for goal (R, C_0)	Other SLG-trees
	$\mathrm{root}(R; C_0)$	
Clause resolution $R \leftarrow D, B_1, \ldots, B_k \in P$ $C_1 := C_0 \wedge D$	$\cdots \quad | \quad \cdots$	
	$\mathrm{body}(R; B_1, \ldots, B_k; C_1)$	
Query projection $\exists_{B_1}.C_1 \equiv C_1^1 \vee \ldots \vee C_1^k$	$\cdots \quad | \quad \cdots$	
	$\mathrm{goal}(R; B_1, C_1^i; B_2, \ldots, B_k; C_1) \xrightarrow{C_1^i \leq_C C_1'} \mathrm{root}(B_1; C_1')$	SLG-tree
Answer propagation Let $C_2 := C_1 \wedge A_1$	$\cdots \quad | \quad \cdots$	
	$\mathrm{body}(R; B_2, \ldots, B_k; C_2) \xleftarrow{\text{new } A_1} \cdots \mathrm{ans}(B_1; A_1) \cdots$	
$\vdots$	$\vdots$	
	$\mathrm{goal}(R; B_k, C_k'; ; C_k) \xrightarrow{C_k^i \leq_C C_k'} \mathrm{root}(B_k; C_k')$	SLG-tree
Answer propagation Let $C_{k+1} := C_k \wedge A_k$	$\cdots \quad | \quad \cdots$	
	$\mathrm{body}(R; ; C_{k+1}) \xleftarrow{\text{new } A_k} \cdots \mathrm{ans}(B_k; A_k) \cdots$	
Answer projection $\exists_R.C_{k+1} \equiv A_1 \vee \ldots \vee A_l$	$\cdots \quad | \quad \cdots$	
	$\mathrm{ans}(R; A_i)$	

Figure 1. SLG^C Evaluation of goal R w.r.t. a constraint C_0.

Proof: *By induction on stages of* TP. *Let* $G\vartheta \in \mathrm{TP}^i(\emptyset)$ *and* $\vartheta \models C$. *The claim holds vacuously for* $i = 0$. *Let* $i > 0$. *Then there is a clause* $G \leftarrow D, B_1, \ldots, B_k \in P$ *and an extension* θ *of* ϑ *such that* $\theta \models D$ *and* $B_i\theta \in \mathrm{TP}^{i-1}(\emptyset)$. *We can construct a path in* $\mathrm{slg}(G, C)$ *that ends with a node* $\mathrm{ans}(G; A')$ *such that* $\vartheta \models A'$. *Using the assumption* $\vartheta \models C$ *we have* $\theta \models C \wedge D$ *(this corresponds to the application of the* Clause Resolution *rule). Thus,* $\theta \models C_1'$ *for at least one element* C_1' *of* $\exists_{B_1} C \wedge D$. *By the inductive hypothesis* $\theta \in \| \mathrm{ans}(B_1, C_1') \|$. *This fact in turn yields a node* $\mathrm{ans}(B_1; A_1) \in \mathrm{slg}(B_1, C_1')$ *such that* $\theta \models A_1$. *Again, using the previous assumptions,* $\theta \models C \wedge D \wedge A_1$. *In general, let* C_i' *be an element of* $\exists_{B_i}.C \wedge D \wedge A_1 \wedge \ldots \wedge A_{i-1}$. *Clearly, by* $i-1$ *applications of the induction hypothesis,* $\theta \models C_i'$. *Then by induction hypothesis on* B_i *we have* $\theta \in \| \mathrm{ans}(B_i, C_i') \|$. *This exactly corresponds to an application of the* Query Projection *and* Answer Propagation *rules from Definition 13.*

After k *steps we have* $\theta \models C \wedge D \wedge A_1 \wedge \ldots \wedge A_k$. *Thus,* $\vartheta \models A'$ *for some element* A' *of* $\exists_G.C \wedge D \wedge A_1 \wedge \ldots \wedge A_k$ *(this is achieved by the* Answer Projection *rule), and therefore* $\vartheta \in \| \mathrm{ans}(G, C) \|$.

In the actual algorithm, the application of the Answer Propagation *rule does not necessarily use the tree* $\mathrm{slg}(B_i, C_i')$ *for answer resolution. However, if a different tree* $\mathrm{slg}(B_i, C_i'')$ *is used then it is always the case that* $C_i' \leq_C C_i''$. *Thus, by Lemma 20,* $\| \mathrm{ans}(B_i, C_i') \| \subseteq \| \mathrm{ans}(B_i, C_i'') \|$ *and no answers can possibly be lost.* ∎

109

```
(1)    root(tc(X,Y);[X = b])                                              initial query node
(2)      ├body(tc(X,Y);tc(X,Z),tc(Z,Y);[X = b])
(4)      │ └goal(tc(X,Y);tc(X,Z),[X = b];tc(Z,Y);[X = b])                 get results for X = b
(8)      │   ├body(tc(X,Y);tc(Z,Y);[X = b,Z = c])                         answer from node (7)
(9)      │   │ └goal(tc(X,Y);tc(Z,Y),[Z = c];;[X = b,Z = c])             get results for X = c (→ 10)
(18)     │   │   ├body(tc(X,Y);;;[X = b,Z = c,Y = b]                      answer from node (17)
(20)     │   │   │ └ans(tc(X,Y);[X = b,Y = b])                            new answer for X = b
(31)     │   │   ├body(tc(X,Y);;;[X = b,Z = c,Y = c]                      answer from node (30)
(33)     │   │   │ └ans(tc(X,Y);[X = b,Y = c])
(41)     │   │   └body(tc(X,Y);;;[X = b,Z = c,Y = d]                      answer from node (40)
(44)     │   │     └ans(tc(X,Y);[X = b,Y = d])                            new answer for X = b
(21)     │   ├body(tc(X,Y);tc(Z,Y);[X = b,Z = b])                         answer from node (20)
(22)     │   │ └goal(tc(X,Y);tc(Z,Y),[Z = b];;[X = b,Z = b])            get results for X = b
(23)     │   │   ├body(tc(X,Y);;;[X = b,Z = b,Y = c]                      answer from node (7)
(25)     │   │   │ └ans(tc(X,Y);[X = b,Y = c])
(24)     │   │   ├body(tc(X,Y);;;[X = b,Z = b,Y = b]                      answer from node (20)
(26)     │   │   │ └ans(tc(X,Y);[X = b,Y = b])
(46)     │   │   └body(tc(X,Y);;;[X = b,Z = b,Y = d]                      answer from node (44)
(54)     │   │     └ans(tc(X,Y);[X = b,Y = d])
(45)     │   └body(tc(X,Y);tc(Z,Y);[X = b,Z = d])                         answer from node (44)
(48)     │     └goal(tc(X,Y);tc(Z,Y),[Z = c];;;[X = b,Z = d])           get results for X = d (→ 49)
(3)      └body(tc(X,Y);e(X,Y);[X = b])
(5)        └goal(tc(X,Y);e(X,Y),[X = b];;[X = b])
(6)          └body(tc(X,Y);;;[X = b,Y = c])
(7)            └ans(tc(X,Y);[X = b,Y = c])                                new answer for X = b

(10)   root(tc(X,Y);[X = c])                                              subquery from (9)
(11)     ├body(tc(X,Y);tc(X,Z),tc(Z,Y);[X = c])
(13)     │ └goal(tc(X,Y);tc(X,Z),[X = c];tc(Z,Y);[X = c])                 get results for X = c
(19)     │   ├body(tc(X,Y);tc(Z,Y);[X = c,Z = b])                         answer from node (17)
(27)     │   │ └goal(tc(X,Y);tc(Z,Y),[Z = b];;[X = c,Z = b])            get results for X = b
(28)     │   │   ├body(tc(X,Y);[X = c,Z = b,Y = c]                        answer from node (7)
(30)     │   │   │ └ans(tc(X,Y);[X = c,Y = c])                            new answer for X = c
(29)     │   │   ├body(tc(X,Y);[X = c,Z = b,Y = b]                        answer from node (20)
(34)     │   │   │ └ans(tc(X,Y);[X = c,Y = b])
(47)     │   │   └body(tc(X,Y);[X = c,Z = b,Y = d]                        answer from node (44)
(55)     │   │     └ans(tc(X,Y);[X = c,Y = d])
(32)     │   ├body(tc(X,Y);tc(Z,Y);[X = c,Z = c])                         answer from node (30)
(35)     │   │ └goal(tc(X,Y);tc(Z,Y),[Z = c];;[X = c,Z = c])            get results for X = c
(36)     │   │   ├body(tc(X,Y);[X = c,Z = c,Y = b]                        answer from node (17)
(38)     │   │   │ └ans(tc(X,Y);[X = c,Y = b]
(37)     │   │   ├body(tc(X,Y);[X = c,Z = c,Y = c]                        answer from node (30)
(39)     │   │   │ └ans(tc(X,Y);[X = c,Y = c])
(42)     │   │   └body(tc(X,Y);[X = c,Z = c,Y = c]                        answer from node (40)
(56)     │   │     └ans(tc(X,Y);[X = c,Y = c])
(43)     │   └body(tc(X,Y);tc(Z,Y);[X = c,Z = d]                          answer from node (40)
(57)     │     └goal(tc(X,Y);tc(Z,Y),[Z = d];;[X = c,Z = b])
(12)     └body(tc(X,Y);e(X,Y);[X = c])
(14)       └goal(tc(X,Y);e(X,Y),[X = c];;[X = c])
(15)         ├body(tc(X,Y);;;[X = c,Y = b])
(17)         │ └ans(tc(X,Y);[X = c,Y = b])                                new answer for X = c
(16)         └body(tc(X,Y);;;[X = c,Y = d])
(40)           └ans(tc(X,Y);[X = c,Y = d])                                new answer for X = c

(49)   root(tc(X,Y);[X = d])                                              subquery from (48)
(50)     ├body(tc(X,Y);tc(X,Z),tc(Z,Y);[X = d])
(52)     │ └goal(tc(X,Y);tc(X,Z),[X = d];tc(Z,Y);[X = d])
(51)     └body(tc(X,Y);e(X,Y);[X = d])                                    answer from node (40)
(53)       └goal(tc(X,Y);e(X,Y),[X = d];;[X = d])
```

The First column indicates the order, in which the individual nodes have been created, the second column shows the SLG-trees generated, and the last column describes how answers have been generated by the SLG-trees; the relation e represents the edges in the graph $a \rightarrow b \overset{\rightarrow}{\leftarrow} c \rightarrow d$.

Figure 2. Annotated SLG evaluation of query $tc(X,Y)$ for $X = b$.

By composing the previous Lemmas we have:

Theorem 22 (Soundness and Completeness) *Let* (G, C, P) *be a query tuple. Then for all valuations ϑ such that $\vartheta \models C$*

$$G\vartheta \in \mathrm{TP}^\omega(\emptyset) \iff \vartheta \in \|\operatorname{ans}(G, C)\|.$$

Proof: *Soundness follows from Lemmas 18 and 19, completeness from Lemma 21.* ∎

The soundness and completeness proof is based on the reduction to the fixpoint computation on *ground* instances. However, to prove termination of the query evaluation algorithms (in both the bottom-up and top-down cases) a finite encoding of a potentially infinite result of the evaluation is needed [19, 30]:

Theorem 23 (Termination) *Let C be a constraint-compact class. Then the SLG^C evaluation terminates for all queries (G, C, P).*
Proof: *Let C be a constraint-compact class of constraints. Then:*

1. *The number of trees in the SLG-forest $\mathrm{SLG}(G, C)$ is finite, as there are only finitely many predicate symbols $G' \in P$ and for every predicate symbol the set $\{C_i : \text{root } (G', C_i) \in \mathrm{SLG}(G, C)\}$ is finite by Definitions 3 and 13.*

2. *Every root node has finitely many children, as there are only finitely many clauses in P.*

3. *Every body node has finitely many children, as the set $\exists_G . C$ is finite for any $C \in C$.*

4. *Every goal node as only finitely many children, as there are only finitely many elements in the set $\operatorname{ans}(G', C')$ for any atom G' and $C' \in C$ by Definition 3.*

5. *Every $\mathrm{slg}(G, C)$ has finite depth, because of finite number of subgoals in the bodies of each clause in P.*

Therefore the rules from Definition 13 can be applied only finitely many times. ∎

The termination of the Constraint Memoing algorithm is guaranteed in all cases when the bottom-up algorithm terminates computing a finite interpretation $\mathrm{TP}^\omega_C(\emptyset)$. Moreover, it is usually easy to *decompose* the original bottom-up evaluation procedure and extract the elementary operations on constraints needed for Constraint Memoing (Definition 2).

3.1. Optimization

To reduce the overhead introduced by the SLG^C resolution (in comparison to standard SLD resolution) we explore several possibilities:
1. Solving more general goals than necessary:

Action/Node	Children	Conditions
Query projection		
$\mathrm{body}(G; B_1, \ldots, B_k; C)$	$\begin{cases} \mathrm{goal}(G; B_1, C_1; B_2, \ldots, B_k; C) \\ \quad \vdots \\ \mathrm{goal}(G; B_1, C_l; B_2, \ldots, B_k; C) \end{cases}$	$\exists_{B_1}.C \supset C_1 \vee \ldots \vee C_l$ for some $C_1, \ldots, C_l$

111

This modification may reduce the number of SLG-trees in the SLG-forest (in the cases where $|\exists_{B_1}.C| > l$). However, the propagation of constraints *at the time of goal resolution* is reduced. The soundness and completeness properties are preserved by Lemma 20. The termination is guaranteed similarly to Theorem 23. In [7] the following version of such a modification was considered:

Action/Node	Children	Conditions
Query projection		
$\text{body}(G; B_1, \ldots, B_k; C) \rightarrow \text{goal}(G; B_1, \text{true}; B_2, \ldots, B_k; C)$		none

In this case, there is only one SLG-tree per predicate symbol. On the other hand, no constraints are propagated at the time of goal resolution—the constraints are used merely to restrict the returned answers. Thus, the computation essentially computes all answers to an *uninstantiated* query similarly to the bottom-up algorithm, and the performance suffers: The performance is approximately the same as evaluating the uninstantiated query.

2. Mixed SLG and SLD resolution (by memoing only a subset of the predicate symbols present in the program).

Action/Node	Children	Conditions
Non-tabled resolution		
$\text{body}(G; B_1, \ldots, B_k; C) \dashv$	$\begin{cases} \text{body}(G; B_1^1, \ldots, B_{k_1}^1, \\ \quad B_2, \ldots, B_k; C \wedge D^1) \\ \quad\quad\vdots \\ \text{body}(G; B_1^l, \ldots, B_{k_l}^l, \\ \quad B_2, \ldots, B_k; C \wedge D^l) \end{cases}$	for B_1 not tabled goal $B_1 \leftarrow D^i, B_1^i, \ldots, B_{k_i}^i \in P$ and $C \wedge D^i$ satisfiable

This is a different way of reducing the number of SLG-trees generated by the algorithm: SLG-trees are generated only for a subset of the predicate symbols in P. The remaining symbols are always resolved using program clauses, similarly to SLD-resolution. Again, soundness and completeness are preserved (by simple modification of Theorem 22). Termination is guaranteed if and only if at least one predicate is resolved by the SLG^C resolution for every cycle in the dependency graph of P (this follows by an easy extension of Theorem 23). Otherwise, an infinite branch may appear in some of the SLG-trees. This may lead to non-termination similarly to the case of SLD-resolution.

Also, as there is only a bounded number of SLD resolution steps between any two SLG^C resolution steps, the bodies of the non tabled clauses can be *unfolded* in the bodies of their callers. This transformation completely eliminates the need for non tabled resolution steps.

3. Program transformation similar to supplementary magic [17]. The previous folding transformation may introduce unnecessary recomputation of conjunctions of goals. This can be avoided by a technique that *folds* common parts of bodies of the clauses and creates separate clauses. Note that the recomputation is avoided by making the heads of such clauses tabled—resolved by the SLG^C resolution.

The last two optimizations are based on program transformations. However, in contrast to the Magic Transformation, these two transformations are completely query-independent.

4. Magic Templates Transformation for $\mathcal{C}$ (MT$^{\mathcal{C}}$)

This section describes a simple version of the program transformation approach to the goal-oriented query evaluation in constraint deductive databases—the Magic Templates transformation (in the constraint setting the difference between Magic Sets and Magic Templates is blurred). The transformation has to be slightly modified in the context of constraint databases.

Algorithm 24 (MT program transformation)

$$\begin{aligned}
\mathrm{mst}(G, C, P) = \{ \, & A \leftarrow D, \mathrm{magic}A, B_1, \ldots, B_k, \\
& \mathrm{magic}B_1 \leftarrow D, \mathrm{magic}A, \\
& \qquad \vdots \\
& \mathrm{magic}B_k \leftarrow D, B_1, \ldots, B_{k-1}, \mathrm{magic}A : \; A \leftarrow D, B_1, \ldots, B_k \in P \} \\
& \cup \{ \, \mathrm{magic}G \leftarrow C_i : C_i \in \exists_G C \}
\end{aligned}$$

where $\mathrm{magic}A, \mathrm{magic}B_1, \ldots, \mathrm{magic}B_k$ are the magic atoms for $A, B_1, \ldots, B_k$, respectively.

Again, for simplicity, only the left-to-right SIPS is used. This corresponds to the selection rule used in Constraint Memoing. In both cases, different selection rules may improve the efficiency of query evaluation [17]. However, in the case on MT, the SIPS is fixed during the *program transformation* phase and there are technical difficulties with combining different SIPS in one program. In the case of SLG$^{\mathcal{C}}$ evaluation, the selection rule can be adjusted during the evaluation process dynamically while preserving correctness of the answers.

The Magic Templates transformation is often preceded by an *adornment* transformation [17]. The adornment phase is designed to partition the search space according to (the statically derivable) information about free and bound arguments of the literals. The purpose of this transformation is threefold:

1. The original purpose of the adornments was to project out all the arguments that are not bound and thus guarantee that only ground tuples are generated (in the constraint setting this is not needed).

2. The other important consequence of using adornments is the possibility to reduce the arity of literals in the bodies of clauses. This leads to more efficient bottom-up evaluation: reduction of arity by one may cause linear speedup [12].

3. The adornment partially factors the search space and allows to propagate only the needed restrictions.

In the SLG$^{\mathcal{C}}$ case the first use of adornments is not needed (similarly to the bottom-up procedure for constraints: Algorithm 9). Thus we implemented the MT without the adornment phase. The second and third uses are also partially achieved in the top-down evaluation: The factoring technique uses a static prediction of binding patterns of literals to reduce their arity. However, at the runtime, these literals have to follow this prediction and thus the effect of factoring is partially achieved using the *subsumption check*. Moreover, the run-time check detects *all* possible factoring opportunities (for the particular evaluation

We test the relative performance of the evaluation methods by computing paths in various graphs.

```
tc(X,Z):-tc(X,Y),tc(Y,Z).        path(X,Z):-X<Y<Z,path(X,Y),path(Y,Z).
tc(X,Y):-e(X,Y).                 path(X,Y):-e(X,Y).
```

In the gap-order case (path) we only look for paths where all edges lead from nodes with lower number to a node with higher number. We use the tc and path programs to find paths in the following graphs:

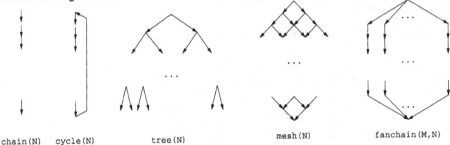

  chain(N)   cycle(N)   tree(N)   mesh(N)   fanchain(M,N)

The nodes of the graphs are numbered by integers from top to bottom. In the case of gap-order Datalog, the integers are represented using constraints (e.g., i is represented by $i - 1 < x < i + 1$). Note that in the case of acyclic graphs the parent nodes are always labeled with a smaller integer.

Figure 3. Test Programs

order) while the static methods can predict only a subclass of them. Also in many cases, the top-down method groups the answers to particular goals according the bindings present in these goals. This way it propagates only the relevant bindings (in the bottom-up method this effect could be achieved by building an goal-based index on the magic atoms). Note that this grouping of answers can not be achieved by using adornments as it depends on the actual data in the constraint database.

5. Performance

In this section, the analytical complexity bound for the Constraint Memoing evaluation is discussed. The complexity of the top-down evaluation depends on the particular class of constraints C; our analysis is based on the relative comparison to the (time- and space-) complexity of the bottom-up evaluation procedure. The analytical results are confirmed by experimental results that show the performance gains achieved by Constraint Memoing.

5.1. Theory

We show that the complexity of Constraint Memoing is no worse than complexity of the bottom-up evaluation:

Theorem 25 *Let* $\mathrm{TP}_C^\omega(\emptyset)$ *be the result of the bottom-up evaluation of the query* (G, C, P) *and* $f(n)$ *a function such that* $|\mathrm{TP}_C^\omega(\emptyset)| \in O(f(|P|))$. *Then*

1. *the SLG-forest* $\mathrm{SLG}(G, C)$ *has at most* $O(f^2)$ *nodes.*
2. *there are at most* $O(f^2)$ *applications of the* SLG^C *rules in the evaluation of the query.*

Proof: *(1) follows from the observation that every SLG-tree in the SLG forest has at most* $O(f)$ *leaves and thus also at most* $O(f)$ *nodes as the height of the trees is fixed by the number of subgoals in the clauses of P, and there are at most* $O(f)$ *different SLG trees in the SLG-forest as the size of* $\mathrm{TP}_C^\omega(\emptyset)$ *limits the number of possible roots of the SLG-trees. (2) follows immediately from (1) as every application of a rule creates at least one new node in the SLG-forest.* ∎

A careful implementation needs to store only a single path (of fixed length) in every SLG-tree in the SLG forest. Thus, the space requirements can be reduced to $O(f)$. On the other hand, the quadratic number of rule applications cannot be avoided in general. However, by analysis of the bottom-up algorithm the number of applications of *clauses* in P is also quadratic with respect to f (the bottom-up algorithm can recompute the same element of the interpretation several times, even if it is added only once to the interpretation $\mathrm{TP}_C^\omega(\emptyset)$).

5.2. *Implementation*

We have implemented experimental versions of the following deductive query evaluation algorithms:

1. the Naive Bottom-up: a straightforward implementation of Algorithm 9,
2. the Semi-naive Bottom-up: a modification of Algorithm 9 [31],
3. the Semi-naive Bottom-up with MT^C, and
4. the Constraint Memoing algorithm SLG^C.

The implementation of each of the evaluation algorithms is parametrized on the underlying class of constraints. For each constraint class we provide elementary operations on the constraint representation (cf. Definition 2) together with a few additional auxiliary operations:

constraint_new(N,C): Given a number N it returns C as the representation of the constraint *true* over N variables. This operation is used to create a *fresh* environment for constraints, present during the evaluation of the individual clauses of the Datalog^C program.

constraint_and(G,C,CO,CN): This operation computes the constraint conjunction of the constraint CO with the constraint C where all the variables in C are renamed with respect to the variables of the atom G. This operation is used when a constraint derived by a subgoal of a clause is "and"-ed to the overall constraint over the variables in the body of the clause. The operation produces only consistent constraints; if the conjunction is not satisfiable, the operation fails.

constraint_qe(G,C,Cn): Let G be an atom. Then Cn is a finite set (list) of constraints equivalent to the constraint C after all variables not in G are eliminated. This operation is used in the *Query Projection* rule, where we project the constraint on the free variables of the goal to be resolved, and the *Answer Projection* rule, where we eliminate all variables not present in the head of the clause.

constraint_subsumes (C1, C2) is the subsumption checking procedure. The operation succeeds if C1 subsumes C2. We can assume that the constraints C1 and C2 are over the same set of variables: we only use this operation to decide if a new constraint atom has been derived by the particular method or if a new SLG-tree is needed.

The last two operations are just for the convenience of the user of the system:

constraint_pp (C) allows "pretty printing" of the results of the evaluation, and

constraint_read (T, G, C) allows entering the constraints as formulas, rather than as the actual representation as Prolog terms.

In addition, we need to specify the Datalog^C programs that we intend to evaluate. Note that we use the *same* implementation of the operations on constraints for *all* the evaluation algorithms. Thus the relative performance of these algorithms is not caused by more sophisticated way of manipulating the constraint representation in one of the algorithms.

5.3. Experimental Results

Both the bottom-up (including the MT optimization) and the Constraint Memoing algorithms have been implemented in Prolog. We would like to emphasize that neither of the implemented evaluation algorithms takes an advantage of Prolog's top-down evaluation strategy—all the algorithms are implemented as meta-interpreters operating on a common ground representation of constraints (note that our top-down technique could have gained

Query	Data	Naive Bottom-up	Semi-naive Bottom-up	Semi-naive with MT	Top-down
tc(X,Y)	chain(32)	64590	40470	78790	29780
tc(1,32)	chain(32)	64250	40310	65910	2720
tc(1,24)	cycle(24)	108860	88040	102860	5740
tc(1,48)	tree(64)	48570	32120	70910	6730
tc(1,36)	mesh(6)	44370	19920	31940	1600
tc(0,37)	fanchain(2,18)	37560	17080	35400	1520
tc(0,37)	fanchain(6,6)	3530	2220	7330	610
tc(0,37)	fanchain(18,2)	1260	840	3200	490
path(X,Y)	chain(16)	16280	9790	31510	10780
path(1,16)	chain(16)	16300	9980	22020	5500
path(0,13)	fanchain(2,6)	16420	10300	37830	2700
path(0,17)	fanchain(4,4)	20390	10950	26230	2990
path(0,13)	fanchain(6,2)	5260	3480	14130	1790

Figure 4. Running times of test queries for various evaluation procedures (in msec).

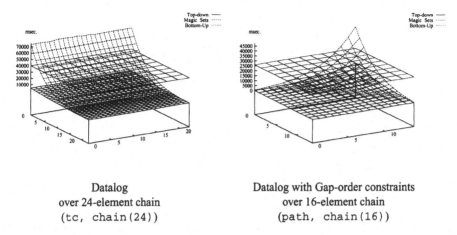

Datalog	Datalog with Gap-order constraints
over 24-element chain	over 16-element chain
(tc, chain(24))	(path, chain(16))

We measure the elapsed time to verify if there is a path from node i (x-axis) to node j (y-axis). The elapsed time is plotted on the z-axis. Note that in the ordered case (right graph), the constraint propagation allows more efficient pruning than in the case of standard Datalog (left graph). Thus the use of constraints may improve efficiency even for standard queries.

Figure 5. Elapsed time of query evaluation for all possible paths.

a considerable advantage by using Prolog's evaluation strategy). Figure 4 summarizes the running time of queries over graphs in Figure 3. The first line shows the performance for the uninstantiated case. In the constraint cases (path) the integers in the queries are expressed using constraints similarly to constants in Figure 3. The examples of the instantiated queries are those, where the optimization achieves the *least* effect (in all cases). The results show that while the implementation of the various evaluation methods are comparable (the results on uninstantiated queries are approximately the same), the evaluation of instantiated queries is much more efficient using the Constraint Memoing algorithm. The boost is inherent to the top-down evaluation method is not caused by using a more sophisticated implementation. The other two experiments (Figures 5 and 6) show that the query evaluation on constraints generally follows the patterns of query evaluation on ground representation:

- for all possible queries over a given graph (Figure 5 plots the elapsed time for all ground queries $tc(i, j)$ over a n-element chain. Similar graphs can be produced for the other structures in Figure 3), and

- for all *shapes* of the given graph (Figure 6 plots the elapsed time for graphs with varying fanout/fanin and chain lengths of $fanchain(x, y)$ defined in Figure 3).

Thus we can expect very efficient Constraint Memoing-based query evaluation engines for constraint extensions of Datalog whose performance will be comparable to the top-down engines for ground Datalog [25, 26].

117

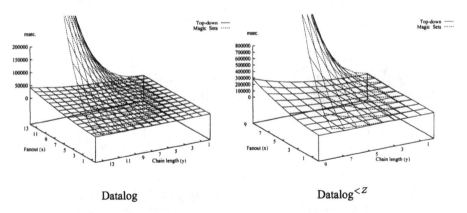

The above graphs plot the elapsed time to find a path in the fanchain(x,y) graph from the top-most node to the bottom-most node (cf. Figure 3). On the x and y axes we plot the parameters of the used graph: the fanout on the x-axis and the chain length on the y-axis. The elapsed time is plotted on the z-axis.

Figure 6. Elapsed time for varying fanout and chain length.

6. Conclusion

We have proposed a practical approach to query evaluation for generalized constraint databases. Both the analytical and the empirical results show that Constraint Memoing is no worse than comparable bottom-up methods and in many cases the practical perfor-mance is much better even when using a very naive implementation. The performance of the Constraint Memoing can be boosted by utilizing compilation methods developed in [5, 25, 26, 32] and performance similar to ground Datalog can be expected. In addition, recent work on scheduling of operations in tabling systems [6] shows modifications to the tabling strategy that make it efficient even if external storage is involved. The scheduling strategies are orthogonal to the extensions introduced for handling constraints and thus can be immediately applied to our proposal.

6.1. Related Work

Recently, there have been several other attempts to make query evaluation in the presence of constraints efficient. There are two main directions of this research:

1. The first direction has its roots in the deductive database community: Techniques for pushing constraints present in the query were proposed in [13, 18, 24]. However, the goal of these methods is to *preprocess* the query (i.e., the goal and the rules) with respect to the given constraints for subsequent bottom-up evaluation. We present a completely different evaluation strategy where the constraints are propagated dynamically without the need for the preprocessing of the query. Also, in the standard database approach, the constraints are considered to be mere *conditions* that restrict the otherwise ground

answers. Constraint Memoing uses constraints as a tool for *representing* both the data computed by the queries and stored in the database itself (i.e., non-ground relations are allowed). This dramatically increases the expressive power of the query language while preserving termination and efficiency.

2. The other direction is pursued in the area of (general) Logic Programming: In [7, 9, 14] top-down evaluation for constraint logic programs is proposed. However, in all cases, general constraint solving procedures are used. Thus, these methods are not directly useful for query evaluation in constraint databases: termination of queries cannot be guaranteed. The closest to our work is [7]. However, the method proposed there allows propagation of constants only (i.e., constraints of the form $x = a$); the *constraint* part of the query is essentially computed bottom-up. Our approach allows full propagation of all possible constraints during the whole evaluation process.

6.2. Directions of Future Research

Future research in this area needs to focus on the following issues:

1. Compilation of constraints. To achieve an efficient implementation of Constraint Memoing, data structures for efficient representation of the constraints have to be developed. There are two main differences to be addressed:

   • In most cases, the size of the constraint representation is bounded with respect to the arity of a literal. However, general Logic Programming engines allow unbounded terms to be built. Exploring this property may lead to an efficient *stack*-based implementation (i.e., without a heap) of the evaluation procedure.
   • On the other hand, classical Logic Programming assumes that every (logical) variable is either free or bound to a single term (and this binding can be changed only by backtracking). This assumption is no longer valid in the presence of constraints as more restrictive conditions may be derived after a variable is originally bound. Also, the constraints specify complex relations *between* the individual variables, which is not possible in the standard approach.

   Development of such a representation enables building of very efficient query evaluation engines based on partial evaluation of the atomic constraints in a given class, similarly to the WAM abstract code [32].

2. Analysis of binding patterns. Similarly to the MT transformation, the queries can be analyzed to determine the *flow of information* in clause bodies [17]. This is a considerably more complicated task in the presence of constraints: it is no longer sufficient to focus on single variables; the relationships between groups of variables have to be taken into consideration (as noted in Section 4). Also, the assumption that all EDB relations are ground (i.e., after resolution of an EDB goal all variables are bound to constants) is no longer valid—the generalized relations store representation of sets of tuples that may be infinite. Such an analysis can be used for several purposes: query optimization (MT-like rewriting), optimization of access to the constraint database (indexing), goal reordering, etc.

3. Interface to an existing RDBMS. As the constraints can be finitely encoded, their representation can be stored as tuples in a standard relational database system. However, query evaluation has to be carried out with respect to the semantics of such encoding (i.e., to perform, e.g., a join of two constraint relations, we can not use the join operation of the underlying RDBMS directly). We propose the top-down evaluation procedure to be used as a front-end built on top of a standard relational DBMS. Similar approach was proposed in [5, 6] for the XSB deductive system. The proposed techniques can be directly applied in the constraint setting.

4. Negation. Adding negation to $Datalog^C$ in such a way that termination is preserved, is a nontrivial task: adding negation often leads immediately to Turing completeness. Essentially, adding negation (and preserving termination) would require the constraint class to be closed under negation (complementation) while preserving constraint-compactness. This condition is easy to satisfy in the case of finite domain constraints. For infinite constraint classes we sometimes need to restrict the class of allowed $Datalog^C$ programs to those, where termination can be guaranteed [20]. [29] presents an extension of Constraint Memoing to $Datalog^C$ programs with negation under the well founded semantics. However, the constraint class is required to be both constraint compact and closed under complementation.

5. Storage and access methods. To achieve an efficient implementation of constraint databases, new storage management techniques have to be developed: access methods suitable for fast retrieval of the stored information, efficient updates of generalized relations, indexing techniques [11], etc.

6. Benchmarks. The performance of various implementations of Logic Programming languages (e.g., Prolog) is often judged by the performance on a standard benchmarks (e.g., nrev). We propose to develop similar benchmarks for query evaluation methods in constraint databases. The benchmarks should be independent of the particular class of constraints. Such test suite would allow us to compare performance of various query evaluation methods.

References

1. S. Abiteboul, R. Hull & V. Vianu. (1995). *Foundations of Databases*. Addison-Wesley.
2. F. Bancilhon, D. Maier, Y. Sagiv & J. Ullman. (1986). Magic Sets and Other Strange Ways to Implement Logic Programs. In *ACM Symposium on Principles of Database Systems*, pages 1–16.
3. W. Chen & D.S. Warren. (1993). Query evaluation under the well-founded semantics. In *ACM Symposium on Principles of Database Systems*, pages 168–179.
4. W.F. Clocksin & C.S. Mellish. (1987). *Programming in Prolog*, 3rd edition. Springer, Berlin.
5. J. Freire, T. Swift & D.S. Warren. (1996). Beyond depth-first: Improving tabled logic programs through alternative scheduling strategies. In *Programming Languages: Implementations, Logics, and Programs*, LNCS 1140, pages 234-258.
6. J. Freire, T. Swift & D.S. Warren. (1997). Taking i/o seriously: Resolution reconsidered for disk. In *International Conference on Logic Programming*.
7. H. Gao & D.S. Warren. (1993). A powerful evaluation strategy for CLP programs. In *PPCP'93: First Workshop on Principles and Practice of Constraint Programming*, Providence RI, pages 90-97.
8. J. Jaffar & M. Maher. (1994). Constraint logic programming: A survey. *Journal of Logic Programming* 19:503–581.

9. M. Johnson. (1993). Memoization in constraint logic programming. In *PPCP'93: First Workshop on Principles and Practice of Constraint Programming*, Providence, RI, pages 130-138.

10. P. Kanellakis, G. Kuper, and P. Revesz. (1995). Constraint Query Languages. *Journal of Computer and System Sciences* 51:26–52.

11. P. Kanellakis, S. Ramaswamy, D. Vengroff & J. Vitter. (1993). Indexing for Data Models with Constraints and Classes. In *ACM Symposium on Principles of Database Systems*, pages 233–243.

12. D. Kemp, K. Ramamohanarao & Z. Somogyi. (1990). Right-, left-, and multi-linear transformations that maintain context information. In *International Conference on Very Large Data Bases*, pages 380–391.

13. D.B. Kemp & P.J. Stuckey. (1993). Analysis based constraint query optimization. In D.S. Warren, editor, *International Conference on Logic Programming*, pages 666–682.

14. P. Lim & P. Stuckey. (1990). Meta programming as constraint programming. In *North American Conference on Logic Programming*, pages 416–430.

15. J. Lloyd. (1987). *Foundations of Logic Programming*, 2nd edition Springer-Verlag.

16. M. Maher. (1993). A logic programming view of clp. In *International Conference on Logic Programming*, pages 737–753.

17. R. Ramakrishnan. (1991). Magic Templates: A Spellbinding Approach to Logic Programs. *Journal of Logic Programming* 11:189–216.

18. R. Ramakrishnan & D. Srivastava. (1993). Pushing Constraint Selections. *Journal of Logic Programming* 16:361–414.

19. P. Revesz. (1993). A Closed-Form Evaluation for Datalog Queries with Integer (Gap)-Order Constraints. *Theoretical Computer Science* 116:117–149.

20. P.Z. Revesz. (1995). Safe Stratified Datalog with Integer Order Programs. In *International Conference on Constraint Programming*, LCNS 1000, pages 154-169.

21. K.F. Sagonas, T. Swift and D.S. Warren. (1994). XSB as an efficient deductive database engine. In Snodgrass, R. T. and Winslett, M., editors, *ACM SIGMOD International Conference on Management of Data*, pages 442–453.

22. D. Srivastava. (1993). Subsumption and Indexing in Constraint Query Languages with Linear Arithmetic Constraints. *Annals of Mathematics and Artificial Intelligence* 8:315–343.

23. D. Srivastava, R. Ramakrishnan & P. Revesz. (1994). Constraint Objects. In A. Borning, editor, *PPCP'94, Second International Workshop on Principles and Practice of Constraint Programming*, LNCS 874, pages 181–192.

24. P.J. Stuckey & S. Sudarshan. (1994). Compiling query constraints. In *ACM Symposium on Principles of Database Systems*, pages 56–67.

25. T. Swift & D.S. Warren. (1994a). An abstract machine for SLG resolution: definite programs. In *Logic Programming - Proceedings of the 1994 International Symposium*, pages 633–652.

26. T. Swift & D.S. Warren. (1994b). Analysis of SLG-WAM evaluation of definite programs. In *Logic Programming - Proceedings of the 1994 International Symposium*, pages 219–235.

27. S. Tamaki & T. Sato. (1986). OLD Resolution with Tabulation. In *International Conference on Logic Programming*, pages 84–98.

28. D. Toman. (1995). Top-Down Beats Bottom-Up for Constraint Based Extensions of Datalog. In *International Logic Programming Symposium*, pages 189–203.

29. D. Toman. (1997). Computing the Well-founded Semantics for Constraint Extensions of Datalog¬. In *Constraint Databases and Applications*, LNCS 1191, pages 64–79.

30. D. Toman, J. Chomicki & D. Rogers. (1994). Datalog with Integer Periodicity Constraints. In *International Logic Programming Symposium*, pages 189–203.

31. J. Ullman. (1989). *Principles of Database and Knowledge-Base Systems*, volume 2. Computer Science Press.

32. D.H.D. Warren. (1983). An Abstract PROLOG Instruction Set. Technical Report 309, Artificial Intelligence Center, Computer Science and Technology Division, SRI International, Menlo Park, CA.

33. H. Williams. (1976). Fourier-Motzkin Elimination Extension to Integer Programming Problems. *Journal of Combinatorial Theory A* 21:118–123.

Constraints, 2, 361–375 (1997)

Refining Restriction Enzyme Genome Maps

PETER Z. REVESZ

revesz@cse.unl.edu

Department of Computer Science and Engineering, University of Nebraska-Lincoln,
Lincoln, NE 68588-0115, USA

Abstract. A genome map is an ordering of a set of clones according to their believed position on a DNA string. Simple heuristics for genome map assembly based on single restriction enzyme with complete digestion data can lead to inaccuracies and ambiguities. This paper presents a method that adds additional constraint checking to the assembly process. An automaton is presented that for any genome map produces a refined genome map where both the clones and the restriction fragments in each clone are ordered satisfying natural constraints called step constraints. Any genome map that cannot be refined is highly likely to be inaccurate and can be eliminated as a possibility.

Keywords: constraint query languages, set constraints, genome mapping

1. Introduction

Deoxyribonucleic acid or DNA, the genetic material that encodes the blueprint of any living organism, is composed of a string of nucleotides that are adenine (A), thymine (T), cytosine (C), and guanine (G). Clones are copies of random substrings of a given DNA string. Clones may overlap in a clone database.

Restriction enzymes are enzymes that cut a nucleotide string always at specific sites.[1] Each different restriction enzyme cuts the nucleotide string at different sites. After cutting all information about the original order of the small fragments is lost, because the small fragments just float randomly in the solution.[2] In this paper we assume that each clone is cut at all restriction sites that are specific for the enzyme applied. This is called complete digestion. Clones can be copied easily and completely digested by various enzymes and the lengths of the fragments after the digestion can be measured.

A genome map is a sequence of clones $c_1, \ldots, c_n$ of some DNA string such that the left end of c_i precedes the left end of c_{i+1} on the DNA string. A refined genome map according to a specific enzyme is a genome map where the restriction fragments of each clone are also ordered from left to right according to their position on the DNA string. We can summarize the problem of genome map assembly with single enzyme complete digestion as follows:
INPUT: For an enzyme and for each of a set of N clones of the same DNA string the approximate fragment lengths after complete digestion of the clone by the enzyme.
OUTPUT: All possible genome maps compatible with the input.

For example, the following may be an input to the genome map assembly problem:

The unit of measurements in the above table is one hundred base pairs. For any fragment its measurement can be off by a few nucleotides from its actual length. Small errors can be eliminated from consideration by rounding the measurements to the nearest tenths or hundreds of nucleotides.

Table 1. A sample input
database with nine clones.

Clone	Fragment Lengths
C1	5,10,15,25,30,35
C2	5,10,15,20,35,40
C3	5,20,25,30,45,50
C4	5,10,20,25,30,45
C5	5,10,15,20,25,35
C6	8,15,20,25,40
C7	15,20,25,30,45,50
C8	8,20,25,35,40
C9	15,40,45,50

There are some good heuristics for assembling genome maps, although the problem is known to be NP-complete in the number of restriction fragments in the clones (Gillett, 1992; Karp, 1993). However, the simple heuristics often lead to incorrect maps or ambiguities. The refinement method introduced in this paper aims to correct inaccuracies and eliminate ambiguities in genome maps.

In this paper we devise a nondeterministic automaton that refines genome maps. This automaton is nondeterministic on the transitions from a state to itself, although it will be normally deterministic on the transitions from a state to another state. Given any unrefined genome map (derived using some simple heuristic), the automaton decides whether it can be refined, that is, whether the restriction fragments can be ordered in each clone in a way that the orderings in the individual clones are compatible. If a refinement is not possible then the unrefined genome map assembly is highly likely to be invalid.

The automaton can be implemented in programming languages that provide (1) representation of sets, (2) representation and solving of set constraints, and (3) recursion. One such language is provided in the DISCO database system (short for *Datalog with Integer and Set order COnstraints*), which is currently implemented at the University of Nebraska (Byon and Revesz, 1995). We expressed the automaton in DISCO and tested it on small sample problems.

The paper is organized as follows. Section 2 describes heuristics for the genome map assembly problem. Section 3 presents an automaton for refining genome maps. Section 4 provides implementation in DISCO of the automaton and some sample results. Section 5 discusses related work. Section 6 presents some conclusions and open problems.

Note: An earlier version of this paper was presented at the CP'96 workshop on constraints and databases (Revesz 1996).

2. Basic Genome Map Assembly Heuristics

The basic strategy of the solution is the following. We try to find the order of the clones according to the position of their left ends on the DNA string. Then we walk through from left to right on the clones. That is we pick our best guess for the leftmost clone. Then we try to identify the next leftmost clone and so on until we reach the end of the DNA string. Next we consider several heuristics for choosing the next clone.

Threshold Heuristic: If $A = \{a_1, \ldots, a_m\}$ is the current clone, choose as the next clone out of the yet unused ones the clone B_i such that the cardinality of $A \cap B_i$ is above a certain constant threshold.

For our example, the cardinality of the intersections considering the enzyme discussed are the following:

Table 2. The overlap matrix. Since the matrix is symmetric, only the upper triangular part is shown.

	C2	C3	C4	C5	C6	C7	C8	C9
C1	4	3	4	5	2	3	2	1
C2		2	3	5	3	2	3	2
C3			5	3	2	5	2	2
C4				4	2	4	2	1
C5					3	3	3	1
C6						3	4	2
C7							2	3
C8								1

Maximal Overlap Heuristic: This is a heuristic that we introduce and use in this paper. This extends the previous heuristic with the following. In case several clones could be chosen according to the enzyme threshold heuristic, then choose the one with the highest overlap.

Suppose we know that clone 8 is the leftmost clone on the DNA string. Then using the maximal overlap heuristic, we obtain for our example the search tree shown in Figure 1. The search tree shows that there is some ambiguity in the genome map assembly. We have seven possible genome maps to consider.

3. A Refined Genome Map Assembly Automaton

In the refined genome map assembly problem we are not only interested in the order of the clones, but also the order and alignment of the restriction fragments in each clone. Sometimes, it is hard to know how to align two clones even when we know that they overlap. Suppose that the cardinality of the intersection of clones A and B is 4. Then we can be fairly sure that these two overlap if our threshold value is 3.[3]

But do they overlap on each of the four segments that they have in common, or only on three, two or one of them? The maximal alignment seems the most reasonable assumption under the following conditions, which we assume to hold in the rest of this paper:

(1) No clone contains another clone.

(2) No clone contains two different restriction fragments with the same length. However, different clones may contain different restriction fragments that have the same length.[4]

(3) Each restriction fragment is contained in at most k clones, where k is some fixed number.

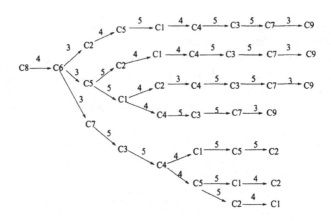

Figure 1. The search tree using the maximal overlap heuristic

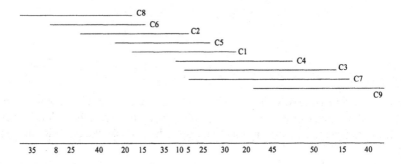

Figure 2. A refined genome map.

(4) The right end of each clone overlaps the left end of at least one other clone when they are mapped to their correct positions on the DNA string.

Note that all the unrefined genome maps that we want to check and refine further, if we can, will automatically satisfy (4). To solve the example in the previous sections, we test each of the seven genome maps in Figure 1 separately. Out of the seven only one, namely the genome map corresponding to the topmost branch of the tree, can be refined with maximal alignment as shown in Figure 3. Hence this genome map is the most likely to reflect the real order of clones on the DNA string.

In Figure 3 we present a non-deterministic refinement automaton, named NRA, that tests whether a candidate unrefined genome map is valid or not under the assumptions listed above. The basic idea behind the NRA is to build a staircase like the one shown in Figure 2.[5] The staircase shows a refinement of the candidate unrefined genome map that is the topmost branch of the search tree in Figure 1.

We call any subset of the staircase with $k + 1$ clones a *window*. As we refine the genome map this window will move to the right and down the staircase. Let at all times the elements of the window be called $A_1, \ldots, A_{k+1}$ in order.

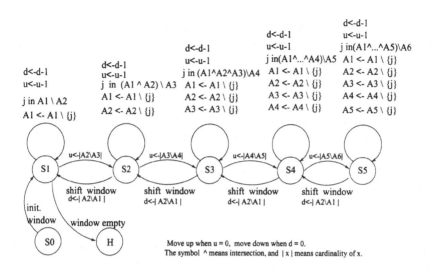

Figure 3. The automaton for $k = 5$.

We say that a clone is active if it must contain the element that we pick next. At any time one to k clones are active. The main idea in the automaton is to have a separate state i for the case when i clones are active. We also keep two counters, d and u to signal that we must move to a lower or higher state. When $d = 0$ we will move to a lower state. Moving to a lower state is needed when we read the last item from the leftmost clone $A1$. Moving to a lower state occurs again after picking cardinality of $A2 \setminus A1$ number of items, because then we will read the last item of $A2$. Hence when we move to a lower state we set the counter d to $card(A2 \setminus A1)$. When moving to a lower state we also advance the window one step downward. This means that we assign to A_i the previous value of A_{i+1} for each $1 \le i \le k$ and assign to a_{k+1} the next clone of the genome map that we wanted to refine. If no next clone exists, that is, when we are reading the last few clones in the genome map, then the value of A_{k+1} will be the empty set.

Similarly, when $u = 0$ we move to a higher state. Moving from state i to state $i + 1$ is needed when we already picked all items in $A_i \setminus A_{i+1}$. Moving to a higher state occurs again after picking all items in $A_{i+1} \setminus A_{i+2}$, because then we read all items in A_{i+1} which don't occur in A_{i+2}. Hence when we move to a higher state we set the counter u to $card(A_{i+1} \setminus A_{i+2})$.

Finally, there are transitions from each state i to itself. On these transitions we pick a value from the leftmost i clones in the window. On each self-transition, we also decrease by one the counters d and u.

Let d_1 be the number of fragments in c_1, and let d_i be the cardinality of $c_i \setminus c_{i-1}$ for $1 < i \le n$. Let u_i be the cardinality of $c_i \setminus c_{i+1}$ for each $1 \le i < n$, and let u_n be the cardinality of c_n. Let $\alpha(c_i)$ be the number of elements picked from clone c_i.

LEMMA 1 *Suppose that the automaton reaches the halt state given a genome map $c_1, \ldots, c_n$. Then the following must be true for each $1 < i < n$:*

$$\alpha(c_{i+1}) = \alpha(c_i) + d_{i+1} - u_i$$

Proof: When the automaton moves from a lower state to a higher state and starts picking items from c_i it sets $u = u_i$ and does not move to a higher state until u_i number of items are picked from c_i that are not in c_{i+1}. After that the automaton moves to a higher state and starts picking items from c_{i+1}. But while it picks items from c_{i+1} it must also pick simultaneously the same items from c_i until shifting c_i out from the window. When shifting c_i out from the window the automaton sets $d = d_{i+1}$ and does not shift out c_{i+1} also until d_{i+1} number of items are picked from c_{i+1}. These three facts imply that $\alpha(c_{i+1}) = \alpha(c_i) + d_{i+1} - u_i$. ∎

Next we prove that to reach the halt state the automaton must pick all the items from each clone. At first, note the following identity (*) for each $1 < i < n$:

$$card(c_{i+1}) = card(c_i) + card(c_{i+1} \setminus c_i) - card(c_i \setminus c_{i+1}) = card(c_i) + d_{i+1} - u$$

LEMMA 2 *Suppose that the automaton reaches the halt state given a genome map $c_1, \ldots, c_n$. Then the following must be true for each $1 \leq i \leq n$:*

$$\alpha(c_i) = card(c_i)$$

Proof: We prove the Lemma by induction on i. When moving from state s_0 to s_1 the automaton sets $d = d_1$ and does not shift out c_1 from the window until d is zero, and at each decrement of d a new item is picked and removed from c_1. Hence d_1 items are picked from c_1. By definition $d_1 = card(c_1)$, hence $\alpha(c_1) = card(c_1)$ and the lemma is true for $i = 1$.

Now assume that the lemma is true for i and prove for $i + 1$. By Lemma 1 we know that $\alpha(c_{i+1}) = \alpha(c_i) + (d_{i+1} - u_i)$ holds. By the induction hypothesis, we know that $\alpha(c_i) = card(c_i)$. Hence $\alpha(c_{i+1}) = card(c_i) + d_{i+1} - u_i$. This last equation and the identity (*) above imply that $\alpha(c_{i+1}) = card(c_{i+1})$. This proves the lemma. ∎

For each adjacent pair of clones c_i, c_{i+1} we call the requirement that the items in $c_i \setminus c_{i+1}$ precede the items in $c_i \cap c_{i+1}$ which are aligned and precede the items in $c_{i+1} \setminus c_i$ the *i*th *step constraint*. We say that a genome map is consistent with a refined genome map if they have the same sequence of clones, and the sequence of restriction fragments in the refined genome map satisfies all the step constraints.

For example, the first branch of the tree in Figure 1 is a genome map that is consistent with the refined genome map shown in Figure 2. However, the second topmost branch in Figure 1 is a genome map that is not consistent with any refined genome map. The main problem is with the subsequence $C5, C2, C1$. We can show that no genome map containing this subsequence can be refined.

A refined genome map containing $C5, C2, C1$ would have to satisfy the step constraint between $C5$ and $C2$ as well as the step constraint between $C2$ and $C1$. The first step constraint implies that item 25 precedes items $5, 10, 15, 20, 35$ in $C5$, items $5, 10, 15, 20, 35$ precede item 40 in $C2$ and the items $5, 10, 15, 20, 35$ are aligned in $C5$ and $C2$. The second step constraint implies that items $20, 40$ precede items $5, 10, 15, 35$ in $C2$, items $5, 10, 15, 35$ precede items $25, 30$ in $C1$ and the items $5, 10, 15, 35$ are aligned in $C2$ and $C1$. Here the first step constraint implies that 5 precedes 40, while the second step constraint implies that 40 precedes 5 in $C2$. Clearly this is impossible. Similar failure can be shown for the lower branches. Next we prove that the NRA correctly distinguishes between the refinable and the unrefinable candidate genome maps.

THEOREM 1 *The non-deterministic automaton NRA reaches the halt state if and only if the input genome map can be refined such that all step constraints are satisfied.*

Proof: (if) Suppose that the input genome map can be refined such that the refinement satisfies all step constraints. We have to show that the automaton can reach the halt state.

Let the refined genome map be $c_1, \ldots, c_n$ where the refinement consist of picking the restriction fragments in the order $r_1, \ldots, r_m$.

We prove that the automaton can reach the halt state by induction on m. For $m = 1$, we can have only one clone because no clone contains another. The initial values when moving from state s_0 to s_1 will be $u = d = 1$, and after one transition from state s_1 to itself both $u = d = 0$. At this point the automaton can move to the halt state.

Now assume that we can always reach the halt state for problem sizes of length m, and prove for $m + 1$. Having an extra restriction fragment means that we have a sequence of restriction fragments $r_0, r_1, \ldots, r_m$ that satisfies all step constraints. Then we have one of the following subcases.

Case (i): There is a new restriction fragment r_0 added to clone c_1. Since $r_0, r_1, \ldots, r_n$ satisfies all step constraints, it must be the case that r_0 in not in clone c_2. In this case we have to increase by one the values of d_1 and u_1. Then the automaton can move from state s_0 to state s_1 and set $d = d_0$ and $u = u_1$. Then it can make a transition from state s_1 to itself while reading restriction fragment r_0 from clone c_0. After that the automaton can run as before. Obviously, this run of the automaton would still satisfy all step constraints.

Case (ii): There is a new clone c_0 added to the beginning of the genome map and r_0 is contained in clone c_0 but not in clone c_1. In this case let d_0 be the cardinality of c_0 and d_1 be the cardinality of $c_1 \setminus c_0$.

In this case, the automaton can move from state s_0 to s_1, and set $d = d_1$ and $u = 1$ by definition. Then the automaton can read restriction fragment r_0 from clone c_0. At that point it can enter state s_2 and start reading $r_1, \ldots, r_{d_0-1}$. It is apparent from the structure of the automaton that while reading these items, the automaton can run as before the extension except for being in one higher numbered state than before. After picking r_{d_0-1} the automaton can make a downward transition and run perfectly the same way as before. This run of the automaton would satisfy all previous step constraints as well as the new step constraint 0.

(only if) Suppose that the automaton reaches the halt state. We have to show that the fragments picked by the automaton form a refinement of the input genome map in which each step constraint i is satisfied.

Let $c_1, \ldots, c_n$ be the input genome map and let c_i be any arbitrary clone in it. Just before picking the first item from c_i, the automaton moves to a higher state and sets $u = u_i$ which is exactly the cardinality of $c_i \setminus c_{i+1}$. The automaton does not move again from a lower to a higher state until $u = 0$, that is after we picked u_i number of elements from c_i that are not in c_{i+1}. Therefore, the first u_i picks of the automaton after setting $u = u_i$ must be exactly the elements of $c_i \setminus c_{i+1}$. Then until the automaton shifts c_i out of the window, it picks items that are in $c_i \cap c_{i+1}$. After shifting c_i out of the window, the automaton sets $d = d_{i+1}$ and does not shift out c_{i+1} until d_{i+1} elements are picked from c_{i+1}. If the automaton picks all elements in $c_i \cap c_{i+1}$, then these last d_{i+1} elements picked must be in $c_{i+1} \setminus c_i$. By Lemma 2 the automaton picks all items from each clone. Hence the ith step constraint must be satisfied by the order of the restriction fragments picked by the automaton. Since we can reason similarly for each c_i, each step constraint must be satisfied. ∎

The NRA is non-deterministic only on the transitions from a state to itself, and when both d and u are 0. Therefore, it is easy to convert the automaton into a deterministic automaton, called DRA, as follows. For each self-transition of state s_i instead of taking away only one item, we take away the set of all items that could be picked. That is, change $j \in (A_1 \cap \ldots \cap A_i) \setminus A_{i+1}$ into $J \neq \emptyset$ and $J \leftarrow (A_1 \cap \ldots \cap A_i) \setminus A_{i+1}$ and change $A_m \leftarrow A_m \setminus \{j\}$ into $A_m \leftarrow A_m \setminus J$ for each $m \leq i$. Further, delete all constraints in which u or d occurs, and add instead on the down transitions the constraint $A_1 = \emptyset$ and on the up transitions the constraints $A_i \subseteq A_{i+1}$ and $A_1 \neq \emptyset$.

COROLLARY 1 *The automaton DRA is deterministic and reaches the halt state if and only if the input genome map can be refined such that all step constraints are satisfied.*

Proof: At first we show that DRA is deterministic. When we are in any state s_i for $i > 0$, then making a down transition requires that $A_1 = \emptyset$. Making an up transition requires that $A_i \subseteq A_{i+1}$ and $A_1 \neq \emptyset$. Making a self-transition requires that $(A_1 \cap \ldots \cap A_i) \setminus A_{i+1}$ is non-empty, which implies that $A_i \not\subseteq A_{i+1}$ and $A_1 \neq \emptyset$. From this follows that no two transitions can be possible at the same time. Also, the transition from s_0 to s_1 is also deterministic. Therefore DRA is a deterministic automaton.

To show the second part of the Corollary, by Theorem 1 it is enough to show that the DRA halts exactly when there is a run of the NRA that halts. Therefore it is enough to show by induction on the number of transitions in the DRA, that if we go from one state a to another state b in the DRA, then we can also go from a to b in the NRA using one or more transitions. Suppose that this hypothesis is true for the kth transition of the DRA. There are the following cases for the $k + 1$st transition.

We move in the DRA from state s_i to state s_{i+1}. Then $A_i \subseteq A_{i+1}$ must be true. When $A_i \subseteq A_{i+1}$, then $u = 0$ must be true in the NRA, because by Lemma 2 all elements of A_i are picked, and the last time u was set to $card(A_i \setminus A_{i+1})$, and every time an element of

A_i is picked the value of u is decreased. Therefore, we can also move in the NRA from state s_i to state s_{i+1}.

We move in the DRA from state s_i to state s_{i-1}. Then $A_1 = \emptyset$ must be true. When $A_1 = \emptyset$, then $d = 0$ must be true in the NRA, because by Lemma 2 all elements of A_1 are picked, and the last time d was set to $card(A_1 \setminus B)$, where B is the clone that moved out of the window last time we moved down, and every time an element of A_1 is picked the value of d is decreased. Therefore, we can also move in the NRA from state s_i to state s_{i-1}.

We move in the DRA from state s_i to itself. Then $(A_1 \cap \ldots \cap A_i) \setminus A_{i+1} = J$ is non-empty. Let $J = \{a_1, \ldots a_n\}$. In this case we can clearly move in the NRA from state s_i to itself n times, by picking $j = a_m$ for the mth self-transition for $1 \leq m \leq n$. This shows that whichever state we reach after $k + 1$st transition in the DRA, we can also reach the same state after a sequence of transitions in the NRA. Moreover, the same window will remain in both the DRA and the RNA. This proves that whenever the DRA reaches the halt state h, there is a run of the RNA which also reaches h. ∎

4.   An Implementation of the Automaton

We chose for implementation the NRA automaton because it could be easily expressed in the DISCO constraint database system. Constraint databases generalize the relational data model by describing extensional database predicates using constraint tuples, with each constraint tuple being a quantifier-free conjunctive formula of atomic constraints in some constraint theory. Constraint query languages (Kanellakis et al., 1995) map input constraint databases to output constraint databases. This is important because in the DISCO solution we are interested in obtaining an output database which will describe the refined genome map. A genome biologist would very likely be interested in the refined genome map, not only whether the input candidate genome map could be refined. Therefore some type of database solution seems natural to this problem.

The advantages of constraint database systems over relational database systems include the flexibility of implicit representation of data, the compact representation of large and possibly infinite relations, the more efficient pruning of the search space, and a higher expressive power of queries. The last advantage means that it is possible to express and solve many problems in constraint database systems that traditional database systems cannot handle. Byon and Revesz (1995) present some example queries that cannot be expressed in relational database systems without constraints.

4.1.   The DISCO Query Language

The syntax of the query language of DISCO, denoted $Datalog^{<z, \subseteq P(z)}$, is that of traditional Datalog (Horn clauses without function symbols) where the bodies of rules can also contain a conjunction of integer or set order constraints. That is, each program is a finite set of rules of the form: $R_0 :\!— R_1, R_2, \ldots, R_l$. The expression R_0 (the rule *head*) must be an atomic formula of the form $p(v_1, \ldots, v_n)$, and the expressions $R_1, \ldots, R_l$ (the rule *body*) must be atomic formulas of one of the following forms:

1. $p(v_1, \ldots, v_n)$ where p is some predicate symbol.

2. $v\theta u$ where v and u are integer variables or constants and θ is a relational operator $=, \neq, <, \leq, >, \geq, <_g$ where g is any natural number. For each g the atomic constraint $v <_g u$ is used as shorthand for the expression $v + g < u$.

3. $V \subseteq U$ or $V = U$ where V and U are set variables or constants.

4. $c \in U$ or $c \notin U$ where c is an integer constant and U is a set variable or constant.

Atomic formulas of the form (2) above are called gap-order constraints and of the form (3-4) are called set order constraints. In this paper we will always use small case letters for integer variables and capital letters for set variables. Set variables always stand for a finite or infinite set of integers.

Let $\mathcal{M}$ be the set of all possible ground tuples over the integers and sets of integers. Let P be a $Datalog^{<z, \subseteq P(z)}$ program and d be a constraint database. Let $\mathcal{D}$ be the set of ground tuples implied by d. The function T_P from and into $\mathcal{M}$ is defined as follows.

$T_P(\mathcal{D}) = \{t \in \mathcal{M} :$ there is a rule $R_0 :\!- R_1, \ldots, R_k$ in P and an instantiation θ such that

$R_0\theta = t$, and $R_i\theta$ holds if R_i is a constraint and $R_i\theta \in \mathcal{D}$ otherwise for each $1 \leq i \leq k$. $\}$

It is shown by Byon and Revesz (1995) that $Datalog^{<z, \subseteq P(z)}$ queries have a fixpoint model which coincides with the least model. It was also shown in (Revesz, 1995) that the data complexity of DISCO queries is DEXPTIME-complete. Therefore DISCO can express a wide variety of combinatorial and logical problems. For example, DISCO can express the basic NP-complete problem of testing the satisfiability of a propositional formula in conjunctive normal form by a fixed query and a variable size database (Byon and Revesz, 1995).

4.2. Expressing the Refinement Automaton in DISCO

We start by expressing the clone data by the input database relation:

$clone(1, \{5, 10, 15, 25, 30, 35\})$.
$clone(2, \{5, 10, 15, 20, 35, 40\})$.
$clone(3, \{5, 20, 25, 30, 45, 50\})$.
$clone(4, \{5, 10, 20, 25, 30, 45\})$.
$clone(5, \{5, 10, 15, 20, 25, 35\})$.
$clone(6, \{8, 15, 20, 25, 40\})$.
$clone(7, \{15, 20, 25, 30, 45, 50\})$.
$clone(8, \{8, 20, 25, 35, 40\})$.
$clone(9, \{15, 40, 45, 50\})$.

We define the $card\_diff(a, b, k)$ relation in the input database to be true if the cardinality of the difference of the elements of clones a and b is k. We define $card(a, k)$ to be true if the cardinality of clone a is k. We also define the relation $next$ that allows us to count from 0 to the largest k in the previous two relations.

$next(0, 1).$

$\vdots$

$next(6, 7).$

The candidate genome map assembly that we would like to refine is represented by the input relation $next\_clone(a, b)$ which is true if after clone a the next clone is clone b, and the relation $first(a)$ which is true if a is the first clone. We also add a dummy clone $C10$ to the end of the list with empty set of fragments and declare $next\_clone(10, 10)$ to be a true fact in the database.

Let L be the set of length values that occur in any of the clones. In the example of Figure 2 the set L is $\{5, 8, 10, 15, 20, 25, 30, 35, 40, 45, 50\}$. Only the values in L need to be tested for membership in sets. Hence for each constant $c \in L$ we add the following constraint tuples to the input database:

$$in(c, X) \quad :\!\!- \quad c \in X.$$
$$not\_in(c, X) :\!\!- \quad c \notin X.$$

We define the relation $cut(i, X, Y)$ which means that $Y \subseteq X \setminus \{i\}$ as follows.

$$cut(i, X, Y) :\!\!- Y \subseteq X, not\_in(i, Y).$$

To express the automaton, we keep the configuration of the automaton in the relation $si(j, a_1, A_1, \ldots, a_k, A_k, d, u)$. This configuration indicates that we are in state i, the current window is the remaining parts $A_1, \ldots, A_k$ of the clones $a_1, \ldots, a_k$, and if $j \neq -1$, then j was the last item picked, otherwise we just made a transition from another state to state i. The transitions from state i to itself for each $1 \le i \le 5$ can be expressed as follows.

$$\begin{aligned} s_i(j, a_1, B_1, \ldots, a_k, A_k, d_1, u_1) :\!\!- \quad & s_i(j_1, a_1, A_1, \ldots, a_k, A_k, d, u), \\ & in(j, A_1), \ldots, in(j, A_i), not\_in(j, A_{i+1}), \\ & cut(j, A_1, B_1), \ldots, cut(j, A_i, B_i), \\ & next(d_1, d), next(u_1, u). \end{aligned}$$

The transitions from lower states to higher states can be expressed as:

$$\begin{aligned} s_{i+1}(-1, a_1, A_1, \ldots, a_k, A_k, d, u) :\!\!- \quad & s_i(j, a_1, A_1, \ldots, a_k, A_k, d, 0), \\ & card\_diff(a_{i+1}, a_{i+2}, u). \end{aligned}$$

The transitions from higher states to lower states can be expressed as:

$$\begin{aligned} s_{i-1}(-1, a_2, A_2, \ldots, a_{k\,|\,1}, A_{k\,|\,1}, d, u) :\!\!- \quad & s_i(j, a_1, A_1, \ldots, a_k, A_k, 0, u), \\ & card\_diff(a_2, a_1, d), \\ & next\_clone(a_k, a_{k+1}), \\ & clone(a_{k+1}, A_{k+1}). \end{aligned}$$

Finally, the initial transition from state 0 to state 1 and the final transition from state 1 to state h can be expressed as:

$$h(a_1, \ldots, a_k) \qquad\qquad :\!\!- \quad s1(j, a_1, \{\}, \ldots, a_k, \{\}, 0, u).$$

$$\begin{aligned} s0(-1, a_1, A_1, \ldots, a_k, A_k, d, u) :\!\!- \quad & first(a_1), \\ & next\_clone(a_1, a_2), \ldots, next\_clone(a_{k-1}, a_k), \\ & clone(a_1, A_1), \ldots, clone(a_k, A_k), \\ & card(a_1, d), card\_diff(a_1, a_2, u). \end{aligned}$$

4.3. Testing on a Sample Data

We tested the algorithm on the sample data shown in Table 1. Below Table 3 shows one sequence of partial tuples (only seven out of sixteen arguments are shown) found by the DISCO system. In the actual implementation, we added an extra sixteenth temporal argument t which was initialized to 0 and was increased by 1 for each transition from state i to itself. This helped us to keep track of the order of the tuples and to check the correctness of the program. In the future, we will add a trace routine by which DISCO will be able to print out the proof trees.

Table 3. The execution steps of the automaton on the first genome map (i.e., C8,C6,C2,C5,C1,C4,C3,C7,C9) of the sample input database.

S	j	A1	A2	A3	A4	A5	A6
1		8,20,25,35,40	8,15,20,25,40	5,10,15,20,35,40	C5	C1	C4
1	35	8,20,25,40	8,15,20,25,40	5,10,15,20,35,40	C5	C1	C4
2		8,20,25,40	8,15,20,25,40	5,10,15,20,35,40	C5	C1	C4
2	8	20,25,40	15,20,25,40	5,10,15,20,35,40	C5	C1	C4
2	25	20,40	15,20,40	5,10,15,20,35,40	C5	C1	C4
3		20,40	15,20,40	5,10,15,20,35,40	C5	C1	C4
3	40	20	15,20	5,10,15,20,35	C5	C1	C4
4		20	15,20	5,10,15,20,35	C5	C1	C4
4	20		15	5,10,15,35	5,10,15,25,35	C1	C4
3		15	5,10,15,35	5,10,15,25,35	C1	C4	C3
4		15	5,10,15,35	5,10,15,25,35	C1	C4	C3
4	15		5,10,35	5,10,25,35	5,10,25,30,35	C4	C3
3		5,10,35	5,10,25,35	5,10,25,30,35	C4	C3	C7
3	35	5,10	5,10,25	5,10,25,30	C4	C3	C7
4		5,10	5,10,25	5,10,25,30	C4	C3	C7
4	10	5	5,25	5,25,30	5,20,25,30,45	C3	C7
5		5	5,25	5,25,30	5,20,25,30,45	C3	C7
5	5		25	25,30	20,25,30,45	20,25,30,45,50	C7
4		25	25,30	20,25,30,45	20,25,30,45,50	C7	C9
5		25	25,30	20,25,30,45	20,25,30,45,50	C7	C9
5	25		30	20,30,45	20,30,45,50	15,20,30,45,50	C9
4		30	20,30,45	20,30,45,50	15,20,30,45,50	15,40,45,50	
4	30		20,45	20,45,50	15,20,45,50	15,40,45,50	
3		20,45	20,45,50	15,20,45,50	15,40,45,50		
3	20	45	45,50	15,45,50	15,40,45,50		
4		45	45,50	15,45,50	15,40,45,50		
4	45		50	15,50	15,40,50		
3		50	15,50	15,40,50			
3	50		15	15,40			
2		15	15,40				
2	15		40				
1		40					
1	40						
h							

In the last three columns of the above table $C1, C3, C4, C7$ and $C9$ stand for the set of items in clones $1, 3, 4, 7$ and 9 respectively. The table does not show the value of j

when it is -1, because that indicates only the initialization and transitions between states. From the table one can read out the sequence from top to bottom in the second column: $35, 8, 25, 40, 20, 15, 35, 10, 5, 25, 30, 20, 45, 50, 15, 40$. In the example, the order of the restriction fragments with lengthes 8 and 25 in clone 8 could be reversed, leading to another solution, which is also computed by DISCO. On this problem DISCO was run on a SUN sparc 2 workstation in 579 CPU seconds.

We also implemented recently the automaton in C++. It gave us a faster solution. We could run an example with a hundred clones within 1.75 cpu seconds. However, debugging the C++ code took a much longer time than debugging the DISCO code. The main advantage of the DISCO implementation was a fast prototyping. The second advantage is the easier understandability and modifiability of the code.

5. Related Work

There are many variations of the genome map assembly problem besides the one we considered in the paper. One other version called the probed partial digestion problem is considered in (Tsur et al., 1994). Here the task is to align a number of DNA fragments each of which overlaps the same small piece of the DNA string. This is different from our problem, where some pairs of clones (for example in Figure 2 clones C8 and C9) do not overlap. The probed partial digestion problem is solved using the deductive database system LDL (Tsur and Zaniolo, 1986).

In a second version of the genome mapping problem, the clones do not all overlap and the information of overlap derives from probe data and not from restriction fragment length similarities as in our problem. This problem was considered for example in (Harley et al., 1996). Here a rough map is constructed first and refined by considering certain graph properties that must hold to make a map linear.

A third version of the mapping problem considered in (Dix and Yee, 1994; Yap, 1993) relies on multiple restriction enzyme data. In this version, we are given for three copies A, B, and C of the same DNA string the following information: For A the set of fragment lengths that are obtained after enzyme one is applied, for B the lengths after enzyme two is applied, and for C the lengths when the two enzymes are applied together. The problem is to order the restriction fragments in the three copies in parallel such that every time there is a cut in copy A or in copy B, there is also a cut in copy C. This problem is solved in (Yap, 1993) using the constraint logic programming system CLP(R) described in (Jaffar et al., 1992).

The DISCO constraint database system is related to several other systems that allow some type of set constraints (Dovier and Rossi, 1993; Gervet, 1994; Legeard and Legros, 1991; Ramakrishnan et al. 1992; Srivastava et al. 1994). The automaton described in Section 3 can be implemented in these systems as well. However, the running times and scaling for larger size problems could be very different in these systems because they use different methods for solving set constraints.

6. Conclusions and Open Problems

As is apparent, there are several variations on the genome map assembly problem. These variations suggest that modifications may be necessary in tayloring any algorithm to particular applications. For example, we also plan to modify our (DISCO) solution by adding probe data information and use them together with restriction fragment lengths information.

In the solution to the genome map refinement problem, the constraint automaton was a useful tool. It should be explored whether a similar automaton can be used to solve other problems that may or may not be related to the the the topic of genomes.

Acknowledgments

The author would like to thank Roy French, from the Department of Plant Pathology, University of Nebraska, for helpful comments on a previous draft of this paper. This work was supported by NSF grants IRI-9625055 and IRI-9632871.

Notes

1. For example, one restriction enzyme may cut the DNA at each occurrence of the substring GTTAAC (from left to right or right to left, it does not matter for the enzyme) into GTT and AAC.
2. The only exception is that we may identify the two ending fragments of each clone and take out these from each clone (Olson et al., 1986). Hence only fragments that are cut at both ends by the restriction enzyme are considered.
3. The threshold value is also influenced by the accuracy of the measurements. For example, some of the 5s in the table in the introduction may reflect measurements of 495, or 502. The restriction fragments measured as 495 and 502 may or may not be actually equivalent. In general, the more accurate the measurements, the smaller threshold values we need (Lander and Waterman, 1988).
4. It is possible to detect repetitions of same lengths. If a repetition is detected within any clone, then we try another restriction enzyme.
5. Any set of clones satisfying conditions (1) and (4) can be arranged into a staircase. Just sort the clones according to the position of their left endpoints on the DNA string. The sorted order forms a staircase because condition (1) implies that if the left end of clone A precedes the left end of clone B, then the right end of clone A also precedes the right end of clone B and condition (4) ensures that the adjacent clones overlap.

References

1. J. Byon & P.Z. Revesz. (1995). DISCO: A constraint database system with sets. In *Proc. Workshop on Constraint Databases and Applications*, pages 68–83, Springer-Verlag,Berlin/Heidelberg/New York.
2. T.I. Dix& C.N. Yee. (1994). A restriction mapping engine using constraint logic programming, In *Proceedings of 2nd International Conference on Intelligent Systems for Molecular Biology*, pages 112-120, AAAI Press.
3. A. Dovier& G. Rossi. (1993). Embedding extensional finite sets in CLP. In *International Logic Programming Symposium*, MIT Press, Cambridge,MA.
4. C. Gervet. (1994). Conjunto: Constraint logic programming with finite set domains. In *Proc. International Logic Programming Symposium*, pages 339–358, MIT Press, Cambridge, MA.
5. W. Gillett. (1992). DNA mapping algorithms: Strategies for single restriction enzyme and multiple restriction enzyme mapping. Washington Univ. Tech. Report WUCS-92-29.

6. E. Harley, A. Bonner & N. Goodman. (1996). Good maps are straight. *Proc. 4th Int. Conf. on Intelligent Systems for Molecular Biology*, p. 88-97.

7. J. Jaffar, S. Michaylov, P. J. Stuckey & R.H.C. Yap. (1992). The CLP(*R*) language and system. In *ACM Transactions on Programming Languages and Systems*, Vol. 14, pages 339-395, ACM Press, New York.

8. P.C. Kanellakis, G.M. Kuper & P.Z. Revesz. (1995). Constraint query languages. *Journal of Computer and System Sciences* 51:26–52.

9. R.M. Karp. (1993). Mapping the genome: some combinatorial problems arising in molecular biology. In *Proc. 25th ACM Symp. on Theory of Computing*, pages 278-285, ACM Press, New York.

10. E.S. Lander & M.S. Waterman. (1988). Genomic mapping by fringerprinting random clones: A mathematical analysis. *Genomics* 2:231-239.

11. B. Legeard & E. Legros. (1991). Short overview of the CLPS System. In *Proc. PLILP*.

12. M.V. Olson et al. (1986). Random-clone strategy for genomic restriction mapping in yeast. *Genomics* 83:7826–7830.

13. R. Ramakrishnan, D. Srivastava & S. Sudarshan. (1992). CORAL: Control, relations and logic. In *Proc. VLDB*.

14. P.Z. Revesz. (1993). A closed-form evaluation for datalog queries with integer (gap)-order constraints. *Theoretical Computer Science* 116:117-149.

15. P.Z. Revesz. (1995). Datalog queries of set constraint databases, In *Fifth International Conference on Database Theory*, pages 425–438, Springer-Verlag, Berlin/Heidelberg/New York.

16. P.Z. Revesz. (1996). Genomic database applications in DISCO, In *Proc. CP'96 Workshop on Constraints and Databases*, pages 234–245, Springer-Verlag, Berlin/Heidelberg/New York.

17. D. Srivastava, R. Ramakrishnan & P.Z. Revesz. (1994). Constraint objects. In *Proc. 2nd Workshop on Principles and Practice of Constraint Programming*, pages 274–284, Springer-Verlag, Berlin/Heidelberg/New York.

18. S. Tsur & C. Zaniolo,. (1986). LDL: A logic-based data-language. In *Proc. VLDB*, pages 33-41.

19. S. Tsur, F. Olken & D. Naor. (1994). Deductive databases for genome mapping. Technical Report LBL-29577, Lawrence Berkeley Laboratiry, Berkeley, CA.

20. R.H.C. Yap. (1993). A constraint logic programming framework for constructing DNA restriction maps, *Artificial Intelligence in Medicine* 5:447–464.

Constraints: An International Journal, 2, 377–399 (1997)

Maintaining Global Integrity Constraints in Distributed Databases

NAM HUYN   huyn@cs.stanford.edu

Department of Computer Science, Stanford University, Stanford, California, 94305, USA

Abstract. Given some integrity constraints over a distributed database, we consider the problem of incrementally checking global consistency in response to updates made to the base relations but without accessing all these base relations. In many application areas such as collaborative design, mobile computing and enterprise information systems, total data availability cannot be assumed. Even if all the base data is available, some of it may incur such a high cost that its use should only be considered as a last resort. Without looking at all the relations that participate in the constraint, how can one meaningfully check a constraint for violation? When the constraint is known to be satisfied prior to the update, the state of the relations that are available (aka local) can in principle be used to infer something about the relations that are not available (aka remote). This observation is the basis for the existence of tests that guarantee that global consistency is preserved under a given update, without looking at all the base data. In order to make consistency maintenance *practical*, the challenge is to find those tests that are *most general* (we call *Complete Local Tests*) and that are *efficient* to generate and execute. This paper addresses the problem of finding efficient complete local tests for an important class of constraints that are very common in practice: constraints expressible as conjunctive queries with negated subgoals. For constraints where the predicates for the remote relations do not occur more than once, we present complete local tests under insertions and deletions to the local relations. These tests can be expressed as safe, nonrecursive Datalog¬ queries against the local relations. These results also apply to other constraints with negation that are not conjunctive.

Keywords: Integrity constraints, consistency maintenance, distributed databases

1. Introduction

In applications such as collaborative design, mobile computing, and enterprise information systems, information is often distributed but subject to global integrity constraints that must be maintained. When updates are made to some data, we must check if all the data under constraint remains consistent. Incremental consistency checking usually involves accessing all the data whose consistency might be affected. Yet, accessing all this data may not always be desirable or even possible: for instance, it may be more efficient to check for potential constraint violations using only local data if possible, before extending the check to remote data; information access may be restricted for security reasons; remote data sources may be disconnected temporarily due to mobility requirements.

Thus, incrementally checking integrity constraints using only a subset of the participating relations is an important problem to consider. But without looking at all the base relations, how can we guarantee a given update does not violate the constraints? While we may not be able to provide this guarantee in all situations, there are many situations where it is possible to infer that the update is consistent. The following example illustrates this point.

EXAMPLE: Consider a university information system, distributed in four different sites as shown in Figure 1. While the databases are independently managed at their own site, they are subject to a global integrity constraint that students may not enroll in a course unless

139

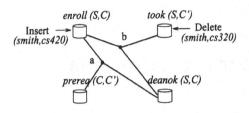

Figure 1. University information system.

they have either taken all the prerequisites for the course or obtained a special approval from the dean to enroll. This enrollment policy can be stated by the following integrity constraint:

$$(\forall\, S, C, C')\ enroll(S, C) \wedge prereq(C, C') \Rightarrow took(S, C') \vee deanok(S, C) \qquad (1)$$

The databases may be disconnected due to network failure during which updates are allowed as long as the system remains globally consistent. Consider the insertion of a new tuple *enroll*(*smith*, *cs*420). Let us see how we can guarantee that the insertion does not violate the global constraint in each of the following three scenarios.

1. Node *a* fails and relation *prereq* becomes inaccessible. It is consistent to enroll *smith* in *cs*420 if he already has approval from the dean. Alternatively, consider the students who were enrolled in *cs*420 without using dean's approval (assuming there is one). Anyone of these students must have satisfied all the prerequisites for *cs*420. All these prerequisites must be among $\mathcal{P}$, the courses that all these students have taken. $\mathcal{P}$ is shown in Figure 2 with hashed lines. If *smith* has taken all courses in $\mathcal{P}$, he must have satisfied all the prerequisites for *cs*420.

2. Node *b* fails and relation *took* becomes inaccessible. Again, approval from the dean is one way to enroll *smith* consistently. Alternatively, we want to make sure *smith* has taken all the prerequisite courses for *cs*420. Obviously, we cannot check this condition directly since relation *took* is not available. Fortunately, there is an indirect method that considers the prerequisites for all courses *smith* was enrolled in without using the dean's approval. If these prerequisites include all of *cs*420's prerequisites, we can conclude that *smith* has indeed taken all *cs*420's prerequisites. Figure 2 illustrates this test.

3. Both nodes fail and none of the relations *prereq*, *took*, and *deanok* is accessible. There is no way to ensure *smith*'s enrollment is legitimate.

□

While these tests obviously guarantee that data integrity is preserved under a given update, we also wish them to be as general as possible. Indeed, a degenerate test procedure that always results in predicting potential violation is certainly sound but too conservative to be of practical use. The challenge is to find the *most general* of these tests when they exist.

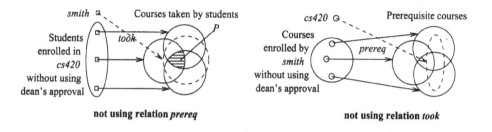

Figure 2. Preserving global consistency under different scenarios.

Such most general tests, called *Complete Local Tests* (or CLT's in short), can be defined as follows:

- A CLT only looks at the instance of the local [1] base relations and the update instance.

- When the test is satisfied, global consistency is guaranteed to be preserved, regardless of the instance of remote relations. When it is not satisfied, there is some instance of the remote relations such that global consistency is not preserved.

Constraints of the form $(\forall \bar{U})(g_1 \wedge \ldots \wedge g_m \Rightarrow h_1 \vee \ldots \vee h_n)$, such as (1), are very common in practice. These constraints are used to specify that for a combination of data $(\bigwedge_i g_i)$ to be legitimate, it must have a "cover" among the h_j's (i.e., a tuple in the relation for some h_j that legitimizes the combination). These constraints have an equivalent query form in which the database is queried for violations, i.e., combinations of data that have no cover. The database is consistent if the constraint query returns no answers. In query form, the constraints of interest are represented as Datalog queries of the form

$$inconsistent :- g_1, \ldots, g_m, \neg h_1, \ldots, \neg h_n.$$

where *inconsistent* is a special 0-ary predicate. For this reason, we call them *Conjunctive-Query Constraints with Negation*, or CQC$^{\neg}$'s in short. Besides the query form for CQC$^{\neg}$'s, the logic form will also be used to explain our reasoning.

This paper mainly considers the problem of finding not only most general tests for constraints whose query involves negation in general and for CQC$^{\neg}$'s in particular, but also tests that can be *efficiently* implemented such as first order queries. The CQC$^{\neg}$ class is shown in Figure 3 as the shaded oval. Because of the presence of negation in the query, many questions that have practical significance are not immediately obvious. Do CQC$^{\neg}$'s admit test procedures that are complete and that can be efficiently generated? Do CQC$^{\neg}$'s admit CLT's that can be efficiently executed, i.e., in time polynomial in the size of the local relations? Can these CLT's be expressed as first order queries so they can be executed using conventional query-evaluation engines? In this paper, we establish the following results:

- For CQC$^{\neg}$'s with single occurrences of the remote predicates (constraints shown in Figure 3 as the area bordered by a dashed arc labeled "Our work"), there are complete local tests that check for consistency of insertions and deletions to the local relations and that are expressible in safe, nonrecursive Datalog with negation.

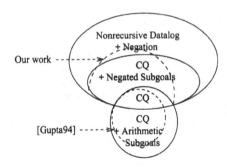

Figure 3. Constraint classes for the CLT problem

- All solution CLT's can be generated at compile time. The time to generate them and their size are linear in the size of the constraints in the best case, and exponential in the worst case. We give the solutions in a form that makes their expression in (safe) nonrecursive Datalog⁻ (and other traditional query languages such as SQL) straightforward.

- These results also apply to other constraints with negation that are not conjunctive.

1.1. Related Work

The notions of local tests and their completeness were first introduced in [4], [1], and [3], and were embodied in an actual system supporting collaborative design in building construction [9]. The most powerful result for CLT's that can be found in [1] applies to a subset of conjunctive-query constraints with arithmetic comparisons but with no negation, and handles only insertion updates to the local relations (shown as a dashed circle in Figure 3). Negation was considered in [1] but only for local tests that are not complete. The approach used in [1] for finding complete tests is based on containment of conjunctive queries with arithmetic comparisons, and only in some restricted cases, a closed form solution for the CLT's (as queries) can be obtained by expanding and simplifying the containment tests. In [8] a larger class of Datalog programs with negation was considered, but for a different though closely related problem: the problem of detecting queries independent of updates not looking at any base relations. The problem of consistency maintenance considered in this paper is also closely related to the problem of view self-maintenance (see [10], [2], and [6]) as follows: checking CQC⁻ constraints reduces to checking if a given view instance is independent of a given update, but the latter problem is still open for CQ views with negation and with an arbitrary number of remote predicates. In fact, a subclass of this problem, namely that of checking if a given view instance gains new tuples under a given update to some local relation, reduces to our problem and can be solved using the results presented in this paper. Finally, this paper extends earlier results we presented in [7] to checking consistency of arbitrary sets of local deletions.

1.2. Paper Outline

The rest of this paper is organized as follows. In the next section, we provide some basic concepts on maintaining CQC¬ constraints, state assumptions and present our notation and terminology conventions. In Section 3, we illustrate our approach to the problem of finding complete local tests by showing the concepts and the reasoning used in deriving complete local tests for our running example. We then present the complete local tests for the general case in Section 4 and describe their complexity in Section 5. In Section 6, we summarize our results and discuss future work.

2. Preliminaries

2.1. Datalog¬

In this paper, integrity constraints (and their complete tests if any) are modeled as queries expressed by nonrecursive Datalog¬ programs. A Datalog¬ program is a collection of Horn rules that may have negated subgoals in their bodies. These rules are assumed to be *safe* (see [11]): variables that appear in a rule's head or in a negated subgoal must also appear in a non-negated subgoal. The predicates used in a Datalog¬ program are partitioned into EDB predicates and IDB predicates. EDB predicates are those that only occur in rule bodies and represent base relations that are under constraint. Among the IDB predicates, there is a distinguished predicate called the *query predicate* that generates answers for the query. The following variable naming convention will be used in all Datalog¬ programs as well as in logic sentences: variable names always start in upper case, constant names in lower case.

2.2. Integrity Constraints

We mainly focus on constraints expressed by conjunctive queries with negation (CQC¬), that is, Datalog¬ programs consisting of a single rule of the form

$$inconsistent :- g_1, \ldots, g_m, \neg h_1, \ldots, \neg h_n,$$

where the g_i's and h_i's denote atoms with EDB predicates. In order to ensure safe use of negation, variables used in the h_i's must occur among the g_i's. The body in the rule above is called the *constraint query*. When the constraint query has an answer, the constraint is violated.

Since the EDB relations can be either local or remote, we introduce a notation that makes the local vs. remote distinction explicit. This notation also makes it explicit which variables are used in the subgoals. Thus, for the remainder of this paper, CQC¬'s are represented as

$$inconsistent :- P(\bar{X}, \bar{Y}), \bigwedge_{i \in L} \neg Q_i(\bar{X}_i, \bar{Y}_i, \bar{Z}_i), \bigwedge_{j \in M} \neg Q_j(\bar{X}_j, \bar{Y}_j, \bar{Z}_j), R(\bar{Y}, \bar{Z}). \quad (2)$$

- $P(\bar{X}, \bar{Y})$ denotes a conjunction of zero or more positive local subgoals (i.e., subgoals with local predicates), and $R(\bar{Y}, \bar{Z})$ a conjunction of zero or more positive remote subgoals. $\bar{X}$ denotes the (ordered) set of variables that are used in positive local subgoals but not in positive remote subgoals, $\bar{Y}$ denotes the set of variables used in some positive local subgoal and some positive remote subgoal, and $\bar{Z}$ denotes the set of variables that are used in positive remote subgoals but not in positive local subgoals. Thus $\bar{X}$, $\bar{Y}$, and $\bar{Z}$ are mutually disjoint. Note the use of **boldface** in the constraint query (2) to emphasize the fact that the predicates in R's subgoals are remote.

- The negated subgoals are partitioned into two subsets indexed by L and M: L indexes the negated local subgoals, that is, for $i \in L$, $Q_i(\bar{X}_i, \bar{Y}_i, \bar{Z}_i)$ denotes a subgoal with some local predicate; M indexes the negated remote subgoals, that is, for $j \in M$, $\mathbf{Q}_j(\bar{X}_j, \bar{Y}_j, \bar{Z}_j)$ denotes a subgoal with some remote predicate. Obviously, we assume that L and M are disjoint. Also note the use of **boldface** in (2) for the remote Q's.

- $\bar{X}_i \subseteq \bar{X}$, $\bar{Y}_i \subseteq \bar{Y}$, $\bar{Z}_i \subseteq \bar{Z}$ are assumed for all $i \in L$ and $i \in M$ to ensure safe use of negation. We use $\bar{x}$ (resp. $\bar{y}$, $\bar{z}$) to denote a vector of constants of the same arity as $\bar{X}$ (resp. $\bar{Y}$, $\bar{Z}$). When $\bar{X}_i \subseteq \bar{X}$, $\bar{x}_i$ denotes the projection of $\bar{x}$ onto the variables in $\bar{X}_i$. When $\bar{x}$ and $\bar{x}'$ are two vectors of constants of the same arity as $\bar{X}$, we will use $\bar{x} =_M \bar{x}'$ as a shorthand for $\bigwedge_{j \in M} \bar{x}_j = \bar{x}'_j$, representing the fact that the two vectors agree over the variables in each $\bar{X}_j$, $j \in M$.

- We use the following terminology for the subqueries in the constraint: we call P and the Q_i's for $i \in L$ the *local queries*, R and the Q_j's for $j \in M$ the *remote queries*.

2.3.   Complete Local Tests

We now give a more precise definition of complete local tests (abbreviated CLT's). Given

- A constraint represented by a query Q that tests the local and remote databases D_{local} and D_{remote}) for violations, as in (2), and

- An update U on D_{local},

a CLT is a condition that characterizes the following

$$(\forall D_{remote}) \ Q(D_{local}, D_{remote}) = \emptyset \Rightarrow Q(U(D_{local}), D_{remote}) = \emptyset. \qquad (3)$$

That is, when the constraint is not violated prior to the update, it is not violated after the update. This condition guarantees that the update preserves global consistency regardless of the instance of the remote database. Note that a CLT is a function of only the constraint definition, the given instance of D_{local}, and the given update instance U. As a consequence, if the CLT evaluates to *true*, we are guaranteed that the system remains consistent after the update if it is consistent before. If the CLT evaluates to *false*, such a guarantee cannot be provided, because D_{remote} may be in a state such that the system is globally consistent prior to the update but becomes inconsistent after the update. CLT represents the best we can do with only the given information.

   Throughout the rest of this paper, given a constraint and an instance of the local relations, an update is said to be *consistent* if it preserves global consistency independently of the instance of the remote relations.

2.4. *Alternative to a containment-based approach*

Query containment (see [11]) is an implication problem that is commonly encountered in database work. Given two queries $\mathcal{P}$ and $\mathcal{Q}$ over some database D, we say that $\mathcal{P}$ is *contained* in $\mathcal{Q}$, written as $\mathcal{P} \subseteq \mathcal{Q}$, if the answer to $\mathcal{P}$ is a subset of the answer to $\mathcal{Q}$, for every instance of D.

Consistency checking, as defined by (3), can be reduced to the problem of testing query containment. For example, maintaining the constraint

$$inconsistent :- l(X), \neg g(X, Z), \neg h(X, Z), r(Z)$$

under insertion of $l(a)$ reduces to testing containment of the following boolean queries:

$\mathcal{P} :$ $inconsistent :- \neg g(a, Z), \neg h(a, Z), r(Z)$

$\mathcal{Q} :$ $inconsistent :- l(X), \neg g(a, Z), \neg h(a, Z), r(Z)$

Since the extensions L and G of local predicates l and g are known, we can eliminate these predicates from the queries. We can expand query $\mathcal{P}$ to:

$$inconsistent :- \neg h(a, Z), r(Z), \bigwedge_{(x,z)\in G} (a \neq x \vee Z \neq z)$$

and expand $\mathcal{Q}$ to the union, over tuples $t \in L$, of the following queries

$$inconsistent :- \neg h(t, Z), r(Z), \bigwedge_{(x,z)\in G} (t \neq x \vee Z \neq z)$$

Thus, maintaining CQC$^\neg$ constraints reduces to testing containment of unions of conjunctive queries with negation and $\neq$ comparisons. Levy [8] gave an algorithm for testing such containments, which unfortunately has a complexity exponential in the size of the given relations in our problem (the queries have an exponential number of rules, and the rules have a number of subgoals the size of the given relations). Whether such containment problem has a polynomial-time solution remains open. It is even less clear whether the containment problem can always be expressed as a first order query on the local predicates.

While a containment-based approach cannot be easily applied to efficiently maintain CQC$^\neg$'s, the "university" example used earlier seems to suggest that an alternative but more direct approach can be used instead to find CLT's. The approach we offer in this paper essentially amounts to compile-time generation of runtime query tests.

3. Extended example

In this section, we will go through the process of finding a complete local test for our running example. We will present the formal results for the general case in the next section. Recall from Section 1 the problem of finding complete tests for constraint (1) repeated here for convenience

$$(\forall\, S, C, C')\ enroll(S, C) \wedge prereq(C, C') \Rightarrow took(S, C') \vee deanok(S, C) \qquad (4)$$

when relation *prereq* is remote. We first consider a simple insertion and later a simple deletion.

3.1. Characterizing when a simple insertion is consistent

Suppose we want to insert *enroll*(*smith*, *cs*420). To enroll *smith* in *cs*420 without violating the constraint, we must ensure that he has either obtained approval from the dean or taken all the prerequisites. In other words, a *cover* for any pair of tuples *enroll*(*smith*, *cs*420) and *prereq*(*cs*420, C') must be found. This condition is formalized as follows (by substituting *smith* for S and *cs*420 for C in (4)):

$$[(\forall C')\, prereq(cs420, C') \Rightarrow took(smith, C')] \vee deanok(smith, cs420) \qquad (5)$$

The problem is that relation *prereq* is not available and we cannot directly look up the prerequisites for *cs*420. In order to eliminate the "unknown" *prereq*(*cs*420, C') from (5), we must be able to "bound" *cs*420's prerequisites or else, our "adversary" will be able to prevent *smith* from legally enrolling in *cs*420 by inventing prerequisites *smith* never took. We have just used a simple *adversary argument* to deal with the unknown, in which an imaginary adversary is trying to cause constraint violations by controlling the unknown.

To find the bound, a key observation is that the adversary *is not totally free* to choose a state for *prereq* and must still respect the constraint that all past enrollments in *cs*420 were legal (by substituting *cs*420 for C in (4)):

$$(\forall S)\, [\, enroll(S, cs420) \wedge \neg deanok(S, cs420) \Rightarrow$$
$$(\forall C')\, [prereq(cs420, C') \Rightarrow took(S, C')]] \qquad (6)$$

By exchanging the premises of the two implications in (6), we obtain a bound for the unknown *prereq*(*cs*420, C'). We call this bound *possible-cs420-prereq*(C'), which represents all classes commonly taken by students without using dean's approval and can be formalized as:

$$possible\text{-}cs420\text{-}prereq(C') \stackrel{\text{def}}{\equiv}$$
$$(\forall S)\, [enroll(S, cs420) \wedge \neg deanok(S, cs420) \Rightarrow took(S, C')] \qquad (7)$$

This bound is tight and a complete test under the insertion is obtained by replacing the unknown *prereq*(*cs*420, C') in (5) with the bound *possible-cs420-prereq*(C'):

$$(\forall C')\, [possible\text{-}cs420\text{-}prereq(C') \Rightarrow took(smith, C')] \vee deanok(smith, cs420)$$
$$(8)$$

3.2. Ensuring test is finitely evaluable

Condition (8) would be easy to implement as a Datalog⁻ program (or in any traditional query language) if we know how to *finitely* evaluate *possible-cs420-prereq*(C'). The problem is that the current definition of *possible-cs420-prereq*(C') in (7) is not safe. If every student uses the dean's approval to enroll in *cs*420, then it is consistent that anything could be a prerequisite for *cs*420 and relation *possible-cs420-prereq* would be infinite. Thus, in order for the implication in (8) to hold, it is necessary that the following *boundability condition* also hold:

$$(\exists S)\,[enroll(S, cs420) \wedge \neg deanok(S, cs420)] \tag{9}$$

Under this boundability condition, we can use the following finite bound, instead of *possible-cs420-prereq(C')*, without changing the logical meaning of (8):

$$finite\text{-}cs420\text{-}prereq(C') \stackrel{\text{def}}{\equiv}$$
$$(\exists S)\,[enroll(S, cs420) \wedge \neg deanok(S, cs420) \wedge took(S, C')] \wedge$$
$$(\forall S)\,[enroll(S, cs420) \wedge \neg deanok(S, cs420) \Rightarrow took(S, C')]$$

In summary, a complete test that is both safe and logically equivalent to (8) is given by:

$$[(9) \wedge (\forall C')\,finite\text{-}cs420\text{-}prereq(C') \Rightarrow took(smith, C')] \vee deanok(smith, cs420)$$

This test can be expressed by the following nonrecursive Datalog¬ program using `consistent-insert` as the query predicate:

```
enroll-cs420-no-dean(S) :- enroll(S,cs420),¬deanok(S,cs420).
            union(C') :- enroll-cs420-no-dean(S),took(S,C').
  not-a-cs420-prereq(C') :- union(C'), enroll-cs420-no-dean(S),
                            ¬took(S,C').
  finite-cs420-prereq(C') :- union(C'), ¬not-a-cs420-prereq(C').
             notcovered :- finite-cs420-prereq(C'), ¬took(smith,C').
      consistent-insert :- enroll-cs420-no-dean(S), ¬notcovered.
      consistent-insert :- deanok(smith,cs420).
```

3.3. Deriving complete test for a simple deletion

Now suppose we want to delete *took(smith, cs320)*. For a deletion to be consistent, we want to avoid situations where the tuple to be deleted is the sole way to legitimize the existence of certain tuples in other relations. If *smith* was enrolled in a course that has *cs320* as prerequisite, we must ensure that he was able to do so only with the dean's approval. In other words, any pair of tuples *enroll(smith, C)* and *prereq(C, cs320)*, which uses *took(smith, cs320)* as a cover, must have an *alternative cover* to be found in *deanok*, the only choice of local relations left. This condition is formalized as follows (by substituting *smith* for S and *cs320* for C', and removing *took(smith, cs320)* from (4)):

$$(\forall C)\,[enroll(smith, C) \wedge prereq(C, cs320) \Rightarrow deanok(smith, C)] \tag{10}$$

Since *prereq(C, cs320)* is unknown, the same idea of bounding courses having *cs320* as prerequisite applies here as well, using the fact that prior to the deletion, there was no enrollment violations involving courses having *cs320* as prerequisite:

$$(\forall C)\,[prereq(C, cs320) \Rightarrow (\forall S)\,[enroll(S, C) \Rightarrow took(S, cs320) \vee deanok(S, C)]]$$

The bound, we call *possible-cs320-prereqfor(C)*, is found on the right hand side of the first implication in the last formula:

$$possible\text{-}cs320\text{-}prereqfor(C) \stackrel{\text{def}}{\equiv}$$
$$(\forall S)\,[enroll(S, C) \Rightarrow took(S, cs320) \vee deanok(S, C)] \tag{11}$$

By eliminating unknown $prereq(C, cs320)$ from (10) using its bound (11), we obtain the following complete test for the consistent deletion of $took(smith, cs320)$:

$$(\forall C)\,[enroll(smith, C) \wedge possible\text{-}cs320\text{-}prereqfor(C) \Rightarrow deanok(smith, C)]$$

This test can be directly implemented as the following nonrecursive Datalog⁻ program with `consistent-delete` as the query predicate:

```
            enroll-no-dean(S,C) :- enroll(S,C), ¬deanok(S,C).
                     forbid(C) :- enroll-no-dean(S,C),
                                  ¬took(S,cs320).
     possible-cs320-prereqfor(C) :- enroll-no-dean(S,C),
                     ¬forbid(C).
potentially-inconsistent-delete :- enroll-no-dean(smith,C),
                                   possible-cs320-prereqfor(C).
             consistent-delete :- ¬potentially-inconsistent- delete.
```

4.   Deriving Complete Local Tests

In this section, we consider constraints of the following general form:

$$inconsistent :- P(\bar{X}, \bar{Y}), \bigwedge_{i \in L} \neg Q_i(\bar{X}_i, \bar{Y}_i, \bar{Z}_i), \bigwedge_{j \in M} \neg \boldsymbol{Q_j}(\bar{X}_j, \bar{Y}_j, \bar{Z}_j), \boldsymbol{R}(\bar{Y}, \bar{Z})$$

where L and M are two disjoint sets of indices, $\bar{X}$ and $\bar{Y}$ and $\bar{Z}$ denote disjoint sets of variables, and for each i in L or M, we require that $\bar{X}_i \subseteq \bar{X}$, $\bar{Y}_i \subseteq \bar{Y}$, and $\bar{Z}_i \subseteq \bar{Z}$ in order to ensure safe use of negation. We characterize the different subqueries in the constraint as follows:

- $P(\bar{X}, \bar{Y})$ denotes a *local* query in $\bar{X}$ and $\bar{Y}$. A query is said to be local if it only uses local predicates for its input EDB predicates.

- For each $i \in L$, $Q_i(\bar{X}_i, \bar{Y}_i, \bar{Z}_i)$ denotes a local query in $\bar{X}_i$, $\bar{Y}_i$, and $\bar{Z}_i$.

- $R(\bar{Y}, \bar{Z})$ denotes a *remote* query in $\bar{Y}$ and $\bar{Z}$. A query is said to be remote if it only uses remote predicates for its input EDB predicates. Note the use of **boldface** to indicate that the query is remote.

- For each $j \in M$, $Q_j(\bar{X}_j, \bar{Y}_j, \bar{Z}_j)$ denotes a remote query in $\bar{X}_j$, $\bar{Y}_j$, and $\bar{Z}_j$. Again, note the use of **boldface** to indicate that each of these queries is remote.

For the purpose of this section, the details within each of these subqueries are not important. The subqueries do not even have to be conjunctive. We only require the remote subqueries to have the following property:

- The remote queries must be such that for each $j \in M$, Q_j can be *instantiated arbitrarily*, and R can be *instantiated arbitrarily as a singleton*. That is, given any relation instance I_j for each $j \in M$ and given any tuple t, there is an instance of the remote database over which each Q_j produces I_j exactly and R produces tuple t exactly. This property of the remote queries will be used in proving completeness of the local tests presented later, where we need to show the existence of an instance of the remote database over which the remote queries produce specific answers. A class of remote queries with this property can be described as follows: each Q_j is a positive literal with some remote predicate, R is a conjunction of positive literals with a remote predicate, and no remote predicate occurs more than once among R and the Q_j's. The main result of this paper for conjunctive-query constraints with negation is based on this class of remote queries. Results for other constraint classes can also be obtained if we can identify other classes of remote queries with the property, examples of which will be given in the conclusion.

In the remainder of the paper, we assume that updates are made to the local relations only. We model these updates by their effect on the local queries. That is, we analyze global consistency under insertions or deletions to the relations for the local queries P and Q_i's. We further assume that the insertions and deletions represent net changes to these relations. That is, a tuple is inserted into a relation only if it is not already in the relation, and a tuple is deleted from a relation only if it is already in the relation. No generality is lost by making this assumption since we can always query the local database to find out whether or not a tuple is already in the relation for a local query.

We will successively consider the following three cases: P is absent; R is absent; and both P and R are present.

4.1. Local Tests for Constraints with P absent

When P is absent, the constraint takes on a special form where there are neither X-variables nor Y-variables: $inconsistent :- \bigwedge_{i \in L} \neg Q_i(\bar{Z}_i), \bigwedge_{j \in M} \neg \boldsymbol{Q}_j(\bar{Z}_j), \boldsymbol{R}(\bar{Z})$. Insertions into the local Q_i's are always consistent since the constraint query is antimonotonic in these Q_i's (i.e., the constraint query never gain tuples when tuples are added to the Q_i's).

The following theorem gives a solution CLT under deletions from the local Q_i's when P is absent. Intuitively, to guarantee that a deletion is consistent, we want to make sure that any tuple ($\bar{z}$) in R that uses a deleted tuple as a cover has an alternative cover to be found among the remaining tuples in the local Q_i's. Further, there is no other way to guarantee consistency since we cannot count on the remote Q_j's to provide cover, as their instance is totally controlled by the adversary.

THEOREM 1 (DELETION) *Consider a constraint defined by*

$$inconsistent :- \bigwedge_{i \in L} \neg Q_i(\bar{Z}_i), \bigwedge_{j \in M} \neg \boldsymbol{Q}_j(\bar{Z}_j), \boldsymbol{R}(\bar{Z}).$$

For each $h \in L$, let δQ_h be a set of tuples of the same arity as $\bar{Z}_h$, and let Q_h^- denote the relation for $Q_h - \delta Q_h$. The deletion of δQ_h from Q_h for all $h \in L$ is consistent if and only if

$$(\forall \bar{Z}) \, [\bigvee_{h \in L} \delta Q_h(\bar{Z}_h) \Rightarrow \bigvee_{i \in L} Q_i^-(\bar{Z}_i)]. \tag{12}$$

Proof:

IF: Assume (12) holds. Suppose the deletion violates the constraint. Then, there is a $\bar{z}$ in R that agrees with some deleted tuple (i.e., such that $\bigvee_{h \in L} \delta Q_h(\bar{z}_h)$ holds) but such that $Q_i^-(\bar{z}_i)$ is false for all $i \in L$. But by substituting $\bar{z}$ for $\bar{Z}$ in (12), we infer that $\bigvee_{i \in L} Q_i^-(\bar{z}_i)$ holds. Contradiction!

ONLY-IF: Assume (12) is false, i.e., there is some $\bar{z}$ such that $\bigvee_{h \in L} \delta Q_h(\bar{z}_h)$ holds but $Q_i^-(\bar{z}_i)$ is false for each $i \in L$. Let $R = \{(\bar{z})\}$ and let all remote Q_j's be empty. After the deletion, $R(\bar{z})$ violates the constraint since $Q_i(\bar{z}_i)$ is false for all $i \in L$ (by hypothesis) and $Q_j(\bar{z}_j)$ is false all $j \in M$ (by construction of the remote Q_j's). To verify there is no prior violation, we need to show that there is some $h \in L$ such that $Q_h(\bar{z}_h)$ holds. Indeed, we know there is some $h \in L$ such that $\delta Q_h(\bar{z}_h)$ holds (by hypothesis), and since any deleted tuple is present prior to the deletion, $\bar{z}_h$ must be in Q_h. ∎

4.2. Local Tests for Constraints with **R** absent

When R is absent, the constraint takes on a special form where there are neither Y-variables nor Z-variables: $inconsistent :- P(\bar{X}), \bigwedge_{i \in L} \neg Q_i(\bar{X}_i), \bigwedge_{j \in M} \neg \boldsymbol{Q}_j(\bar{X}_j)$.

The following theorem give a solution CLT under insertions to P and the local Q_i's, when R is absent. Intuitively, when a local cover cannot be found for a tuple $(\bar{x})$ inserted to P, a remote cover must be found, albeit not directly. The trick here is to look for tuples already in P that have no local cover (and thus must have used a remote cover), and that are "indistinguishable" from tuple $(\bar{x})$ from the remote point of view.

THEOREM 2 (INSERTION) *Consider a constraint defined by*

$$inconsistent :- P(\bar{X}), \bigwedge_{i \in L} \neg Q_i(\bar{X}_i), \bigwedge_{j \in M} \neg \boldsymbol{Q}_j(\bar{X}_j).$$

Let δP be a set of tuples of the same arity as $\bar{X}$. For each $i \in L$, let δQ_i be a set of tuples of the same arity as $\bar{X}_i$ and let Q_i^+ denote the relation for $Q_i \cup \delta Q_i$. The insertion of δP to P and of δQ_i to Q_i for all $i \in L$ is consistent if and only if

$$(\forall \bar{X}) \, [\delta P(\bar{X}) \Rightarrow [\bigvee_{i \in L} Q_i^+(\bar{X}_i)] \vee (\exists \bar{X}')[P(\bar{X}') \wedge (\bar{X}' =_M \bar{X}) \wedge \bigwedge_{i \in L} \neg Q_i(\bar{X}_i')]]$$
$$\tag{13}$$

Proof:

IF: Assume (13) holds and that there is no prior violation of the constraint. For each tuple $(\bar{x})$ inserted to P (i.e., such that $\delta P(\bar{x})$ holds), we need to show that $P(\bar{x})$ does not violate the constraint, that is, either $Q_i^+(\bar{x}_i)$ holds for some $i \in L$ or $Q_j(\bar{x}_j)$ holds for some $j \in M$ (remember that the remote queries do not change). If $\bigvee_{i \in L} Q_i^+(\bar{x}_i)$ holds, we are done. Otherwise, from (13), we infer that there is some constant $\bar{x}'$ such that $P(\bar{x}')$ holds and $\bar{x}' =_M \bar{x}$, but $Q_i(\bar{x}_i')$ is false for each $i \in L$. Since $P(\bar{x}')$ does not violate the constraint (by hypothesis), there must be some $j \in M$ such that $Q_j(\bar{x}_j')$ holds. Therefore, $Q_j(\bar{x}_j)$ holds since $\bar{x}_j' = \bar{x}_j$.

ONLY-IF: Assume (13) is false, that is, there is some $\bar{x}$ in δP such that $Q_i^+(\bar{x}_i)$ is false for each $i \in L$, and for any $\bar{x}'s$ in P, either $\bar{x}' \neq_M \bar{x}$ or $Q_i(\bar{x}_i')$ holds for some $i \in L$. We need to construct an instance for the remote Q_j's such that the constraint is satisfied prior to the insertion but violated after. For each $j \in M$, let $Q_j = \{(\bar{x}_j') \mid P(\bar{x}'), \bar{x}_j' \neq \bar{x}_j\}$. To see why $P(\bar{x})$ violates the constraint after the insertion, simply note that no $Q_j(\bar{x}_j)$ can hold for any $j \in M$ (by construction of the remote Q_j's), and furthermore, $Q_i^+(\bar{x}_i)$ is false for each $i \in L$ (by hypothesis). To show that there were no violation prior to the insertion, let $\bar{x}'$ be an arbitrary tuple in P. By hypothesis, either $Q_i(\bar{x}_i')$ holds for some $i \in L$ or $\bar{x}_j' \neq \bar{x}_j$ for some $j \in M$. In the first case, we are done showing that $P(\bar{x}')$ did not violate the constraint. In the second case, $Q_j(\bar{x}_j')$ must hold by construction of the remote Q_j's. So in this case again, $P(\bar{x}')$ did not violate the constraint. ∎

The following theorem give a solution CLT under deletions from P and the local Q_i's, when R is absent. Intuitively, to ensure a deletion is consistent, any tuple $(\bar{x})$ in P^- that uses some deleted tuple (among the δQ_h's) as a cover prior to the deletion and that has no other local covers after the deletion, must have a remote cover which can be indirectly found if we can find some tuple $(\bar{x}')$ in P that has no local cover and that is indistinguishable from $(\bar{x})$ from the remote point of view.

THEOREM 3 (DELETION) *Consider a constraint defined by*

$$inconsistent :\!- P(\bar{X}), \bigwedge_{i \in L} \neg Q_i(\bar{X}_i), \bigwedge_{j \in M} \neg Q_j(\bar{X}_j).$$

Let δP be a set of tuples of the same arity as $\bar{X}$, and let P^- denote the relation for $P - \delta P$. For each $h \in L$, let δQ_h be a set of tuples of the same arity as $\bar{X}_h$, and let Q_h^- denote the relation for $Q_h - \delta Q_h$. The deletion of δP from P and of δQ_h from Q_h for all $h \in L$ is consistent if and only if

$$(\forall \bar{X}) [\ P^-(\bar{X}) \wedge [\bigvee_{h \in L} \delta Q_h(\bar{X}_h)] \wedge \bigwedge_{i \in L} \neg Q_i^-(\bar{X}_i) \Rightarrow$$
$$(\exists \bar{X}') [P(\bar{X}') \wedge (\bar{X}' =_M \bar{X}) \wedge \bigwedge_{i \in L} \neg Q_i(\bar{X}_i')]] \tag{14}$$

Proof:
IF: Assume (14) holds and that there is no constraint violation prior to the deletion. Suppose the constraint is violated after the deletion, i.e., there is a $\bar{x}$ in P^- that agrees with some deleted tuple (i.e., such that $\bigvee_{h \in L} \delta Q_h(\bar{x}_h)$ holds) but such that $Q_i^-(\bar{x}_i)$ is false for all $i \in L$ and $Q_j(\bar{x}_j)$ is false for all $j \in M$. By substituting $\bar{x}$ for $\bar{X}$ in (14), we infer there is some constant $\bar{x}'$ such that $P(\bar{x}')$ holds, no $Q_i(\bar{x}_i')$ holds for $i \in L$, and $\bar{x}_j' = \bar{x}_j$ for each $j \in M$. The latter implies that for each $j \in M$, $Q_j(\bar{x}_j')$ is false, since $Q_j(\bar{x}_j)$ is false. So $P(\bar{x}')$ is in violation of the constraint, which contradicts the hypothesis of no prior violation.
ONLY-IF: Assume (14) is false, that is, there is an $\bar{x}$ such that both $P^-(\bar{x})$ and $\bigvee_{h \in L}$ $\delta Q_h(\bar{x}_h)$ hold, but $Q_i^-(\bar{x}_i)$ is false for each $i \in L$ and the following holds

$$(\forall \bar{X}')[(P(\bar{X}') \wedge \bar{X}' =_M \bar{x}) \Rightarrow \bigvee_{i \in L} Q_i(\bar{X}'_i)]$$

For each $j \in M$, let $Q_j = \{(\bar{x}'_j) \mid P(\bar{x}') \wedge \bar{x}'_j \neq \bar{x}_j\}$. After the deletion, $P^-(\bar{x})$ violates the constraint since $Q_i^-(\bar{x}_i)$ is false for each $i \in L$ (by hypothesis) and $Q_j(\bar{x}_j)$ is false for each $j \in M$ (by construction of the remote Q_j's). To verify there is no prior violation, assume $P(\bar{x}')$ holds. If $\bigvee_{i \in L} Q_i(\bar{x}'_i)$ holds, we are done. Otherwise, there must be some $j \in M$ such that $\bar{x}'_j \neq \bar{x}_j$. Therefore $Q_j(\bar{x}'_j)$ holds (by construction of the remote Q_j's). ∎

4.3. Local Tests for Constraints with both **P** and **R** present

Generalizing on the extended example in Section 3, the following theorem gives a solution CLT under insertions, when both P and R are present. Intuitively, to ensure that an insertion is consistent, any tuple $(\bar{x}, \bar{y}, \bar{z})$ such that $(\bar{x}, \bar{y})$ is inserted to P must have a cover either among the local Q_i's or among the remote Q_j's after the insertion. The existence of a cover among the latter is guaranteed if P has a tuple $(\bar{x}', \bar{y})$ such that the tuple $(\bar{x}', \bar{y}, \bar{z})$ has no local cover and is indistinguishable from $(\bar{x}, \bar{y}, \bar{z})$ from the remote point of view.

THEOREM 4 (INSERTION) *Consider a constraint defined by*

$$inconsistent :- P(\bar{X}, \bar{Y}), \bigwedge_{i \in L} \neg Q_i(\bar{X}_i, \bar{Y}_i, \bar{Z}_i), \bigwedge_{j \in M} \neg \boldsymbol{Q}_j(\bar{X}_j, \bar{Y}_j, \bar{Z}_j), R(\bar{Y}, \bar{Z}).$$

Let δP be a set of tuples of the same arity as $(\bar{X}, \bar{Y})$. For each $i \in L$, let δQ_i be a set of tuples of the same arity as $(\bar{X}_i, \bar{Y}_i, \bar{Z}_i)$ and let Q_i^+ denote the relation for $Q_i \cup \delta Q_i$. The insertion of δP to P and of δQ_i to Q_i for all $i \in L$ is consistent if and only if

$$(\forall \bar{X}, \bar{Y}, \bar{Z}) [\ \delta P(\bar{X}, \bar{Y}) \wedge$$
$$(\forall \bar{X}') [P(\bar{X}', \bar{Y}) \wedge \bar{X}' =_M \bar{X} \Rightarrow \bigvee_{i \in L} Q_i(\bar{X}'_i, \bar{Y}_i, \bar{Z}_i)] \Rightarrow$$
$$\bigvee_{i \in L} Q_i^+(\bar{X}_i, \bar{Y}_i, \bar{Z}_i)] \tag{15}$$

Proof:

IF: Assume (15) holds and that the constraint is satisfied prior to the insertion. To show that the constraint is not violated after the insertion, we need to show the following:

$$(\forall \bar{X}, \bar{Y}, \bar{Z}) \, \delta P(\bar{X}, \bar{Y}) \wedge R(\bar{Y}, \bar{Z}) \wedge \bigwedge_{j \in M} \neg Q_j(\bar{X}_j, \bar{Y}_j, \bar{Z}_j) \Rightarrow \bigvee_{i \in L} Q_i^+(\bar{X}_i, \bar{Y}_i, \bar{Z}_i) \tag{16}$$

To show that (16) holds, it is sufficient to show the following holds

$$(\forall \bar{X}, \bar{Y}, \bar{Z}) \ R(\bar{Y}, \bar{Z}) \wedge \bigwedge_{j \in M} \neg Q_j(\bar{X}_j, \bar{Y}_j, \bar{Z}_j) \Rightarrow$$
$$(\forall \bar{X}') [P(\bar{X}', \bar{Y}) \wedge \bar{X}' =_M \bar{X} \Rightarrow \bigvee_{i \in L} Q_i(\bar{X}'_i, \bar{Y}_i, \bar{Z}_i)], \tag{17}$$

since (16) follows directly from (17) and (15).

We now show (17) holds. Let $\bar{x}$, $\bar{x}'$, $\bar{y}$, and $\bar{z}$ be such that the following holds:

$$R(\bar{y}, \bar{z}) \wedge \bigwedge_{j \in M} \neg Q_j(\bar{x}_j, \bar{y}_j, \bar{z}_j) \wedge P(\bar{x}', \bar{y}) \wedge \bar{x}' =_M \bar{x}$$

It follows that for each $j \in M$, $Q_j(\bar{x}'_j, \bar{y}_j, \bar{z}_j)$ is false since $\bar{x}'_j = \bar{x}_j$. And since the constraint is not violated prior to the insertion, it must be the case that

$$\bigvee_{i \in L} Q_i(\bar{x}'_i, \bar{y}_i, \bar{z}_i)$$

holds, completing the proof of (17).

ONLY-IF: Assume (15) is false, that is, there is a tuple $(\bar{x}, \bar{y})$ in δP and some $\bar{z}$ such that both:

$$(\forall \bar{X}') \, P(\bar{X}', \bar{y}) \wedge \bar{X}' =_M \bar{x} \Rightarrow \bigvee_{i \in L} Q_i(\bar{X}'_i, \bar{y}_i, \bar{z}_i) \tag{18}$$

and

$$\bigwedge_{i \in L} \neg Q_i^+(\bar{x}_i, \bar{y}_i, \bar{z}_i) \tag{19}$$

hold. In the following, we construct an instance for R and for the remote Q_j's such that the constraint is satisfied prior to the insertion but violated after. Consider $R = \{(\bar{y}, \bar{z})\}$ and for each $j \in M$, $Q_j = \{(\bar{x}'_j, \bar{y}_j, \bar{z}_j) \mid P(\bar{x}', \bar{y}), \bar{x}'_j \neq \bar{x}_j\}$. On the one hand, the inserted tuple $P(\bar{x}, \bar{y})$ violates the constraint after the insertion since: $R(\bar{y}, \bar{z})$ holds (by construction of R); for each $j \in M$, $Q_j(\bar{x}_j, \bar{y}_j, \bar{z}_j)$ is false (by construction of the remote Q_j's); and for each $i \in L$, $Q_i^+(\bar{x}_i, \bar{y}_i, \bar{z}_i)$ is false (ref. (19)). On the other hand, to see why the constraint is satisfied prior to the insertion, let $\bar{x}'$ be some arbitrary constant such that $P(\bar{x}', \bar{y})$ holds. If $\bar{x}' =_M \bar{x}$, it follows from (18) that $\bigvee_{i \in L} Q_i(\bar{x}'_i, \bar{y}_i, \bar{z}_i)$ holds, and thus the constraint is satisfied. If $\bar{x}' \neq_M \bar{x}$, there must be some $j \in M$ such that $\bar{x}'_j \neq \bar{x}_j$. By construction of the remote Q_j's, $Q_j(\bar{x}'_j, \bar{y}_j, \bar{z}_j)$ must hold. Thus, the constraint is satisfied. ∎

The following theorem gives a solution CLT under deletions, when both P and R are present. Intuitively, to ensure that the deletion is consistent, any tuple $(\bar{x}, \bar{y}, \bar{z})$ in $P^-(\bar{x}, \bar{y}) \wedge R(\bar{y}, \bar{z})$ that uses some deleted tuple (among the δQ_h's) as a cover prior to the deletion, must have some alternative cover either among the local Q_i's or among the remote Q_j's after the deletion. The existence of a cover among the latter is guaranteed if P has a tuple $(\bar{x}', \bar{y})$ such that $(\bar{x}', \bar{y}, \bar{z})$ has no local cover and is indistinguishable from $(\bar{x}, \bar{y}, \bar{z})$ from the remote point of view.

THEOREM 5 (DELETION) *Consider a constraint defined by*

$$inconsistent :\!- P(\bar{X}, \bar{Y}), \bigwedge_{i \in L} \neg Q_i(\bar{X}_i, \bar{Y}_i, \bar{Z}_i), \bigwedge_{j \in M} \neg \boldsymbol{Q_j}(\bar{X}_j, \bar{Y}_j, \bar{Z}_j), \boldsymbol{R}(\bar{Y}, \bar{Z}).$$

Let δP be a set of tuples of the same arity as $(\bar{X}, \bar{Y})$, and let P^- denote the relation for $P - \delta P$. For each $h \in L$, let δQ_h be a set of tuples of the same arity as $(\bar{X}_h, \bar{Y}_h, \bar{Z}_h)$ and let Q_h^- denote the relation for $Q_h - \delta Q_h$. The deletion of δP from P and of δQ_h from Q_h for all $h \in L$ is consistent if and only if

$$(\forall \bar{X}, \bar{Y}, \bar{Z}) \quad P^-(\bar{X}, \bar{Y}) \wedge [\bigvee_{h \in L} \delta Q_h(\bar{X}_h, \bar{Y}_h, \bar{Z}_h)] \wedge \psi(\bar{X}, \bar{Y}, \bar{Z}) \Rightarrow$$

$$\bigvee_{i \in L} Q_i^-(\bar{X}_i, \bar{Y}_i, \bar{Z}_i) \tag{20}$$

where $\psi(\bar{X}, \bar{Y}, \bar{Z})$ is defined by

$$(\forall \bar{X}') \ P(\bar{X}', \bar{Y}) \wedge \bar{X}' =_M \bar{X} \Rightarrow \bigvee_{i \in L} Q_i(\bar{X}_i', \bar{Y}_i, \bar{Z}_i)$$

Proof:
    IF: Assume (20) holds and that the constraint is satisfied prior to the deletion. To show that the constraint is not violated after the deletion, we need to show the following:

$$(\forall \bar{X}, \bar{Y}, \bar{Z}) \quad P^-(\bar{X}, \bar{Y}) \wedge [\bigvee_{h \in L} \delta Q_h(\bar{X}_h, \bar{Y}_h, \bar{Z}_h)] \wedge$$

$$R(\bar{Y}, \bar{Z}) \wedge \bigwedge_{j \in M} \neg Q_j(\bar{X}_j, \bar{Y}_j, \bar{Z}_j) \Rightarrow$$

$$\bigvee_{i \in L} Q_i^-(\bar{X}_i, \bar{Y}_i, \bar{Z}_i) \tag{21}$$

To show that (21) holds, it is sufficient to show the following holds

$$(\forall \bar{X}, \bar{Y}, \bar{Z}) \ R(\bar{Y}, \bar{Z}) \wedge \bigwedge_{j \in M} \neg Q_j(\bar{X}_j, \bar{Y}_j, \bar{Z}_j) \Rightarrow \psi(\bar{X}, \bar{Y}, \bar{Z}) \tag{22}$$

since (21) follows directly from (22) and (20).
    We now show (22) holds. Let $\bar{x}$, $\bar{x}'$, $\bar{y}$, and $\bar{z}$ be constants such that the following holds:

$$R(\bar{y}, \bar{z}) \wedge \bigwedge_{j \in M} \neg Q_j(\bar{x}_j, \bar{y}_j, \bar{z}_j) \wedge P(\bar{x}', \bar{y}) \wedge \bar{x}' =_M \bar{x}$$

It follows that for each $j \in M$, $Q_j(\bar{x}_j', \bar{y}_j, \bar{z}_j)$ is false since $\bar{x}_j' = \bar{x}_j$. And since the constraint is not violated prior to the deletion, it must be the case that

$$\bigvee_{i \in L} Q_i(\bar{x}_i', \bar{y}_i, \bar{z}_i)$$

holds, completing the proof of (22).
    ONLY-IF: Assume (20) is false, that is, there are constants $\bar{x}$, $\bar{y}$, and $\bar{z}$ such that both:

$$P^-(\bar{x}, \bar{y}) \wedge [\bigvee_{h \in L} \delta Q_h(\bar{x}_h, \bar{y}_h, \bar{z}_h)] \wedge \psi(\bar{x}, \bar{y}, \bar{z}) \tag{23}$$

and

$$\bigwedge_{i \in L} \neg Q_i^-(\bar{x}_i, \bar{y}_i, \bar{z}_i) \tag{24}$$

hold. In the following, we construct an instance for R and for the remote Q_j's such that the constraint is satisfied prior to the deletion but violated after. Consider $R = \{(\bar{y}, \bar{z})\}$ and for each $j \in M$, $Q_j = \{(\bar{x}'_j, \bar{y}_j, \bar{z}_j) \mid P(\bar{x}', \bar{y}), \bar{x}'_j \neq \bar{x}_j\}$. On the one hand, the constraint is violated after the deletion since: $P^-(\bar{x}, \bar{y})$ holds (following (23)); $R(\bar{y}, \bar{z})$ holds (by construction of R); for each $j \in M$, $Q_j(\bar{x}_j, \bar{y}_j, \bar{z}_j)$ is false (by construction of the remote Q_j's); and for each $i \in L$, $Q_i^-(\bar{x}_i, \bar{y}_i, \bar{z}_i)$ is false (ref. (24)).

On the other hand, to see why the constraint is satisfied prior to the deletion, let $\bar{x}'$ be a constant such that $P(\bar{x}', \bar{y})$ holds. If $\bar{x}' =_M \bar{x}$, it follows from $\psi(\bar{x}, \bar{y}, \bar{z})$ that $\bigvee_{i \in L} Q_i(\bar{x}'_i, \bar{y}_i, \bar{z}_i)$ holds, and thus the constraint is satisfied. If $\bar{x}' \neq_M \bar{x}$, there must be some $j \in M$ such that $\bar{x}'_j \neq \bar{x}_j$. By construction of the remote Q_j's, $Q_j(\bar{x}'_j, \bar{y}_j, \bar{z}_j)$ must hold. Thus, the constraint is satisfied. ∎

5. Complexity of the Complete Local Tests

The complete local tests we derived in the previous section can all be generated at compile time, that is, when the constraint is defined. Both the time to generate them and their size are linear in the size of the constraint. Unfortunately, not all these tests can be evaluated safely. While it is easy to see that tests (13) and (14) in Theorem 2 and 3 can be expressed in a straightforward manner in safe, nonrecursive Datalog$^\neg$, it is not immediately obvious that such is the case with tests (12), (15), and (20) in Theorems 1, 4, and 5.

First, let us consider test (12), repeated here for convenience:

$$(\forall \bar{Z}) \, [\bigvee_{h \in L} \delta Q_h(\bar{Z}_h) \Rightarrow \bigvee_{i \in L} Q_i^-(\bar{Z}_i)].$$

If all $\bar{Z}_i$'s are identical, then it is easy to see how to express this test as a safe, nonrecursive Datalog$^\neg$ query whose size is linear in the size of the original constraint. However, in the general case where the $\bar{Z}_i$'s are not necessarily identical, we can still express the test as a safe query but whose size is no longer linear. The following theorem gives us a method to make formulas with a similar form safe.

THEOREM 6 *For each $i \in L$, let $A_i(\bar{Z}_i)$ and $B_i(\bar{Z}_i)$ be safe queries. The first order formula*

$$(\forall \bar{Z}) \, [\bigvee_{h \in L} A_h(\bar{Z}_h) \Rightarrow \bigvee_{i \in L} B_i(\bar{Z}_i)]. \tag{25}$$

is equivalent to the following safe boolean query

$$\bigwedge_{h \in L} (\forall \bar{Z}_h) \, [A_h(\bar{Z}_h) \Rightarrow \bigvee_{i \in L \mid \bar{Z}_i \subseteq \bar{Z}_h} B_i(\bar{Z}_i)]. \tag{26}$$

Proof: Showing (26) $\Rightarrow$ (25) is trivial. To show (25) $\Rightarrow$ (26), assume (25) holds but (26) is false. There is some $h \in L$ and some $\bar{z}_h$ such that $A_h(\bar{z}_h)$ holds but $B_i(\bar{z}_i)$ is false for all $i \in L$ such that $\bar{Z}_i \subseteq \bar{Z}_h$. Let $\bar{z}$ be obtained from $\bar{z}_h$ by extending it with constant symbols that do not occur in the relation for any B_i. Substituting $\bar{z}$ for $\bar{Z}$ in (25), we infer that $\bigvee_{i \in L \mid \bar{Z}_i \not\subseteq \bar{Z}_h} B_i(\bar{z}_i)$ holds, which is impossible since for each of these i's, $\bar{z}_i$ contains some new constant symbols which make $B_i(\bar{z}_i)$ false. ∎

Thus, using Theorem 6, the safe query into which the original unsafe formula is rewritten has a size quadratic in the size of the unsafe formula.

We now turn to tests (15) and (20). The following example shows a test that cannot be evaluated safely and illustrates the method we use later to rewrite it to a safe query.

EXAMPLE: Consider a constraint defined by the following rule

$$inconsistent :- p(X, Y), \neg q_1(X, Z_1), \neg q_2(X, Z_2), r(Y, Z_1, Z_2).$$

Theorem 4 gives the following local test for the insertion of $p(a, b)$:

$$(\forall Z_1, Z_2)\,[(\forall X)\,[p(X, b) \Rightarrow (q_1(X, Z_1) \vee q_2(X, Z_2))] \Rightarrow (q_1(a, Z_1) \vee q_2(a, Z_2))] \quad (27)$$

A naive approach to verifying this condition consists of testing

$$(\forall Z_1, Z_2)\,\alpha(Z_1, Z_2) \Rightarrow \beta(Z_1, Z_2)$$

where α and β are queries defined by:

$$\alpha(Z_1, Z_2) \stackrel{\text{def}}{\equiv} (\forall X)\,[p(X, b) \Rightarrow (q_1(X, Z_1) \vee q_2(X, Z_2))]$$
$$\beta(Z_1, Z_2) \stackrel{\text{def}}{\equiv} q_1(a, Z_1) \vee q_2(a, Z_2)$$

The problem with this approach is that neither α nor β return a finite answer. So, instead of evaluating α directly, the idea is to decompose it into a union of subqueries, each of which generates a finite answer in some variables and a totally arbitrary answer in the remaining variables, so that only the finite portion of the answer needs to be considered. For instance, when $(\exists X)\,p(X, b)$ holds, the following lists all possible ways to satisfy $\alpha(Z_1, Z_2)$:

- Any Z_1 that satisfies the finite query $\varphi_1(Z_1) \stackrel{\text{def}}{\equiv} (\exists X)\,[p(X, b) \wedge q_1(X, Z_1)] \wedge (\forall X)\,[p(X, b) \Rightarrow q_1(X, Z_1)]$, and any Z_2.

- Any Z_2 that satisfies the finite query $\varphi_2(Z_2) \stackrel{\text{def}}{\equiv} (\exists X)\,[p(X, b) \wedge q_2(X, Z_2)] \wedge (\forall X)\,[p(X, b) \Rightarrow q_2(X, Z_2)]$, and any Z_1.

- Any Z_1 and Z_2 that satisfy the finite query $\varphi_{12}(Z_1, Z_2) \stackrel{\text{def}}{\equiv} (\exists X)\,[p(X, b) \wedge q_1(X, Z_1)] \wedge (\exists X)\,[p(X, b) \wedge q_2(X, Z_2)] \wedge \alpha(Z_1, Z_2)$.

In the first case, (27) is reduced to testing the following:

$$(\forall Z_1, Z_2)\, \varphi_1(Z_1) \Rightarrow (q_1(a, Z_1) \vee q_2(a, Z_2))$$

which is equivalent to

$$(\forall Z_1)\, \varphi_1(Z_1) \Rightarrow q_1(a, Z_1)$$

since we cannot satisfy the finite query $q_2(a, Z_2)$ with arbitrary values of Z_2. By treating the other cases in an analogous fashion, we obtain an expression that is both safe and equivalent to (27) as follows:

$$
\begin{aligned}
&(\exists X)\, p(X, b) \\
\wedge\ &(\forall Z_1)\, [\varphi_1(Z_1) \Rightarrow q_1(a, Z_1)] \\
\wedge\ &(\forall Z_2)\, [\varphi_2(Z_2) \Rightarrow q_2(a, Z_2)] \\
\wedge\ &(\forall Z_1, Z_2)\, [\varphi_{12}(Z_1, Z_2) \Rightarrow (q_1(a, Z_1) \vee q_2(a, Z_2))]
\end{aligned}
$$

$\square$

The following theorem gives us a general method to express a class of unsafe formulas as safe queries. We will later show how to recognize these formulas in tests (15) and (20) from Theorems 4 and 5.

THEOREM 7 Let $A(\bar{X})$ be a safe query, and for each $i \in L$, let $B_i(\bar{X}_i, \bar{Z}_i)$ and $C_i(\bar{Z}_i)$ be safe queries, where $\bar{X}_i \subseteq \bar{X}$ and $\bar{Z}_i \cap \bar{X} = \emptyset$. For each nonempty subset I of L, let $\bar{Z}_I$ denote $\bigcup_{i \in I} \bar{Z}_i$. Let $\bar{Z}$ denote $\bar{Z}_L$. The first order formula

$$(\forall \bar{Z})\, [(\forall \bar{X})\, [A(\bar{X}) \Rightarrow \bigvee_{i \in L} B_i(\bar{X}_i, \bar{Z}_i)] \Rightarrow \bigvee_{i \in L} C_i(\bar{Z}_i)] \tag{28}$$

is equivalent to the following safe boolean query

$$\bigvee_{i \in L \,|\, \bar{Z}_i = \emptyset} C_i() \vee [(\exists \bar{X})\, A(\bar{X}) \wedge \bigwedge_{I \neq \emptyset} (\forall \bar{Z}_I)(\varphi_I(\bar{Z}_I) \Rightarrow \bigvee_{i \in I \,|\, \emptyset \neq \bar{Z}_i \subseteq \bar{Z}_I} C_i(\bar{Z}_i))] \tag{29}$$

where $\varphi_I(\bar{Z}_I)$ is defined by

$$[\bigwedge_{i \in I} (\exists \bar{X})\, A(\bar{X}) \wedge B_i(\bar{X}_i, \bar{Z}_i)] \wedge (\forall \bar{X})\, A(\bar{X}) \Rightarrow \bigvee_{i \in I} B_i(\bar{X}_i, \bar{Z}_i)$$

Proof: Since all the $C_i(\bar{Z}_i)$'s in (29) with $\bar{Z}_i = \emptyset$ can be factored out, no generality is lost if we show (28) $\Leftrightarrow$ (29) under the assumption that no $\bar{Z}_i$ is empty.

(28) $\Rightarrow$ (29): Assume (28) holds. Then $(\exists \bar{X})\, A(\bar{X})$ must hold since otherwise, (28)'s LHS becomes vacuously true, and (28) becomes false. Let I be a nonempty subset of L and let $\bar{z}_I$ be some vector of constants that makes $\varphi_I(\bar{z}_I)$ true. Let $\bar{z}$ be obtained from $\bar{z}_I$ by extending it with constant symbols that do not occur in any relation C_i. Since $\varphi_I(\bar{z}_I)$ holds, $\bar{z}$ makes (28)'s LHS true. And since (28) holds, its RHS must also hold. Finally, since

$\bigvee_{i\in I \mid \bar{Z}_i \not\subseteq \bar{Z}_I} C_i(\bar{z}_i)$ is false (by construction of $\bar{z}$), it follows that $\bigvee_{i\in I \mid \emptyset \neq \bar{Z}_i \subseteq \bar{Z}_I} C_i(\bar{Z}_i)$ holds.

(29) $\Rightarrow$ (28): Assume (29) holds. Let $\bar{z}$ be a vector of constants that makes (28)'s LHS true. Let us define $I_0 = \{i \in L \mid (\exists \bar{X}) A(\bar{X}) \wedge B_i(\bar{X}_i, \bar{z}_i)\}$. Since (28)'s LHS holds for $\bar{z}$, $[(\forall \bar{X}) A(\bar{X}) \Rightarrow \bigvee_{i\in I_0} B_i(\bar{X}_i, \bar{z}_i)]$ must also hold, and I_0 cannot be empty (otherwise $(\exists \bar{X}) A(\bar{X})$ would have been false). As a result, $\varphi_{I_0}(z_{I_0})$ holds. Since (29) holds (by hypothesis), it follows that $\bigvee_{i\in I_0 \mid \emptyset \neq \bar{Z}_i \subseteq \bar{Z}_{I_0}} C_i(\bar{z}_i)$ also holds, and $\bar{z}$ makes (28)'s RHS true. ∎

As a corollary of Theorem 7, the complete local tests from Theorems 4 and 5 can always be expressed as a safe query.

COROLLARY 1 *Tests (15) and (20) from Theorems 4 and 5 can always be rewritten as queries in safe, nonrecursive Datalog⁻.*

Proof:

We show how to rewrite each of (15) and (20) in such a way that the unsafe portion of the formula can be identified as having the form of (28).

First, (15) can be written as

$$(\forall \bar{X}, \bar{Y}) \left[\delta P(\bar{X}, \bar{Y}) \Rightarrow \alpha(\bar{X}, \bar{Y})\right] \tag{30}$$

where $\alpha(\bar{X}, \bar{Y})$ is

$$(\forall \bar{Z}) \left[\; (\forall \bar{X}') \left[P(\bar{X}', \bar{Y}) \wedge \bar{X}' =_M \bar{X} \Rightarrow \bigvee_{i\in L} Q_i(\bar{X}'_i, \bar{Y}_i, \bar{Z}_i)\right] \Rightarrow \right.$$
$$\left. \bigvee_{i\in L} Q_i^+(\bar{X}_i, \bar{Y}_i, \bar{Z}_i)\right]$$

If we treat $\bar{X}$ and $\bar{Y}$ as constants in $\alpha(\bar{X}, \bar{Y})$, then the latter is a formula of the form (28) and can be rewritten as a safe query. Since both $\bar{X}$ and $\bar{Y}$ are range restricted in (30), it follows that (30) can be rewritten as a safe query.

Second, (20) can be written as

$$\bigwedge_{h\in L} (\forall \bar{X}, \bar{Y}, \bar{Z}_h) \left[P^-(\bar{X}, \bar{Y}) \wedge \delta Q_h(\bar{X}_h, \bar{Y}_h, \bar{Z}_h) \Rightarrow \beta(\bar{X}, \bar{Y}, \bar{Z}_h)\right] \tag{31}$$

where $\beta(\bar{X}, \bar{Y}, \bar{Z}_h)$ is

$$(\forall \bar{Z}') \left[\; \bar{Z}'_h = \bar{Z}_h \wedge (\forall \bar{X}') \left[P(\bar{X}', \bar{Y}) \wedge \bar{X}' =_M \bar{X} \Rightarrow \bigvee_{i\in L} Q_i(\bar{X}'_i, \bar{Y}_i, \bar{Z}'_i)\right] \Rightarrow \right.$$
$$\left. \bigvee_{i\in L} Q_i^-(\bar{X}_i, \bar{Y}_i, \bar{Z}'_i)\right]$$

If we treat $\bar{X}$, $\bar{Y}$, and $\bar{Z}_h$ as constants in $\beta(\bar{X}, \bar{Y}, \bar{Z}_h)$, then the latter is a formula of the form (28) and can be rewritten as a safe query. Since $\bar{X}$, $\bar{Y}$, and $\bar{Z}_h$ are range restricted in (31), it follows that (31) can be rewritten as a safe query. ∎

Theorem 7 rewrites a general first order formula of the form (28) to a safe query of the form (29). Since the query considers every subset I of L, its size is exponential in the size of input formula. As a consequence, (safe) complete local tests for constraints with both P and R present also have a size exponential in the size of the constraints. However, there are nontrivial subclasses of constraints (with both P and R present) that admit linear-size local tests. In the future, more work is needed to identify other subclasses of constraints with polynomial-size solutions. In the following, we show three interesting special cases with a linear-size solution. The results are obtained by specializing Theorems 4 and 5, and are shown here without proof. We use the same notation as in the theorems.

- When all the local negated subgoals of the constraint in Theorems 4 and 5 use the same Z-variables (say $\bar{Z}_i = \bar{Z}'$ for each $i \in L$), the complete local test for insertions degenerates to the following safe query:

$$(\forall \bar{X}, \bar{Y}) \, \delta P(\bar{X}, \bar{Y}) \Rightarrow \varphi(\bar{X}, \bar{Y})$$

where $\varphi(\bar{X}, \bar{Y})$ is defined to be

$$(\forall \bar{Z}') \, [\, (\forall \bar{X}') \, [P(\bar{X}', \bar{Y}) \wedge \bar{X}' =_M \bar{X} \Rightarrow \bigvee_{i \in L} Q_i(\bar{X}'_i, \bar{Y}_i, \bar{Z}')] \Rightarrow$$
$$\bigvee_{i \in L} Q_i^+(\bar{X}_i, \bar{Y}_i, \bar{Z}')]$$

and the complete local test for deletions is given by the following safe query

$$\bigwedge_{h \in L} (\forall \bar{X}, \bar{Y}, \bar{Z}') \, P^-(\bar{X}, \bar{Y}) \wedge \delta Q_h(\bar{X}_h, \bar{Y}_h, \bar{Z}') \Rightarrow \psi(\bar{X}, \bar{Y}, \bar{Z}')$$

where $\psi(\bar{X}, \bar{Y}, \bar{Z}')$ is defined to be

$$(\forall \bar{X}') \, [P(\bar{X}', \bar{Y}) \wedge \bar{X}' =_M \bar{X} \Rightarrow \bigvee_{i \in L} Q_i(\bar{X}'_i, \bar{Y}_i, \bar{Z}')] \Rightarrow \bigvee_{i \in L} Q_i^-(\bar{X}_i, \bar{Y}_i, \bar{Z}')$$

Note that the complexity due to the need for checking all subsets of L is totally eliminated.

- When each X-variable used in the constraint in Theorems 4 and 5 is also used by some remote negated subgoal (i.e., $\bar{X} = \bigcup_{j \in M} \bar{X}_j$), the complete local test for insertions degenerates into the following safe query

$$(\forall \bar{X}, \bar{Y}) \, [\delta P(\bar{X}, \bar{Y}) \Rightarrow [\bigvee_{i \in L \, | \, \bar{Z}_i = \emptyset} Q_i^+(\bar{X}_i, \bar{Y}_i)]]$$

and the complete local test for deletions degenerates into the following safe query

$$\bigwedge_{h \in L} (\forall \bar{X}, \bar{Y}, \bar{Z}_h) \, [P^-(\bar{X}, \bar{Y}) \wedge \delta Q_h(\bar{X}_h, \bar{Y}_h, \bar{Z}_h) \Rightarrow \bigvee_{i \in L \, | \, \bar{Z}_i \subseteq \bar{Z}_h} Q_i^-(\bar{X}_i, \bar{Y}_i, \bar{Z}_i)]$$

- When the constraint in Theorems 4 and 5 has no local negated subgoals (i.e., $L = \emptyset$), the complete local test for insertions degenerates into the following safe query

$$(\forall \bar{X}, \bar{Y})\, [\delta P(\bar{X}, \bar{Y}) \Rightarrow (\exists \bar{X}')\, [P(\bar{X}', \bar{Y}) \wedge \bar{X}' =_M \bar{X}]]$$

and obviously, deletions are always consistent.

6. Conclusion

This paper considers the problem of determining whether an update to a distributed database preserves global consistency, when not all the underlying relations are accessible and when the update is made to the relations that are accessible. We solve this problem for integrity constraints on the database that are conjunctive queries with negation (CQC⁻'s). This contribution is important because previous work has only considered constraints without negation, and integrity constraints in distributed databases often involve negation. Note that if the query that defines a constraint has both recursion and negation, the problem becomes undecidable.

More specifically, for a CQC⁻, insertions to (resp. deletions from) the local relations always result in insertions to (resp. deletions from) the local queries in the constraint. Thus, the main result of this paper, which can be obtained by specializing the more general results from Sections 4 and 5, can be summarized as follows:

- For CQC⁻'s where the remote predicates do not occur more than once, consistency of local insertions and local deletions can be tested completely in time polynomial in the size of the local relations and updates. Further, these tests can be generated at compile time in the form of safe, nonrecursive Datalog⁻ (or SQL) queries, whose size is linear in the size of the constraint in the best case and exponential in the worst case.

The result we just stated is not limited to CQC⁻'s but also applies to other constraints of the form

$$inconsistent :- P(\bar{X}, \bar{Y}), \bigwedge_{i \in L} \neg Q_i(\bar{X}_i, \bar{Y}_i, \bar{Z}_i), \bigwedge_{j \in M} \neg \boldsymbol{Q}_j(\bar{X}_j, \bar{Y}_j, \bar{Z}_j), \boldsymbol{R}(\bar{Y}, \bar{Z})$$

as long as updates to the local relations result in either insertions to or deletions from the local queries, and the remote queries have the property mentioned at the beginning of Section 4 (i.e., that each remote Q_j can be instantiated arbitrarily and R instantiated arbitrarily as singleton). For example:

- If the local updates are restricted to either insertions or deletions, then P and the local Q_i's may be *any* local query that is monotonic in the local relations.

- A remote $Q_j(\bar{X}_j, \bar{Y}_j, \bar{Z}_j)$ may even have existential variables, that is, it may be defined to be $(\exists \bar{T})\, S(\bar{X}_j, \bar{Y}_j, \bar{Z}_j, \bar{T})$ where S is a remote query. Remote Q_j's of this form arise in constraints that are inclusion dependencies or more general tuple generating dependencies.

- R may be any union of conjunctive queries over remote relations where no remote predicates occur more than once.

Throughout this paper, we have assumed single occurrences of the remote predicates in the constraint query. If this restriction is ignored, all the CLT's we presented remain sound but may no longer be complete. Indeed, if we allow multiple occurrences of the remote predicates, new dependencies are created within and among the instances of R and Q_j's. This observation suggests that for a test to be complete, the dependencies, induced by the particular structure of the remote queries on their results, must be embodied in the test's condition. Further work is needed to lift the restriction of no repeated remote predicates. Preliminary results have been obtained in [5].

Acknowledgments

This work was supported by ARO grant DAAH04-95-1-0192. We thank Jeff Ullman and Serge Abiteboul for their valuable comments regarding both technical contents and presentation of an earlier version of this paper.

Notes

1. For the rest of this paper, we choose to use the local/remote terminology purely to keep it consistent with [1]. We say that a relation is "local" merely to indicate that it is available for use but not necessarily that is is physically local. Similar, "remote" is synonymous to "not available" for use.

References

1. A. Gupta. (1994). Partial Information Based Integrity Constraint Checking. Ph.D. Thesis, Stanford University.
2. A. Gupta & J.A. Blakeley. (1995). Using Partial Information to Update Materialized Views. *Information Systems*, 20:641–662.
3. A. Gupta, Y. Sagiv, J.D. Ullman & J. Widom. (1994). Constraint Checking with Partial Information. *Proc. 13th ACM Symp. on Principles of Database Systems*, pages 45–55.
4. A. Gupta & J. Widom. (1993). Local Verification of Global Integrity Constraints in Distributed Databases. *Proceedings of the ACM SIGMOD International Conf. on Management of Data*, pages 49–58.
5. N. Huyn. (1996). Testing CQC¬ constraints under limited data access. Technical Report available as URL http://www-db.stanford.edu/pub/papers/cqcnclt-tr.ps.
6. N. Huyn. (1996). Efficient View Self-Maintenance. *Proc. ACM Workshop on Materialized Views*, pages 17–25.
7. N. Huyn. (1997). Efficient Complete Local Tests for Conjunctive-Query Constraints with Negation. *Proc. Int. Conf. Database Theory*, pages 83–97, Delphi, Greece.
8. A. Levy & Y. Sagiv. (1993). Queries Independent of Updates. *Proc. 19th International Conf. on Very Large Data Bases*, pages 171–181.
9. S. Tiwari & H.C. Howard,. (1993). Constraint Management on Distributed AEC Databases. *Fifth International Conf. on Computing in Civil and Building Engineering*, ASCE, pages 1147–1154.
10. F.W. Tompa, & J.A. Blakeley. (1988). Maintaining Materialized Views Without Accessing Base Data. *Information Systems*, 13:393–406.
11. J.D. Ullman. (1989). *Principles of Database and Knowledge-Base Systems*, Volumes 1 and 2, Computer Science Press.

Constraints: An International Journal, 2, 401–427 (1997)

Implementation and Evaluation of Decision Trees with Range and Region Splitting

YASUHIKO MORIMOTO   morimoto@trl.ibm.co.jp

TAKESHI FUKUDA   fukudat@trl.ibm.co.jp

SHINICHI MORISHITA   morisita@trl.ibm.co.jp

TAKESHI TOKUYAMA   ttoku@trl.ibm.co.jp

IBM Tokyo Research Laboratory,
1623-14, Shimo-tsuruma, Yamato City, Kanagawa Pref, 242, JAPAN

Abstract. We propose an extension of an entropy-based heuristic for constructing a decision tree from a large database with many numeric attributes. When it comes to handling numeric attributes, conventional methods are inefficient if any numeric attributes are strongly correlated. Our approach offers one solution to this problem. For each pair of numeric attributes with strong correlation, we compute a two-dimensional association rule with respect to these attributes and the objective attribute of the decision tree. In particular, we consider a family $\mathcal{R}$ of grid-regions in the plane associated with the pair of attributes. For $R \in \mathcal{R}$, the data can be split into two classes: data inside R and data outside R. We compute the region $R_{opt} \in \mathcal{R}$ that minimizes the entropy of the splitting, and add the splitting associated with R_{opt} (for each pair of strongly correlated attributes) to the set of candidate tests in an entropy-based heuristic.

We give efficient algorithms for cases in which $\mathcal{R}$ is (1) x-monotone connected regions, (2) based-monotone regions, (3) rectangles, and (4) rectilinear convex regions. The algorithm has been implemented as a subsystem of SONAR (System for Optimized Numeric Association Rules) developed by the authors. We have confirmed that we can compute the optimal region efficiently. And diverse experiments show that our approach can create compact trees whose accuracy is comparable with or better than that of conventional trees. More importantly, we can grasp non-linear correlation among numeric attributes which could not be found without our region splitting.

Keywords: decision trees, multivariate tests, range splitting, region splitting

1. Introduction

Decision Trees

Constructing an efficient decision tree is a very important problem in data mining[2, 3, 5, 16, 23]. For example, an efficient computer-based diagnostic medical system can be constructed if a small decision tree can be automatically generated for each medical problem from a database of health-check records for a large number of patients.

Let us consider the attributes of tuples in a database. An attribute is called boolean if its range is $\{0, 1\}$, categorical if its range is a discrete set $\{1, .., k\}$ for some natural number k, and numeric if its range is the set of real numbers.

Each data tuple t has $m + 1$ attributes A_i, for $i = 0, 1, .., m$. We treat one boolean attribute (say, A_0) as special, denote it by W, and call it the *objective attribute*. The other attributes are called *conditional attributes*.

The decision tree problem is as follows: A set U of tuples is called "positive" (resp. negative), if for a tuple t, the probability that $t[W]$ is 1 (resp. 0) is at least θ_1 (resp. θ_2) in U, for given thresholds θ_1 and θ_2. We would like to classify the set of tuples into positive subsets

163

Table 1. Health Check Records

Patient	BP	C	S	Diseased
0001	140	+	+	O
0002	120	−	+	O
0003	110	−	−	×
0004	80	−	−	×
0005	90	−	+	×
0006	120	+	+	O
0007	90	+	−	O
0008	100	−	−	×
0009	100	−	+	O
0010	120	−	−	×
⋮	⋮	⋮	⋮	⋮

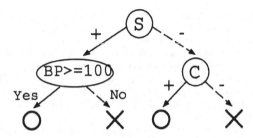

Figure 1. Decision Tree

and negative subsets by using tests with conditional attributes. For a boolean (conditional) attribute, a test is in the form of "$t[A_i] = 1$?". For a categorical attribute, a traditional test is "$t[A_i] = l$?". For a numeric attribute, a traditional test is "$t[A_i] < Z$?" for a given value Z.

Let us consider a rooted binary tree, each of whose internal nodes is associated with a test that has attributes. We associate each leaf node with the subset (called leaf-cluster) of tuples satisfying all tests on the path from the root to the leaf. Every leaf-cluster is labeled as either positive or negative on the basis of the class distribution in the leaf-cluster. Such a tree-based classifier is called a *decision tree*.

For example, assume that we have a database of health-check records, shown in Table 1, for a large number of patients with geriatric diseases. Consider a set of health-check items; say, systolic blood pressure (BP), cholesterol level (C), and urine sugar (S). We would like to decide whether a patient needs a detailed health check for a geriatric disease (say, apoplexy). Suppose that blood-pressure is a numeric attribute, and that urine sugar and cholesterol level are boolean (+ or −) attributes in the health check database. Figure 1 shows an example of a decision tree which decides whether a patient is diseased or not from these health-check items.

We want to construct a compact decision tree. Unfortunately, if we want to minimize the total sum of the lengths of exterior paths, the problem of constructing a minimum decision tree which completely classify a given data is known to be NP-hard [14, 13]. It is also believed that it is NP-hard if the minimized objective is the "size," i.e., number of nodes of the tree. However, in practical applications classification accuracy for unseen data is more important than the complete classification of a given data. Therefore, despite the NP-hardness of the problem, many practical solutions [5, 21, 24, 23] have been proposed in the literature. Among them, the C4.5 program [23] applies an entropy heuristic, which greedily constructs a decision tree in a top-down, breadth-first manner according to the "entropy of splitting." At each internal node, the heuristic examines all the candidate tests, and chooses the one for which the associated splitting of the set of tuples attains the minimum entropy value.

If each test attribute is boolean or categorical, those practical approaches work well, and SLIQ [16] gives an efficient scalable implementation, which can handle a database with 10 million tuples and 400 attributes. SLIQ uses the GINI function instead of entropy.

Handling Numeric Attributes

To handle a numeric attribute, one approach is to make it categorical, by subdividing the range of the attribute into smaller intervals. Another approach is to consider a test of the form $t[A_i] > Z$ or $t[A_i] < Z$, which is called a "guillotine cutting," since it creates a "guillotine-cut subdivision" of the Cartesian space of ranges of attributes. C4.5 and SLIQ adopt the latter approach.

However, [23] pointed out that this approach has a serious problem if a pair of attributes are correlated. For example, let us consider two numeric attributes, "height (cm)" and "weight (kg)," in a health check database. Obviously, these attributes have a strong correlation. Indeed, the region $0.85 * 22 * height^2 < weight < 1.15 * 22 * height^2$ and its complement provide a popular criterion for separating healthy patients from patients who need dietary cures. In the left chart of Figure 2, the gray region shows the "healthy" region. However, if we construct a decision tree for classifying patients by using guillotine cutting, its subdivision is complicated and the size of the tree becomes very large, and hence, it becomes hard to recognize the substantial rule (see the right chart of Figure 2).

Therefore, it is very important to propose a better scheme for handling numeric attributes with strong correlations in order to make an efficient diagnostic system based on a decision trees.

One approach is as follows: Consider each pair of numeric attributes as a two-dimensional attribute. Then, for each such two-dimensional attribute, compute a line partition of the corresponding two-dimensional space so that the corresponding entropy is minimized. One (minor) defect of this method is that it is not cheap to compute the optimal line. Although some work has been done on this problem in computational geometry [4, 8], the worst time complexity remains $O(n^2)$ if there are n tuples. Another (major) defect is that the decision tree may still be too large even if we use line partition. Although some multivariate decision tree classifiers [5, 6] can find multivariate tests in more practical ways, the latter problem, which is inherent in linear partitioning methods, still remains.

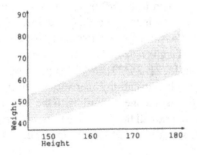 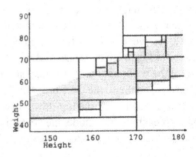

Figure 2. Healthy Region and Guillotine-cut Subdivision

Main Results – Splittings with Respect to Regions

In this paper, we propose the following scheme, applying the two-dimensional association rules, region rules in short, of [10, 11] and an image segmentation algorithm of [1]. The scheme has been implemented as a subsystem of SONAR, which stands for System for Optimized Numeric Association Rules, developed by the authors [12].

Let n be the number of tuples in the database. First, for each numeric attribute, we create an equi-depth bucketing so that tuples are uniformly distributed into $N \leq \sqrt{n}$ ordered buckets according to the values of the attribute.

Next, we find all pairs of strongly correlated numeric attributes. For each such pair A and A', we create an $N \times N$ pixel grid G according to the Cartesian product of the bucketing of each numeric attribute. We consider a family $\mathcal{R}$ of grid regions; in particular, we consider the set $\mathcal{R}(Xmono)$ of all *x-monotone* connected regions and $\mathcal{R}(Base)$ of all *based-monotone* (i.e., bounded by an x-monotone grid curve) regions. Here, a grid region is a union of pixels of G, and it is x-monotone if its intersection with each column of G is either empty or a vertical strip. A grid curve consists of edges of the pixel grid G, and is x-monotone if its intersection with each vertical line is either a point or an interval. Figure 3 shows instances of a based monotone region and an x-monotone region. A based-monotone region may be disconnected, as shown in Figure 3, since the bounding grid curve may contain segments of the upper or lower boundary of G. Note that a connected based-monotone region is an x-monotone region. We also deal with the family of rectangles and the family of rectilinear convex polygonal regions.

Regarding the pair of attributes as a two-dimensional attribute, we compute the region R_{opt} in $\mathcal{R}$ that minimizes the entropy function, and consider the decision rule $(t[A], t[A']) \in R_{opt}$. We present algorithms for computing R_{opt} in worst case times of $O(nN)$ and $O(nN^2)$ for $\mathcal{R}(Base)$ and $\mathcal{R}(Xmono)$, respectively. Moreover, in practical instances, our algorithms run in $O(N^2)$ time and $O(N^2 \log n)$ time. Since $N \leq \sqrt{n}$, the time complexities are $O(n)$ and $O(n \log n)$, respectively. For rectangles and rectilinear convex polygonal regions, the time complexity increases to $O(nN^3)$ in the worst case and $O(N^3 \log n)$ in practice.

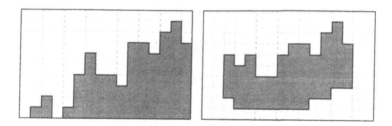

Figure 3. Based Monotone Region (left) and X-monotone Region (right).

Now, we add these rules for all pairs (A, A') of correlated attributes, and construct a decision tree by applying entropy-based heuristic. As a special case of region rules, we also consider rules of the form $(t[A] \in I)$ for an interval I in order to develop our system.

Since the regions separated by guillotine cutting and those separated by line cutting are very special cases of connected based-monotone regions, our method can find a region rule with smaller entropy values at each step of the heuristic. Hence, we can almost always create a smaller tree. In the above example of "height" and "weight," the rule $0.85 * 22 * height^2 < weight < 1.15 * 22 * height^2$ itself defines an x-monotone region, and hence we can create a nice decision tree of height two, i.e., with the root and two leaves.

One defect of our approach is that the decision rule $(t[A], t[A']) \in R$ is sometimes hard to describe. However, we can describe the rule by combining a visualization system. Figure 4 is a graphical view of an x-monotone region rule in a decision tree which was constructed from a "diabetes" diagnosis dataset, which is in the UCI repository [19]. The visualization system uses red color level and brightness to show characteristics of each pixel. The red level indicates the probability of a positive, or negative, patient in each pixel, and the brightness indicates the number of patients in each pixel. The data in the node are partitioned according to whether they are in the x-monotone region R_{opt} or not. In this example, the near-triangle region R_{opt} corresponds to the cluster of patients less likely to be positive for diabetes.

We also discuss the generalization of our method to cases in which the objective attribute is categorical.

2. Entropy-Based Data Segmentation for Decision Trees

2.1. Entropy of a Splitting

Assume that a data set S contains n tuples. To formalize our definition of entropy of splitting, we consider a more general case in which the objective attribute W is a categorical attribute taking values in $\{1, 2, .., k\}$.

The entropy value $Ent(S)$ (with respect to the objective attribute W) is defined as

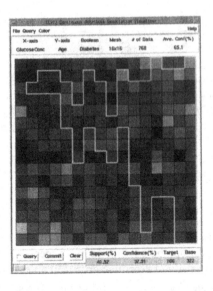

Figure 4. X-monotone Region Splitting

$$Ent(S) = -\sum_{j=1,\ldots,k} p_j \log p_j$$

where p_j is the relative frequency with which W takes the value j in the set S.

We now consider the entropy function associated with a splitting of the data. For example, suppose that the objective attribute has three categories, say C_1, C_2, and C_3, and that each category has 40, 30, and 30 data, respectively.

	C_1	C_2	C_3
100	40	30	30

The value of the entropy of the whole data set is

$$-\frac{40}{100}\log\frac{40}{100} - \frac{30}{100}\log\frac{30}{100} - \frac{30}{100}\log\frac{30}{100} = 1.09.$$

Let us consider a splitting of the data set into two subsets, S_1 and S_2, with n_1 and n_2 data, respectively, where $n_1 + n_2 = n$. The entropy of the splitting is defined by

$$Ent(S_1; S_2) = \frac{n_1}{n}Ent(S_1) + \frac{n_2}{n}Ent(S_2).$$

If we assume that the splitting is as follows:

S_1	C_1	C_2	C_3
60	40	10	10

S_2	C_1	C_2	C_3
40	0	20	20

the entropy index value of the dataset after the splitting is

$$\frac{60}{100}(-\frac{40}{60}\log\frac{40}{60} - \frac{10}{60}\log\frac{10}{60} - \frac{10}{60}\log\frac{10}{60}) + \frac{40}{100}(-\frac{20}{40}\log\frac{20}{40} - \frac{20}{40}\log\frac{20}{40}) = 0.80.$$

Therefore, the splitting decreases the value of the entropy by 0.29.

Let us consider another splitting:

S_1	C_1	C_2	C_3
60	20	20	20

S_2	C_1	C_2	C_3
40	20	10	10

In this case, the value of the associated entropy is 1.075, a decrease of only 0.015.

Let $f(X) = f(x_1, .., x_k) = \sum_{i=1}^{k} x_i \log(x_i/s(X))$, where $s(X) = \sum_{i=1}^{k} x_i$. We have

$$Ent(S) = -f(p_1, ..., p_k) = -\frac{1}{n} f(x_1, .., x_k),$$

where $n = |S|$ and $x_i = p_i n$. Thus,

$$Ent(S_1; S_2) = -\frac{1}{n}\{f(y_1, ..., y_k) + f(x_1 - y_1, ..., x_k - y_k)\},$$

where x_i (resp. y_i) is the number of tuples t in S (resp. S_1) satisfying $t[W] = i$. We use the following property of f:

LEMMA 1 *The function $f(X)$ is convex in the region $X \geq 0$ (i.e., $x_i \geq 0$ for $i = 1, 2, .., k$); that is,*

$$\frac{f(X) + f(X + 2a)}{2} \geq f(X + a)$$

for any vector a satisfying $X > 0$ and $X + 2a > 0$.

Proof: For a vector $\Delta = (\delta_1, ..., \delta_k)$, let $Y(\Delta) = (\Delta, x) = \sum_{i=1}^{k} \delta_i x_i$. In order to show the convexity of $f(X)$, it suffices to show that for any Δ,

$$f''(X) = \frac{\partial^2 f(X)}{\partial Y(\Delta)^2} \geq 0.$$

Since $f'(X) = \frac{\partial f(X)}{\partial Y(\Delta)} = \sum_{i=1}^{k} \frac{\partial f(X)}{\partial x_i} \frac{1}{\delta_i}$,

$$f'(X) = \sum_{i=1}^{k} \delta_i^{-1} \log x_i - s(T) \log s(X),$$

where $T = (\delta_1^{-1}, .., \delta_k^{-1})$. Hence,

$$f''(X) = \sum_{i=1}^{k} \delta_i^{-2} x_i^{-1} - s(T)^2 s(X)^{-1}.$$

Now, it suffices to show that

$$(*) = s(X) \sum_i \delta_i^{-2} x_i^{-1} - s(T)^2 \geq 0.$$

We consider vectors $A = (x_1^{1/2}, .., x_k^{1/2})$ and $B = (x_1^{-1/2}\delta_1^{-1}, .., x_k^{-1/2}\delta_k^{-1})$. Then, from the Cauchy-Schwarz inequality, $(*) = |A|^2|B|^2 - (A, B)^2 \geq 0.$ ∎

2.2. Splittings with Respect to Regions

Given a numeric attribute A, guillotine cutting methods consider the following optimized splitting:

1. Let $S(A > Z) = \{t \in S : t[A] > Z\}$ and $S(A \leq Z) = \{t \in S : t[A] \leq Z\}$ for a real number Z. Compute the value Z_{opt} of Z that minimizes $Ent(S(A > Z); S(A \leq Z))$, and consider the splitting of S into $S(A > Z_{opt})$ and $S(A \leq Z_{opt})$.

   By applying the algorithms of [10], we can extend the above splitting to the following, which is also considered in our decision tree subsystem of SONAR:

2. For an interval I, let $S(A \in I) = \{t \in S : t[A] \in I\}$ and $S(A \in \bar{I}) = \{t \in S : t[A] \notin I\}$. Compute the interval I_{opt} that minimizes $Ent(S(A \in I); S(A \in \bar{I}))$, and consider the associated splitting.

We call the above two kinds of splitting "one-dimensional rules," or "range rules" for short. In this paper, we consider *splittings with respect to grid regions*, which are sometimes called *region rules*.

We specify a number $N \leq \sqrt{n}$, and construct an almost equi-depth ordered bucketing of tuples for each numeric attribute A. That is, we construct buckets $B_1^A, .., B_N^A$ each of which contains approximately n/N tuples, satisfying $t[A] \leq t'[A]$ for every $t \in B_i^A, t' \in B_j^A$ and $i < j$. An efficient randomized algorithm for constructing such a bucketing can be found in [10].

For a pair of numeric attributes A and A', we have a pixel grid G of size $N \times N$ generated as a Cartesian product of bucketings, such that for an (i,j)-th pixel $q(i,j)$, $t \in q(i,j)$ if and only if $t[A] \in B_i^A$ and $t[A'] \in B_j^{A'}$. We denote the pixel containing t as $q(t)$.

We consider a family $\mathcal{R}$ of grid regions of G. For each $R \in \mathcal{R}$, we consider a splitting S into $S(R) = \{t \in S : q(t) \in R\}$ and $S(\bar{R}) = \{t \in S : q(t) \in \bar{R}\}$, where $\bar{R} = G - R$ is the complement of R. Let R_{opt} be the region of $\mathcal{R}$ that minimizes the entropy of the splitting. The region R_{opt} and the associated splitting are called the *optimal region* and the *optimal splitting*, or *region rule*, with respect to $\mathcal{R}$ and the pair of attributes (A, A').

A grid region is called *based-monotone*, if it lies below an x-monotone curve. A grid region is called *x-monotone* if it is a connected region bounded by a pair of x-monotone grid curves. $\mathcal{R}(Base)$ and $\mathcal{R}(Xmono)$ are the sets of all based-monotone and x-monotone regions of G, respectively.

In Section 3, we present efficient algorithms for computing the optimal splitting with respect to certain families of regions, including $\mathcal{R}(Xmono)$ and $\mathcal{R}(Base)$, when the objective attribute W is boolean.

The construction of a decision tree is top-down, starting from its root in breadth-first fashion. When a new internal node is created, the algorithm first computes all one-dimensional rules for singular numeric attributes, and region rules for all pairs of numeric attributes, together with rules associated with boolean or categorical conditional attributes. Then it chooses the rule that minimizes the entropy. The decision made at the node is associated with the splitting.

2.3. Selecting Correlated Attributes

Even if A and A' are not strongly correlated, the region rule associated with the pair (A, A') is better with respect to the entropy value than one-dimensional rules on A and A'. However, it does not necessarily give a better system for users, since a region rule is more complicated than a one-dimensional rule. Indeed, some techniques like a visualization system [11] are necessary to explain a region rule.

Hence, it is desirable that a region rule should only be considered for a pair of strongly correlated conditional attributes. We use the entropy value again to decide whether A and A' are strongly correlated.

For simplicity, we assume that $\mathcal{R}(Xmono)$ is used as the family of regions. We compute R_{opt} for the pair (A, A') and its entropy value $Ent(S(R_{opt}); S(\overline{R_{opt}}))$. We also compute the optimum intervals I and I' to minimize the entropy of the splitting that corresponds to the rules $A(X) \in I$ and $A'(X) \in I'$, respectively.

We give a threshold $\alpha \geq 1$ to decide that A and A' are strongly correlated if and only if

$$\frac{Ent(S) - Ent(S(R_{opt}); S(\overline{R_{opt}}))}{Ent(S) - min\{Ent(S(I); S(\bar{I})), \ Ent(S(I'); S(\bar{I}'))\}} > \alpha$$

The choice of the threshold α depends on the application.

3. Optimization of Splittings

3.1. Naive Hand-Probing Algorithm

From now on, we concentrate on the case in which the objective attribute W is boolean, although our scheme can be extended to the case in which W is categorical. Therefore, the entropy function is written as

$$Ent(S) = -p \log p - (1 - p) \log (1 - p),$$

where p is the frequency with which the objective attribute which has one of the boolean value on the set of tuples.

We consider the problem of computing R_{opt} in several families of grid regions of G. Note that it is very expensive to compute R_{opt} by examining all elements of $\mathcal{R}$, since the set $\mathcal{R}(Base)$, for example, has N^N different regions.

Let n_1 and n_2 be the numbers of tuples t of S satisfying $t[W] = 0$ and $t[W] = 1$, respectively. For a region R, let $x(R)$ and $y(R)$ be the number of tuples t located in the pixels in R that satisfy $t[W] = 0$ and $t[W] = 1$, respectively.

Consider the planar point set $P = \{\iota(R) = (x(R), y(R)) : R \in \mathcal{R}\}$, and its convex hull $conv(P)$. Since $x(R)$ and $y(R)$ are nonnegative integers that are at most n, P contains $O(n^2)$ points, and $conv(P)$ has at most $2n$ points on it. We define

$$E(x, y) = -\frac{f(x, y) + f(n_1 - x, n_2 - y)}{n},$$

using the function f defined in the previous section for $X = (x, y)$. Then, the entropy function $Ent(S(R); S(\bar{R}))$ of the splitting is $E(\iota(R)) = E(x(R), y(R))$.

LEMMA 2 $\iota(R_{opt})$ *must be on* $conv(P)$.

Proof: From Lemma 1, $f(x,y)$ is convex, and hence $E(x,y)$ is a concave function. It is well known that the minimum of a concave function over P is taken at an extremal point, that is, a vertex of $conv(P)$. ∎

Hence, naively, it suffices to compute all the vertices of $conv(P)$ and their associated partition curves. Our problem now resembles global optimization problems [20]. In global optimization, extremal points can be computed by using linear programming. However, we know neither the point set P nor the constraint inequalities defining the convex hull; hence, we cannot use the linear programming approach in a straightforward manner.

Let $conv^+(P)$ (resp. $conv^-(P)$) be the upper (resp. lower) chain of $conv(P)$; Here, we consider that the leftmost (resp. rightmost) vertex of $conv(P)$ belongs to the upper (resp. lower) chain.

Our algorithm is based on the use of what is known in computational geometry as "hand-probing" to compute the vertices of a convex polygon [9]. Hand-probing is based on the *touching oracle*:

> "Given a slope θ, compute the tangent line with slope θ to the upper (resp. lower) chain of the convex polygon together with the tangent point $v^+(\theta)$ (resp. $v^-(\theta)$). If the slope coincides with the slope of an edge of the polygon, the left vertex of the edge is reported as the tangent point."

LEMMA 3 *If a touching oracle is given in* $O(T)$ *time, all vertices of* $conv(P)$ *can be computed in* $O(nT)$ *time.*

Proof: We consider an interval $I = [I(left), I(right)]$ of the upper chain of $conv(P)$ between two vertices $I(left)$ and $I(right)$ in Figure 5. We start with $\theta = \infty$, find the leftmost vertex p_0 and the rightmost vertex p_1 of $conv(P)$, and set $I(left) = p_0$ and $I(right) = p_1$. Let $\theta(I)$ be the slope of the line through points $I(left)$ and $I(right)$. We perform the touching oracle and find $I(mid) = v^+(\theta_I)$. If $I(mid) = I(left)$, we report that I corresponds to an edge of $conv(P)$, and hence no other vertex exists there. Otherwise, we divide I into $[I(left), I(mid)]$ and $[I(mid), I(right)]$, and process each sub-interval recursively. We find either a new vertex or a new edge by executing the touching oracle in the algorithm. Hence, the time complexity is $O(|P|T)$, where $|P| \leq n$ is the number of vertices of P. ∎

LEMMA 4 *For a given* θ, *the touching oracle to* $conv(P)$ *can be computed in* $O(N^2)$ *time, if* $\mathcal{R} = \mathcal{R}(Xmono)$. *If preprocessing takes* $O(N^2)$ *time, it can be computed in* $O(N)$ *time for* $\mathcal{R}(Base)$.

Proof: It suffices to show how to compute $v^+(\theta)$, since $v^-(\theta)$ can be analogously computed. Let $v^+(\theta) = ((x(R_\theta), y(R_\theta))$, and let the tangent line be $y - \theta x = a$. Then, $y(R_\theta) - \theta x(R_\theta) = a$ and $y(R) - \theta x(R) \leq a$ for any $R \in \mathcal{R}$. Hence, R_θ is the region that maximizes $y(R) - \theta x(R)$. Let $g_{i,j}$ be the number of tuples in the (i,j)-th pixel of G, and let $h_{i,j}$ be the number of tuples satisfying $w(t) = 1$ in the (i,j)-pixel. We write $\Phi_{i,j}(\theta) = h_{i,j} - \theta g_{i,j}$. From our definition, $y(R) - \theta(x(R) + y(R)) = \sum_{(i,j) \in R} \Phi_{i,j}(\theta)$.

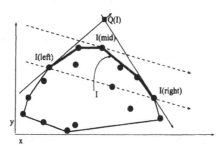

Figure 5. Hand-Probe

If $\mathcal{R} = \mathcal{R}(Xmono)$, R_θ is the *focused region* defined by [10], and can be computed in $O(N^2)$ time by using dynamic programming and fast matrix searching [10, 1].

Let us consider the case in which $\mathcal{R} = \mathcal{R}(Base)$. Since a based-monotone region R is the region below an x-monotone curve, the intersection of R and the j-th column of the grid G forms a half-column below some row index $top_R(j)$, that is, the set of pixels $(1, j), (2, j), ..., (top_R(j), j)$.

We consider the function $\Psi_{j,m}(\theta) = \sum_{i=1}^{m} \Phi_{i,j}(\theta)$ and the index $m_j(\theta)$, which is the value of m that maximizes $\Psi_{j,m}(\theta)$. We can confirm that $top_{R_\theta}(j) = m_j(\theta)$; if not, we can replace the j-th column of R_θ by $(1, j), ..., (m_j(\theta), j)$ to improve the value of $y(R) - \theta(x(R) + y(R))$.

For each θ, it is easy to compute $m_j(\theta)$ in $O(N)$ time, and hence we can compute R_θ in $O(N^2)$ time. Moreover, we can compute the piecewise linear function $\max_m \Psi_{j,m}(\theta)$ in $O(N)$ time, considering θ as a parameter. Using this function, we can query $m_j(\theta)$ in $O(\log N)$ time for a given θ. Hence, the time complexity of computing R_θ is $O(N \log N)$ if preprocessing takes $O(N^2)$ time. We can reduce the $O(N \log N)$ computing time to $O(N)$ by applying the fractional cascading data structure [7].   ∎

We have the following similar results for the family of rectangles and the family of rectilinear convex regions, although the time complexity is increased.

LEMMA 5 *The touching oracle to* $conv(P)$ *can be computed in* $O(N^3)$ *time, if* $\mathcal{R}$ *is either the family of all rectangle grid-regions, or the family of all rectilinear convex grid-regions of* G.

Proof: Using the technique given in [10], an $O(N^3)$-time algorithm can be obtained for the family of rectangles. An $O(N^3)$-time algorithm for the family of rectilinear convex regions can be found in [25].   ∎

Combining Lemmas 2, 3, 4, and 5, we have the following theorem:

THEOREM 1 R_{opt} *can be computed in* $O(nN^2)$ *time for* $\mathcal{R}(Xmono)$, $O(nN)$ *time for* $\mathcal{R}(Base)$, *and* $O(nN^3)$ *time for the family of rectangles and that of rectilinear convex polygons.*

These are the worst case time complexities. In the next section, we further improve the practical time complexity by a factor of $O(n/\log n)$.

3.2. Guided Branch-and-Bound Search

The hand-probing algorithm computes all vertices on the convex hull. However, we only need to compute the vertex corresponding to R_{opt}. Hence, we can improve the performance by pruning unnecessary vertices efficiently. While running the hand-probing algorithm, we maintain the current minimum E_{min} of the entropy values corresponding to the vertices examined so far.

Suppose we have done hand probing with respect to θ_l and θ_r, and next consider the interval $I = [v^+(\theta_l), v^+(\theta_r)] = [I(left), I(right)]$ of $conv^+(P)$. Let $Q(I) = (x_{Q(I)}, y_{Q(I)})$ in the Figure 5 be the point of intersection of the tangent lines whose slopes are θ_l and θ_r. We compute the value $E(Q(I)) = E(x_{Q(I)}, y_{Q(I)})$. If the two tangent lines are parallel, we set $E(Q(I)) = -\infty$.

LEMMA 6 *For any point* $Q' = (x', y')$ *inside the triangle* $I(left)I(right)Q(I)$,

$$E(x', y') \geq \min\{E(Q(I)), E_{min}\}.$$

Proof: Immediate from the concavity of $E(x, y)$. ∎

This lemma gives a lower bound for the values of E at the vertices between $I(left)$ and $I(right)$ in $conv^+(P)$. Hence, we have the following: .

COROLLARY 1 *If* $E(Q(I)) \geq E_{min}$, *no vertex in the interval* I *of* $conv^+(P)$ *corresponds to a region whose associated entropy is less than* E_{min}.

On the basis of Corollary 1, we can find the optimal region R_{opt} effectively by running the hand-probing algorithm together with the branch-and-bound strategy guided by the values $E(Q(I))$. Indeed, the algorithm examines the subinterval with the minimum value of $E(Q(I))$ first. Moreover, during the process, subintervals satisfying $E(Q(I)) \geq E_{min}$ are pruned away.

We maintain the list $\{E(Q(I)) : I \in \mathcal{I}\}$, using a priority queue. Note that E_{min} is monotonically decreased, while Q_{min} is monotonically increased in the algorithm. Most subintervals are expected to be pruned away during the execution, and the number of touching oracles in the algorithm is expected to be $O(\log n)$ in practical instances. We have implemented the algorithm as a subsystem of SONAR, and confirmed the expected performance by experiment as described in Section 4.

Since the touching oracle needs $O(N^2)$ time for $\mathcal{R}(Xmono)$, the algorithm runs experimentally in $O(N^2 \log n)$ time, which is $O(n \log n)$, because $N \leq \sqrt{n}$. Similarly, it runs in $O(N^2)$ time for $\mathcal{R}(Base)$, and in $O(N^3 \log n)$ time for the families of rectangles and rectilinear convex polygonal regions.

4. Experimental Results

4.1. Classification Accuracy

In this subsection, we describe several experimental results to examine classification accuracy of trees with region splitting by using cross-validation test.

Ten fold Cross-Validation Test We performed the following ten fold cross-validation test:

- Randomly divide the original dataset into ten almost equal-sized subsets.

- Take the union of nine subsets and use the union as the training dataset to generate a decision tree that splits data by guillotine cutting, x-monotone regions, rectilinear regions, or rectangular regions.

- Use the remaining one subset as the test dataset to evaluate the decision tree generated by the training dataset. Compute the ratio of the number of test tuples that are misclassified to the number of all data in the test dataset, and call the ratio the *error ratio* of the decision tree *against* the test dataset.

- Repeat the above steps ten times, and then calculate the average of all the error ratios.

Tree Size From a training dataset, we can generate larger decision trees by expanding leaves as much as possible. Larger decision trees can correctly classify data in the training dataset with higher accuracy, but they are likely to *overfit* the training dataset, and therefore provide higher error ratios against the test dataset. We need some criterion for when to stop expanding a decision tree, and we employ the χ^2 test to control tree size [22].

Let us focus on a node X with N tuples. Let p_i denote the relative frequency with which the objective attribute takes the value i. Suppose that the node X is divided into two child nodes named T and F. Let $p_i(T)(resp.p_i(F)$ denote the frequency of the value i in the nodes named by $T(resp.F)$, and let $N_T(resp.N_F)$ be the number of tuples in the node $T(resp.F)$. Let χ^2 denote

$$\sum_i \frac{N_T(p_i(T) - p_i)^2 + N_F(p_i(F) - p_i)^2}{p_i}.$$

Lower χ^2 values support with higher confidence the hypothesis that the data distributions in node X and in X's child nodes are independent. Put another way, lower χ^2 values mean that the splitting at node X is less effective. We therefore give a threshold for χ^2 so that we stop expanding the node X if χ^2 is less than the threshold. Higher thresholds are more likely to stop generating subtrees and thereby producing smaller decision trees. We used thresholds ranging from 0 to 45.

The accuracy critically depends upon the χ^2 critical value that is selected. Unfortunately, we do not have a theoretical method to predict the optimal, or critical, value of χ^2. To the best of our knowledge, this problem is neither solved nor well studied in the literature of research on decision trees. We adopt a naive heuristic method, named *multi-trial method*, in which we construct trees for a few number of χ^2 values, test the trees using the ten fold cross-validation, and select the one with the best accuracy. If the number of categories in the objective attribute is small, say 2 or 3, the efficiency of our algorithms enables this approach practical. Although our method uses a portion, 1/10 in our experiment, of the dataset as the test data for the decision trees, we think it is practically sufficient to use 9/10 of the dataset for the training data of the decision trees.

Pixel Density The average number of tuples in each pixel, which we call the *pixel density*, tends to affect the error ratio of a decision tree. Using a lower pixel density is likely to make decision trees overfit the training dataset, while a coarse grid with a higher pixel density often fails to find variously shaped regions. We empirically found that a pixel density ranging from 5 to 10 gives a lower error ratio for test datasets, and we therefore use a pixel density of 5 or 10. The results for a pixel density of 5 show the effects of relatively fine grid regions, while those for a pixel density of 10 show those of coarse grid regions.

In the process of generating decision trees, at nodes lower in the tree, the number of tuples becomes smaller. In order to guarantee a pixel density of 5 or 10, we are forced to use a coarse grid, say 2×2, which is too rough to generate interesting regions. If we have to use a coarse grid whose size is less than 5×5, we instead employ one-dimensional (range) splitting.

Datasets We used several public datasets, summarized in Table 2, which were acquired from the UCI Machine Learning Repository [19]. Since this experiment was to examine our method for handling numeric rules and its effectiveness, we chose these datasets because all the conditional attributes were numeric. For records that have null value, we assigned the average value of the attribute to those missing values.

If we use small datasets, we have to use small grid matrices, say 5×5 or a little larger. Such small grid matrices are inadequate for comparing various region families. Moreover, such notchy grid regions reduce the accuracy even if they can capture correlations. Therefore, we eliminated small datasets from the repository. However, we included some datasets that are small in the above sense, to obtain as broad an evaluation as possible. Note that numerical values in the "german credit" dataset are discrete.

For the datasets whose number of categories in the objective attribute are more than 3, we employed multidimensional touching oracle, which is mentioned in Section 5, to compute a range and a region.

Classification Capability Figures 6 to 14 show the ten fold cross-validation results of the datasets in Table 2. As regions for splitting datasets, we used x-monotone regions, rectilinear regions, and rectangular regions. The pixel density was set to 5 or 10.

In the figures, lines labeled "Rectilinear (dens5)," for example, show the error ratios against the test dataset of decision trees using rectilinear region splitting with a pixel density of 5, for various χ^2 stopping values ranging from 0 to 45. For smaller χ^2 values, we have decision trees so much larger that their error ratios are relatively high and overfit the training

Table 2. Dataset Summary

Dataset	#categories	#tuples	#attributes
breast-cancer-wisconsin	2	699	9
german credit	2	1000	24
liver disorder	2	345	6
pima diabetes	2	768	8
balance scale	3	625	4
waveform	3	5000	20
waveform-+noise	3	5000	40
vehicle	4	846	18
segmentation	7	2310	19

dataset. In general, we have to make larger decision trees as the number of categories in the objective attribute increases.

In Figure 6, the error ratio of the decision tree for $\chi^2 = 45$ has the lowest value, 4.15%. On the other hand, the lines labeled "guillotine" show the cases in which we use guillotine cutting instead of region splitting. For the "breast-cancer-wisconsin" dataset, the lowest error ratio of those decision trees with guillotine cutting is 5.72%.

The cross-validation results from datasets using diverse conditions can be summarized as follows:

- Table 3 shows that the rectilinear region splitting with pixel density 5 won over the guillotine cutting on eight of nine datasets. Moreover, it won over all of other region splittings except the rectilinear region splitting with pixel density 10 on six data sets.

- The graphs show that if we use x-monotone regions with a low pixel density, it tends to give high error ratio because of overfitting. In contrast to this, rectilinear regions are robust even if we use a low pixel density.

- The χ^2 value giving the minimum accuracy highly depend on both datasets and construction methods.

For each dataset, we compute the lowest error ratio for each type of splitting and the average number of leaves in the accurate trees. Table 3 summarizes the results. In the table, the lowest error ratio for each dataset is underlined. Observe that results of region splitting are more accurate than guillotine cutting in most cases.

4.2. Another Pruning Method

A defect of constructing the decision tree by using χ^2 based pruning together with the multi-trial method is that we need to construct trees for several χ^2 values. In our actual implementation, we first construct the decision tree for the smallest χ^2 value, and then prune it to obtain trees with larger χ^2 values; therefore, construct unnecessarily huge tree for the smallest χ^2 value, and slow down the processing time.

Although it is ideal to find out a more sophisticated method to predict a critical value of χ^2 from the experiment; however, the experimental results, given in Figures 6 to 14,

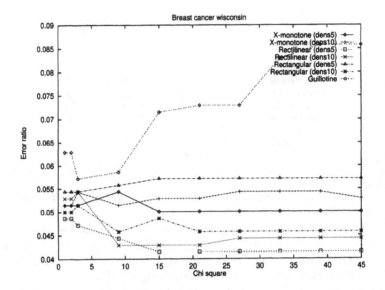

Figure 6. Error Ratios for "breast cancer wisconsin"

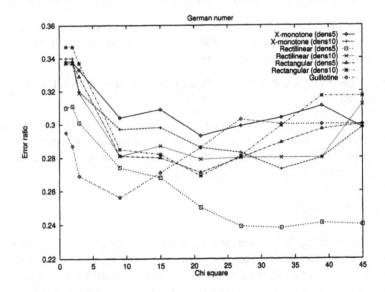

Figure 7. Error Ratios for "german credit"

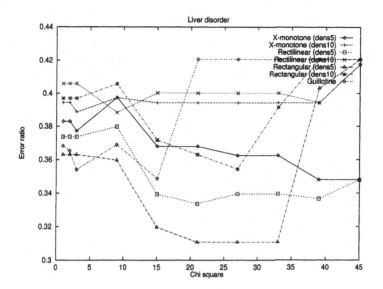

Figure 8. Error Ratios for "liver disorder"

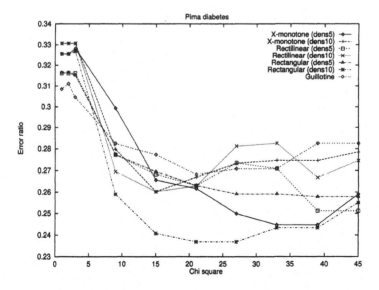

Figure 9. Error Ratios for "pima diabetes"

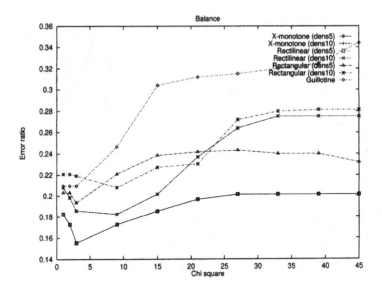

Figure 10. Error Ratios for "balance scale"

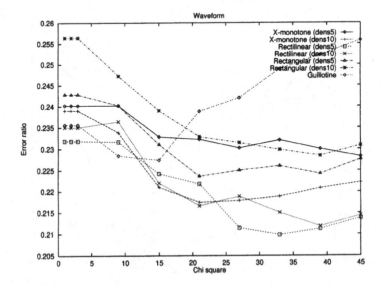

Figure 11. Error ratios for "waveform" dataset

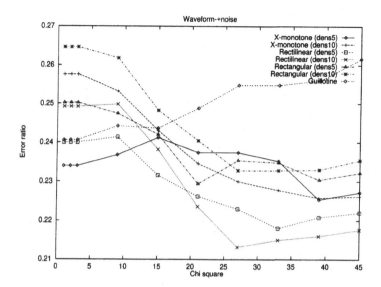

Figure 12. Error Ratios for "waveform-+noise"

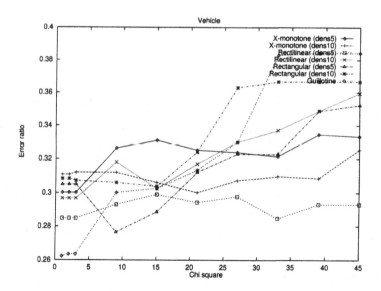

Figure 13. Error Ratios for "vehicle".

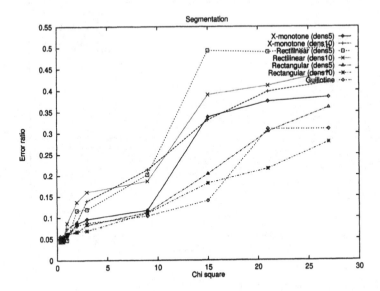

Figure 14. Error Ratios for "segmentation".

| | Rectilinear | | | | X-monotone | | Rectangular | | Guillotine | |
| | dens. 5 | | dens. 10 | | | | | | | |
Dataset	Err(%)	Size	Err(%)	Size	Err(%)	Size	Err(%)	Size	Err(%)	Size
breast-cancer-wisconsin	4.15	3.3	4.29	3.5	5.01	3.4	4.58	4.0	5.72	19.2
german credit	23.80	3.6	27.90	4.3	27.30	3.8	26.90	4.6	25.60	12.8
liver disorder	38.83	3.2	33.36	11.4	34.81	2.0	31.08	2.0	34.87	3.0
pima diabetes	25.12	2.1	26.02	7.0	24.47	4.5	23.69	4.6	26.82	4.4
balance scale	15.52	34.7	18.24	14.5	15.52	34.7	19.34	44.7	20.95	48.8
waveform	20.98	33.2	21.18	27.4	21.74	46.9	22.36	65.1	22.74	91.7
waveform-+noise	21.80	34.6	21.32	38.6	22.54	30.3	22.94	67.7	24.36	91.7
vehicle	28.47	12.2	29.68	77.1	30.02	17.0	27.65	38.9	26.23	94.0
segmentation	4.37	53.7	5.06	58.2	4.81	57.9	4.89	65.3	4.50	71.1

Table 3. Summary of Cross-Validation Results.

Table 4. Cross-Validation Results for Pruned Trees.

Dataset	X-monotone		Rectilinear		Rectangular		Guillotine	
	Err	Size	Err	Size	Err	Size	Err	Size
breast-cancer-wisconsin	3.86	4.0	<u>3.72</u>	4.1	6.14	3.9	7.29	5.6
german credit	28.10	4.2	28.40	4.3	27.60	5.3	<u>26.40</u>	8.2
liver disorder	38.00	2.0	38.00	2.0	38.00	2.0	37.44	4.5
pima diabetes	28.67	5.4	29.59	4.1	29.70	5.0	<u>24.86</u>	8.4
balance scale	<u>19.98</u>	15.8	<u>19.98</u>	15.8	22.40	11.1	26.24	12.5
waveform	<u>23.28</u>	64.5	23.98	65.2	23.84	82.6	29.50	63.4
waveform-+noise	23.82	54.6	<u>22.96</u>	60.5	25.02	66.7	25.08	92.3
vehicle	34.65	17.3	<u>33.69</u>	18.2	33.80	27.5	47.10	11.7
segmentation	24.46	21.4	<u>21.95</u>	22.0	22.12	22.3	32.25	14.2

show that the accuracy curve highly depends on the dataset, and behaves too wild to guess a nice function on the data parameters such as data size, number of attributes, and number of categories, to predict the optimal value of χ^2. The investigation into such a prediction function remains a major open problem in both theory and practice.

In this subsection, we describe our experiment on another pruning strategy, in which we need not construct a unnecessarily huge tree, and compare the accuracy to the multi-trial method.

Training and Validation Set Method   A popular approach for the problem to determine whether to expand a node or not during construction of a decision tree is the *training and validation set* method, in which we separate an available dataset into two distinct subsets and then use one to expand a leaf and the other to evaluate the expansion [18]. Among many possible implementations of the training and validation set method, we adopt the following algorithm:

- We separate the available records into two distinct sets, a training set and a validation set. The validation set contains about one third of all the available records.

- We construct the decision tree on the training set top-down using the entropy heuristic, in which we stop the expansion using the validation given below.

- Suppose that a node (parent node) in the decision tree is split into two children. We compute the number of misclassified records in the validation set for each of the parent node and two children. If the splitting does not reduce the number of misclassified records, then we abandon the splitting and stop expanding at the parent node. Otherwise, we continue expanding the tree recursively.

We evaluate the effectiveness of this approach by using the cross-validation test. Table 4 shows the error ratio and the average number of leaves of the pruned trees. The result shows that although the training and validation set method is sometimes better or competitive, the multiple trial method using χ^2 validation clearly wins on several datasets.

Table 5. Performance in Computing the Optimal Region.

	X-monotone		Rectilinear		Rectangular	
Resolution	sec	#touch	sec	#touch	sec	#touch
10^2	0.08	26	0.05	24	0.01	16
20^2	0.36	27	0.30	24	0.05	23
30^2	1.03	32	1.30	31	0.14	25
40^2	1.78	33	3.19	30	0.37	29
50^2	2.83	34	6.97	31	0.73	30

4.3. Performance Results

In this subsection, we examine several performance experiments. First we examine the time taken to compute the optimal region. After verifying its scalability, we then examine the overall time taken to construct a decision tree with region splitting.

Computing Optimal Regions   The performance of a method for constructing decision trees depends on the time taken to compute the optimal regions for splitting data. Thus the cost of computing one optimal region gives an idea of the method's overall performance in generating one decision tree.

In the first experiments, we generated our test data, in the form of an $N \times N$ grid, as follows: We first generated random numbers uniformly distributed in $[N^2, 2N^2]$ and assigned them to the number of tuples in each pixel. We then assigned a value in $[1, N^2]$ to the number of tuples that take one of the boolean values of the objective attribute, from a corner pixel to the central one, proceeding in a spiral fashion. These test data were generated so that the number of points on the convex hull increases sub-linearly to N, the square root of the number of pixels. We examined the CPU time taken to compute the optimal regions and the number of touching oracles needed to find the regions. All the experiments were performed on an IBM RS/6000 workstation with a 112 MHz PowerPC 604 chip and 512 MB of main memory, running under the AIX 4.1 operating system.

Table 5 shows the time (sec) and the number of touching oracles that were required in the guided branch-and-bound algorithm to find the optimal x-monotone (resp. rectilinear, or rectangular) region that minimizes entropy. It shows that the number of touching oracles increases very slowly thanks to the guided branch-and-bound algorithm. Figure 15 confirms that the CPU time follows our scale estimation. Although the asymptotic time complexity for computing the optimal x-monotone region is better than that for computing the optimal rectilinear region, in practice the optimal rectilinear region is computed faster, because the constant factor is smaller.

At the root of a decision tree, we may need a large number of pixels to guarantee the specified pixel density. The number of tuples, however, decreases in lower parts of the tree, and the number of pixels soon becomes less than 30×30 for most datasets; hence, computing the optimal rectilinear region is not costly, according to Table 5.

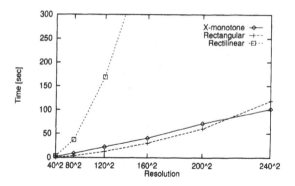

Figure 15. CPU Time for Computing the Optimized Region.

Table 6. Tree Construction Time (1).

#tuples	X-monotone	Rectilinear	Guillotine
1000	58	27	8
2000	163	66	14
3000	273	106	19
4000	425	165	26
5000	613	244	49

Computing Decision Trees   The next experiment examines the overall performance in tree construction. At each node of a decision tree, we first prepare the grid, and then compute the optimal region. The grid preparation is not expensive, because it can be done by scanning all the tuples at a node just once. The problem is that we have to calculate the optimal regions for all pairs (permutations for x-monotone regions) of two distinct numeric attributes. Thus the number of attributes dramatically affects the overall performance.

Table 6 compares the time (sec) taken to construct trees by using datasets with different numbers of tuples. We randomly selected tuples from the "waveform" dataset to generate datasets having different numbers of tuples, and used those datasets to construct decision trees by performing region splitting with a pixel density of 5 and conventional guillotine cutting. We used the first eight numeric attributes as the conditional attributes, in order to simplify the experiment, and compared the time taken to construct pruned trees. The results show that the tree construction time is a little more than our scale estimation, because trees from larger datasets tend to become bigger.

Table 7, on the other hand, compares the performance using datasets with different numbers of attributes. We used 3000 tuples from the "waveform" dataset, and constructed trees using the first N numerical attributes. Observe that the time complexity is almost linear in the square of the number of attributes. In case of guillotine cutting trees, the test optimization cost is so small that time taken to construct a tree depends mainly on its final tree size.

Table 7. Tree Construction Time (2).

#attributes	X-monotone	Rectilinear	Guillotine
4	87	35	14
6	163	70	23
8	273	106	19
10	410	152	15
12	522	204	18

5. Generalizations

5.1. Categorical Objective Attribute

We can extend our scheme to a categorical objective attribute W with k categories $\{1, 2, .., k\}$, where k is a small integer. For a pair of numeric attributes A and A', and a family $\mathcal{R}$ of regions, we consider a splitting of S into $S(R)$ and $S(\bar{R})$, as before. The region R_{opt} is the region that minimizes the entropy $Ent(S(R); S(\bar{R}))$. The only difference is that it is harder to compute R_{opt} than in the boolean objective case.

For a region R, we define $\iota(R) = (x_1(R), ..., x_k(R))$, where $x_i(R)$ is the number of tuples t in $S(R)$ that satisfy $W(t) = i$. Let $P = \{\iota(R) : R \in \mathcal{R}\}$, and consider its convex hull $conv(P)$ in k-dimensional space.

Then, from Lemma 1, we can see that $\iota(R_{opt})$ is on $conv(P)$. Hence, it is enough to examine the vertices of $conv(P)$. We concentrate on the upper part $conv^+(P)$ of $conv(P)$, which consists of facets whose outer normal vector has a positive k-th coordinate, since the lower part $conv^-(P)$ can be treated analogously.

Consider a vector $\Theta = (\theta_1, \theta_2, .., \theta_{k-1}, 1)$, and the hyperplane $H(\Theta)$ tangent to $conv^+(P)$ defined by

$$x_k - \theta_1 x_1 - \theta_2 x_2 - ... - \theta_{k-1} x_{k-1} = c.$$

The k-dim touching oracle is to find the point of $H(\Theta)$ tangent to $conv^+(P)$. The touching point $\iota(R(\Theta))$ corresponds to the region $R(\Theta)$ that maximizes

$$F_\Theta(R) = x_k(R) - \theta_1 x_1(R) - ... - \theta_{k-1} x_{k-1}(R).$$

LEMMA 7 Given Θ, $R(\Theta)$ can be computed in $O(N^2)$ time for $\mathcal{R}(Xmono)$, and in $O(N)$ time with $O(N^2)$ time preprocessing for $\mathcal{R}(Base)$. It can be computed in $O(N^3)$ time for families of rectangles and rectilinear convex regions.

Proof: Once Θ is given, the value of $F_\Theta(i, j)$ at the (i, j)-th pixel of G can be precomputed. Thus, the region $R(\Theta)$ can be computed analogously to Lemmas 4 and 5. ∎

Hence, we can generalize the hand-probing algorithm. For simplicity, we give a brief explanation for the case $k = 3$. Suppose that we have used a 3-dimensional touching oracle for Θ, Θ', and Θ''. Next, we consider the plane through the associated three tangent points, and execute the touching oracle with respect to the slope of this plane. Then, we can find either a new vertex or a new facet of $conv^+(P)$ by executing the touching oracle. We also compute the intersection point Q of three hyperplanes $H(\Theta)$, $H(\Theta')$, and $H(\Theta'')$, and use the value of the entropy function at Q as a lower bound of the entropy values within the simplex defined by Q and the three tangent points. Thus, we can design a hand-probing algorithm, and implement it by using a guided branch-and-bound strategy.

Naive hand-probing requires $O(|P|)$ touching oracles, where $|P|$ is the complexity (total number of faces of all dimensions) of the polygon [9]. This is too expensive, since the number of vertices can be $O(n^{d-1})$, and $|P|$ is only bounded as $O(n^{(d-1)\lfloor d/2 \rfloor})$. However, we expect that the number of touching oracles can be reduced to $O(\log |P|)$ in practice if we use the branch-and-bound algorithm.

5.2. Rule Associated with More Than Two Attributes

Thus far, we have considered regions in a 2-dimensional plane as means for splitting data. In this subsection, we discuss how to use regions in k-dimensional space when $k \geq 3$. Owing to the space limitation, we omit the proofs of theorems in this subsection.

We consider a $N^k = N \times N \times ... \times N$ pixel grid G, associated with k numeric attributes $A_1, ... , A_k$. For a (k-dimensional) pixel region R, we can consider a splitting of tuples inside and outside R. Consider a family $\mathcal{R}$ of (k-dimensional) pixel regions of G, and find R_{opt} whose associated splitting minimizes the entropy.

We denote the coordinate system of G by $(z_1, ..., z_k)$. A region is called a k-*dimensional based-monotone* region if it lies below a k-dimensional monotone surface. A k-dimensional monotone surface is a *lift up* of a $(k-1)$-dimensional based-monotone region in the grid associated with $z_1, ..., z_{k-1}$; that is, its projection to the hyperplane $z_k = 0$ is a $(k-1)$-dimensional based-monotone region, and the projection is one-to-one. Indeed, if $k = 2$, we can obtain a 2-dimensional monotone surface (curve) as a union of horizontal edges of an x-monotone curve.

THEOREM 2 *If $\mathcal{R}$ is the family of all k-dimensional based-monotone regions, then R_{opt} can be computed in a worst case time of $O(\min\{n^2, nN^{k-1}\})$.*

For $k = 3$, we consider another family. A three-dimensional region is an x-monotone terrain if it lies below a three-dimensional grid surface that is a lift-up of a two-dimensional x-monotone region.

THEOREM 3 *If $\mathcal{R}$ is the family of all x-monotone terrains, then R_{opt} can be computed in a worst case time of $O(\min\{n^2, nN^3\})$.*

In practice, both time complexities can be improved by a factor of $n/\log n$.

6. Concluding Remarks

We have proposed an entropy-based greedy method of constructing decision trees by using region rules. Experiments using diverse datasets confirmed that region splitting trees are more accurate than conventional ones, as can be seen in Figures 6 to 14. These show the substantial capability of our method. Moreover, in experiments, the pruned trees shown in Table 4, achieved greater error reduction, especially in cases where there were a sufficient number of records. Although, in order to use the region splitting, we require an additional computation time proportional to the number of numeric conditional attributes, the improvements will be worth the computational cost if there are not too many numeric attributes in many applications.

Another important advantage is the size of the trees, which are much smaller than conventional ones. This makes it easy to grasp the rules affecting the values of the objective attribute. Furthermore, we can recognize many non-linear correlations among conditional attributes, which could not be found without region splitting.

Acknowledgments

This work is based on the extended abstract of "Constructing Efficient Decision Trees by Using Optimized Association Rules" in *Proceedings of the 22nd VLDB Conference*, (Mumbai, India, Sept. 3-6), VLDB Endowment, 1996, pp. 146-155.

This work supported by the Advanced Software Enrichment Project of the Information-Technology Promotion Agency, Japan. We thank Peter Stuckey and Raghu Ramakrishnan for their suggestions and our reviewers whose detailed comments helped improve this paper. Thanks are also due to the maintainers of the UCI machine learning repository.

References

1. T. Asano, D. Chen, N. Katoh & T. Tokuyama. (1996). Polynomial-Time Solutions to Image Segmentations. *Proc. 7th ACM-SIAM Symposium on Discrete Algorithms*, pages 104–113.
2. R. Agrawal, S. Ghosh, T. Imielinski, B. Iyer & A. Swami. (1992). An Interval Classifier for Database Mining Applications. *Proc. 18th VLDB Conference*, pages 560–573.
3. R. Agrawal, T. Imielinski & A. Swami (1993), Database Mining: A Performance Perspective. *IEEE Transactions on Knowledge and Data Engineering* 5& 6:914–925.
4. T. Asano & T. Tokuyama. (1994). Partial Construction of an Arrangement of Lines and Its Application to Optimal Partitioning of Bichromatic Point Set. *IEICE Transactions* E-77-A:595–600.
5. L. Breiman, J. H. Friedman, R. A. Olshen, & C. J. Stone. (1984). *Classification and Regression Tree.* Wadsworth.
6. C. E. Brodley & P. E. Utgoff. (1995). Multivariate Decision Trees. *Machine Learning* 19:45–77.
7. B. Chazelle & L. Guibas. (1986). Fractional Cascading: A Data Structuring Technique. *Algorithmica* 1:133–162.
8. D. Dobkin & D. Eppstein. (1993). Computing the Discrepancy. *Proc. 9th ACM Symposium on Computational Geometry*, pp. 47–52, 1993.
9. D. Dobkin, H. Edelsbrunner & C. Yap. (1986). Probing Convex Polytopes. *Proc. 18th ACM Symposium on Theory of Computing*, pages 387–392.
10. T. Fukuda, Y. Morimoto, S. Morishita & T. Tokuyama. (1996a). Mining Optimized Association Rules for Numeric Attributes. *Proceedings of the Fifteenth ACM SIGACT-SIGMOD-SIGART Symposium on Principles of Database System*, pages 182–191.
11. T. Fukuda, Y. Morimoto, S. Morishita & T. Tokuyama. (1996b). Data Mining using Two-dimensional Optimized Association Rules: Scheme, Algorithms, and Visualization. *Proceedings of the ACM SIGMOD Conference on Management of Data*, pages 13–23.
12. T. Fukuda, Y. Morimoto, S. Morishita & T. Tokuyama. (1996c). SONAR: System for Optimized Numeric Association Rules. *Proceedings of the ACM SIGMOD Conference on Management of Data*, page 553.
13. M. R. Garey & D. S. Johnson. (1979). *Computer and Intractability. A Guide to NP-Completeness.* W. H. Freeman.
14. L. Hyafil & R. L. Rivest. (1976). Constructing Optimal Binary Decision Trees is NP-Complete. *Information Processing Letter* 5:15–17.

15. M. Mehta, J. Rissanen & R. Agrawal. (1995). MDL-based decision tree pruning. *Proceedings of the First International Conference on Knowledge Discovery and Data Mining,* pages 216–221.

16. M. Mehta, R. Agrawal & J. Rissanen. (1996). SLIQ: A Fast Scalable Classifier for Data Mining. *Proceedings of the Fifth International Conference on Extending Database Technology.*

17. D. Michie, D. J. Spiegelhalter & C. C. Taylor. (1984). *Machine Learning, Neural, and Statistical Classification.* Ellis Horwood.

18. T. M. Mitchell. (1997). *Machine Learning.* McGraw-Hill.

19. P. M. Murphy & D. W. Aha. (1994). *UCI Repository of Machine Learning databases.* [http://www.ics.uci.edu/~mlearn/MLRepository.html], University of California, Department of Information and Computer Science, Irvine, CA.

20. P. M. Pardalos & J. B. Rosen (ed.) (1990). *Annals of Operations Research 25, Computational Methods in Global Optimization* J. C. Baltzer AG.

21. J. R. Quinlan. (1986a). Induction of Decision Trees. *Machine Learning,* 1: 81-106.

22. J. R. Quinlan. (1986b). The effect of noise on concept learning. In R. S. Michalski, J. G. Carbonell, and T. M. Mitchell, editors, *Machine Learning An Artificial Intelligence Approach 2,* pages 149–166,.

23. J. R. Quinlan. (1993). *C4.5: Programs for Machine Learning* Morgan Kaufmann.

24. J. R. Quinlan & R. L. Rivest. (1989). Inferring Decision Trees Using Minimum Description Length Principle. *Information and Computation* 80:227–248.

25. K. Yoda, T. Fukuda, Y. Morimoto, S. Morishita & T. Tokuyama. (1997). Computing Optimized Rectilinear Regions for Association Rules. *Proceedings of the Third International Conference on Knowledge Discovery and Data Mining,* (forthcoming).

Table of Contents: Volume 2 (1997)

Numbers 3/4